Cultural Pluralism
and Psychoanalysis

Cultural Pluralism

and Psychoanalysis

The Asian and North American Experience

ALAN ROLAND

ROUTLEDGE
New York and London

Published in 1996 by

Routledge
29 West 35th Street
New York, NY 10001

Published in Great Britain in 1996 by

Routledge
11 New Fetter Lane
London EC4P 4EE

Printed in the United States of America
Design: Jack Donner

Library of Congress Cataloging-in-Publication Data

Roland, Alan 1930–
Cultural pluralism and psychoanalysis :
the Asian and North American experience / Alan Roland
Includes bibliographical references and index.

p.   cm.

ISBN 0–415–91478–7 (cloth). — ISBN 0–415–91479–5 (pbk.)

1. Psychoanalysis and culture.   2. Asian Americans—Psychology.   3. Asians—United
States—Psychology.   4. Individualism—Cross-cultural studies.   5. Cross-cultural counseling.   6. Asian Americans—Counseling of.   I. Title
BF175.4.C84R65   1996
150.19'5'08995073—dc20   96–30239

To Jackie, Tika, and Ariel
and to my patients,
Asian, North American, and Asian-American

Contents

PREFACE   v

PART I: A COMPARATIVE PSYCHOANALYSIS

Chapter One   How Universal Is The Psychoanalytic Self?   3

PART II: THE ASIAN AND AMERICAN INTERFACE

Chapter Two   Walking The Bicultural Tightrope: 25
Indians in the United States

Chapter Three   The Japanese and American Interface   45

Chapter Four   Cultural Hurdles and Inscrutable Muddles   59
LINDA WAI LING YOUNG, Ph.D.

PART III: CLINICAL ISSUES

Chapter Five   Value Issues Involving American Psychoanalysts   71
with Asian Patients

Chapter Six   The Cultural Self, the Personal Self,   83
and Psychological Conflict

Chapter Seven   The Influence of Culture on the Self   101
and Selfobjects Relationships:
An Asian-North American Comparison

Chapter Eight   Psychoanalysis and Psychoanalytic Therapy   117
with Indians and Japanese in the United States

Chapter Nine   Sexuality, the Indian Extended Family, and Hindu Culture   133

Chapter Ten   The Spiritual and the Magic-Cosmic   145
in Psychoanalysis and Psychoanalytic Therapy

Chapter Eleven   The Psychological and the Psychosocial   159
in Indian Organizational Relationships

APPENDICES

Appendix A   Insight-Oriented Psychotherapy and the Chinese Patient   175
MAY TUNG, Ph.D.

Appendix B   Koreans Abroad in Therapy   187
WALTER SLOTE, Ph.D.

REFERENCES   199
INDEX   207

New Orientation to Asians

This book is a broken vow! Having spent almost every spare moment for eleven years working on a previous book (Roland 1988), I swore never to write another one. But a great deal happened over those years, and even more has happened since then. I originally thought there would be little interest in a psychoanalytic understanding of Indians and Japanese, and that a great deal of time and effort would go for nought. A senior editor at a major publishing house commented as much in the early 1980s: "This is too substantial and well-written a manuscript to have so few readers."

Asians were not on the American mind then.[1] When my wife and I were about to depart for India for extended research in 1977, we found that even close friends, well-travelled academics and psychoanalysts, were too embarrassed to ask us anything because they knew nothing about India. It was as though India were off the ends of the earth. A few years later, only a remark by A. K. Ramanujan, a noted Indian poet and linguist at the University of Chicago, shored up my resolve by saying, "When you have important ideas, even if only a few people read it, it will be worthwhile. The ideas will spread."

Then came a dramatic change in the attitudes Americans in the United States have.[2] It was not sufficient for our cultural compass to orient us toward Europe alone. Americans had to become Janus-faced, looking West across the Pacific to Asian societies, and East across the Atlantic to Europe, the Middle East, and Africa.[3] Asians assumed a greater presence in the American mind than ever before and it seemed the global age had clearly arrived.

A number of factors contributed to the increasing Asianization of American consciousness. One is the Japanese economic colossus that challenged American technological and economic competitiveness. This was quickly followed by rapidly expanding economies in China, Korea, Hong Kong, Taiwan, Singapore, and more recently, India: European countries are no longer our only major trading partners. Another factor is expanded media coverage of political events such as Tianenman Square.

Still another is on the level of personal experience where Americans of European, African, and South American origins have increasingly encountered Asian-Americans. By the late 1980s the seeds of the dramatic changes in the Immigration Law of 1965 that opened up our shores to large numbers of Asians began to bear fruit, and by now there are well over eight million Asian-Americans. For the most part, those who came were not "your tired, your poor, your huddled masses yearning to be free," but rather highly educated urban elites from cultures that strongly value disciplined learning.

Thus, in the original Filipino, Indian, and Korean immigration after 1965, especially the latter two, sixty percent or more of the immigrants are college-educated, well over double the average of other Americans, and are able to take advantage of the Immigration Law of 1965 that favored those with education and skills needed in the United States. The 130,000 Vietnamese refugees who came in 1975 were also from these urban educated elites. It is only the Chinese community, the largest Asian-American community in the United States with close to two million, that has half of its immigrants highly educated, and the other half from either working-class backgrounds or relatives of the original immigrants of farmers from Fukien Province. Moreover, our top universities and conservatories are filled with the offspring of these immigrants, as well as with a large number of Asians who expressly come to the United States for graduate school education and then return home. Their numbers comprise approximately 50 percent of graduate students. In contrast to the late 1970s, although encountering some discrimination, these Asian immigrants and the second generation have definitely now established their presence in the United States.

It is from this new orientation to Asia and interest in Asians that I was invited to present a number of papers in remarkably diverse settings. These ranged from usual psychoanalytic meetings such as the American Psychoanalytic Association, the International Congress of Psychoanalysis, the American Academy of Psychoanalysis, Division 39 (Psychoanalysis) of the American Psychological Association, and a number of psychoanalytic institutes; to an annual meeting of the American Philosophical Association and interdisciplinary conferences on the self at the East-West Center in Hawaii and Adelphi University; to Asia Society, Japan Society, and the Institute of Asian Studies in New York City; to the History Colloquium at Rutgers University and various other academic settings; to annual national and regional meetings on South Asia and East Asia, and to university programs in these area studies; to a conference of Rockefeller Fellows of the Asian/American Center at Queens College; to conferences on

Buddhism and psychoanalysis and psychotherapy; and to writing chapters in books that deal with cross-cultural psychological issues. For over five years after 1988, I was writing and presenting one paper after another, each related to my previous book, each developing new themes and contributions.

The vow had been broken. I awakened one day to find this book had been written without my intending it. Much remained to be done, such as the editing out of repetitions, the fleshing out of each chapter with new ideas and particularly with more clinical case examples, and enhancing continuity and integration. But the structure and content of the book was already established.

THE JOURNEY HOME

After returning to New York City from prolonged clinical psychoanalytic research to understand the psychology of Indians and Japanese and how they have been affected by Westernization/modernization, I began reexamining a number of my basic assumptions about American life and culture, myself, and psychoanalysis. I, in effect, was doing what a number of cultural anthropologists have done who have worked in radically different cultures. We were reexamining our own culture, and in my case, our own psychology and psychological theory, psychoanalysis, from cross-civilizational perspectives. This has coincided with a period of intense scrutiny of our Western cultural heritage by those involved with Feminism, Marxism, Social Constructionism, Hermeneutics, and Postmodernism.

I have been particularly drawn to an understanding of our modern Western culture of individualism, and how individualism has affected our whole psychology, and especially, psychoanalytic theory. I have found the work of Louis Dumont (1986), the French anthropologist, to be particularly apropos. He has traversed a related course from an understanding of Indian culture to a journey home to delve into the cultural roots of individualism. As I have tried to understand the psychology of Indians and Japanese within their own cultural framework and history, I wanted to do the same with ourselves. This is not an easy task when one's own cultural heritage is so much a part of one's very self, and deeply embedded in one's bones so to speak. I am convinced that one can only attempt this from a comparative standpoint: the Feminists from gender, the Marxists from class differences, and cultural anthropologists and a handful of psychoanalysts from a cross-civilizational perspective.

At the same time, as I worked with Indians and Japanese in psychoanalysis and psychoanalytic therapy in New York City and observed them interacting with other Americans, I became more and more interested in the interface. Apart from the usual individual differences in persons from any culture, I found definite patterns in these interactions, ones traceable to profound differences, if not at times opposite cultural values and social patterns, which are integral to the psychological makeup of those involved. This cultural/psychological interface is obviously one that immigrants to the United States have faced over a number of generations, but not usually with the degree of difference that Asians have between their original culture and American individualism.

THE CHAPTERS

This book is about culture and psychoanalysis. It is not only related to those from Asian societies—Chinese, Indians, Japanese, and Koreans—but also to North Americans. Culture and sociohistorical change are with rare exceptions the missing dimensions in psychoanalysis. It is not that psychoanalysis has been uninvolved with culture. But it is usually more of a one-way street to see what light psychoanalysis can shed on various areas of culture, rather than how culture influences psychoanalysis in its theory and therapy. These dimensions are especialy relevant to clinicians, whether psychoanalysts, psychologists, or others in one or another mental health field, to enable them to understand what is at stake in working with those from Asia. It is even more relevant than most clinicians realize in working with those from one's own culture, as I intend to demonstrate. The intertwining of culture and psychoanalysis is also pertinent to academics and other interested readers who want to learn more about the psychology of Asians, and how this compares with that of North Americans.

The first chapter, "How Universal is the Psychoanalytic Self?," grew out of two related concerns connected to my journey home. The foremost was to locate psychoanalysis within the culture of individualism, the predominant ethos of modern Western civilization. I see psychoanalysis as a direct outgrowth of individualism, and seminal psychoanalytic thinkers from Freud on in a creative dialogue and dialectic with the culture of individualism: strongly critiquing one or more aspects of individualism, formulating psychological processes and a mode of therapy to enable persons to function better in a culture of individualism, and unreflectingly incorporating considerable assumptions and ways of thinking from individualism. The advent and development of psychoanalysis can be better understood within this cultural/historical perspective.

The other related concern involves the problems of using a psychology such as psychoanalysis, which is so rooted in Western individualism, for understanding Asians. I have critiqued three major paradigms of how psychoanalysis has been applied to Asians—evolutionism, universalism, and relativism—each illustrated by a major proponent, to delineate the strengths and weaknesses of each paradigm. I then formulate my own approach to resolve knotty issues between psychoanalytic universalism and anthropological relativism.

The next section of the book is on the interface of Asians with North Americans, and delving into this subject is a part of my journey home. In the second chapter, "Walking the Bicultural Tightrope: Indians in the United States," I describe the considerable misunderstandings and dissonances that take place between Indian-Americans and other Americans that are largely due to their coming from two vastly different cultural/psychological realms. I particularly emphasize the problems generated by the psychosocial dimensions of Indian hierarchical relationships when they encounter American-style individualism. The delineation of these psychosocial dimensions sets the stage in the next section on the clinical chapters for what takes place in psychoanalytic therapy with Asians. I then depict the travails of both the Indian immigrant and second generation in developing a bicultural self. Problems in the interface for both, as well as by gender, are liberally illustrated by clinical examples and occasionally social ones.

The next chapter on the Japanese and American interface follows the same approach as the previous one by delineating how the three psychosocial dimensions of hierarchical relationships are also present in Japanese but vary significantly from those of Indians. The Japanese psychosocial dimensions then interface differently with American-style individualism. I focus on three major areas of the interface: Japanese corporations in the United States with American support staff, artistic creativity, and recent Japanese-American immigrants involved in marriages and raising families with other Americans. The problems, misunderstandings, and miscommunication are all related with examples to strong differences between the Japanese and American cultural/psychological worlds.

The next chapter in this section, "Cultural Hurdles and Inscrutable Muddles," is by Professor Linda Wai Ling Young, a Chinese-American linguistic anthropologist. I have included her work for three important reasons. Her insights into the radically different linguistic/cultural/philosophical worlds of Chinese and North Americans, which underlie the considerable miscommunications and misunderstandings when they both use English, is extremely relevant to the Asian and North American interface. This Chapter and two others in the Appendix by Dr. May Tung and Dr. Walter Slote expand this book beyond my own work with Indians and Japanese to include those from Chinese and Korean societies. Thirdly, this chapter adds the linguistic dimension, so anchored in culture and philosophy, as essential to understanding Asians and North Americans.

Having established culture as a major factor both in psychoanalysis and in the interface between Asians and North Americans, I then turn in the section on Clinical Issues to describe how culture manifests in a number of ways in working psychoanalytically with Asians but also with North Americans. Since the influence of culture is the most important dimension largely missing in Freudian psychoanalytic theory, regardless of which model is used, and in other North American psychological theories as well, I try to demonstrate its relevance to practicing clinicians in a number of ways and with repeated case vignettes. The whole thrust of the clinical chapters is to examine how culture enters the space of psychoanalytic work with Asians and North Americans.

In the first of the clinical chapters, "Value Issues Involving American Psychoanalysts with Asian Patients," I first focus on the problems an American analyst with European roots faces when working with those from another civilization. The usual ambiguity of psychoanalytic work can dissolve into completely being at sea when one encounters a significantly different normality/psychopathology continuum. Through American therapists becoming more aware of their own values as inherent in the culture of individualism, they can become far more open to other value orientations that stress far greater dependency and deference to authority, an involvement with the spiritual or with personal destiny, very different sources of esteem, and quite different modes of communication. A more culturally aware American analyst can also be more empathically attuned to the conflicts and anguish most Asians experience in encountering the American life-style.

Since returning from my psychoanalytic research in India and Japan, I have not infrequently been asked how this experience impacts on my regular psychoanalytic work. I have become far more aware of how culture and sociohistorical change enters into the psychological makeup of each of my patients, and then manifests itself in the psychoanalytic relationship. With someone from one's own cultural background, this often happens in minor ways; but it can sometimes play a major role in the analytic work.

It is just these concerns that I address in Chapter Six, "The Cultural Self, the Personal Self, and Psychological Conflict." I formulate a cultural self that is integral to the very fabric of our everyday self, but which is invisible unless one has lived in a radically different culture. In psychoanalytic therapy, one must differentiate whether it is cultural factors or idiosyncratic familial ones that generate conflict, either of which can be manifested in the transference. Cultural factors also enter into an ethnic layering of the self, when the second generation internalizes, in childhood, parental values from their original culture, and then gradually incorporates those of American individualism as they grow up. This not infrequently results in psychological conflict. Conflict can also be generated by ethnic encounters within the self from internalized values and attitudes of parents from radically different cultural backgrounds. Sociohistorical trauma is also delineated as is a regional self, where cultural factors from different regions of the United States enter into a person's psychological makeup and conflicts. Case material illustrates all of these points.

In the following chapter, "The Influence of Culture on the Self and Selfobject Relationships: An Asian-North American Comparison," I relate culture in salient ways to self psychology, a major development in Freudian psychoanalysis over the last twenty-five years. The first is to locate the very development of self psychology within North American individualism. The second is delineating the particular relevance of self psychology to Asian psychological makeup and relationships, where there is a strong cultural emphasis on the salience of selfobject relationships and we-self esteem. I then describe different modes and contents of empathic attunement, as well as two kinds of normal idealizations that are present in Asian hierarchical relationships. I posit an additional selfobject relationship to that which is present in North Americans: family and/or group reputation, which strongly affects we-self esteem in Asians.

This cross-civilizational perspective then sheds light on some current theoretical issues in self psychology, such as the need to formulate a greater reciprocity of selfobject relationships, and viewing the separation-individuation process in early childhood as described by ego psychologists as rooted in a particular, culturally influenced selfobject relationship, rather then being seen as antithetical to self psychology. I then turn to problems in Asian selfobject relationships and we-self esteem.

In Chapter Eight, "Psychoanalysis and Psychoanalytic Therapy with Indians and Japanese in the United States," I address three of the major dimensions of clinical psychoanalysis: the psychoanalytic relationship, resistances, and transferences. I detail how the culture of individualism structures the North American psychoanalytic relationship in contrast to how Asians relate psychoanalytically as influenced by the three psychosocial dimensions of hierarchical relationships that I delineated in Chapters Two and Three. I then turn to how resistances are not only idiosyncratic to a given patient, but are also influenced by cultural values and cultural modes of relating and communicating. I address a viewpoint occasionally expressed by some psychoanalysts that culture plays no role in psychoanalytic work once the transferences emerge. I disagree with this position by citing how culture played a central role in the development of intense transferences with both an Indian and a Japanese analysand. I then describe the cases of two Indian immigrant patients seen in psychoanalytic therapy, showing the interface between their experiences in the United States with problems and conflicts from India.

In the last three chapters, I turn to more specialized areas of Asian psychological makeup as compared to North Americans. In Chapter Nine, "Sexuality, the Indian Extended Family, and Hindu Culture," I first contrast the Indian oedipus with the Western one and the cultural influences on women's sexuality. I then turn to a major psychoanalytic theoretical issue involving drive theory and character-formation, demonstrating that drive theory uninformed by cultural influences on the superego and ego ideal and on early object relationships, can be grossly misleading when universally related to character-formation. The chapter concludes with a discussion of the relationship of the erotic to spirituality in Indians.

The following chapter, "The Spiritual and the Magic-Cosmic in Psycho-analysis and Psychoanalytic Therapy," is perhaps the most controversial in the book. With a strong Enlightenment legacy of demystifying religion and the spiritual, and considering the magic-cosmic realm of personal destiny as super-stition, psychoanalysts are usually in a poor position to be attuned to these important areas of psychological functioning in patients from any of the Asian cultures, as well as occasionally in those from various Western societies. I cite some exceptions to the rule among recognized psychoanalysts, as well as among a small but increasingly articulate group of psychoanalysts and psychoanalysts-in-training who are serious practicioners of one or another form of Buddhist meditation.

I posit the spiritual and normality/psychopathology as being on two separate continua, intersecting and interacting in various ways. I go into this interface in a variety of ways in patients, both Asian and American, who are committed to the spiritual quest but are also trying to work out knotty emotional prob-lems in psychoanalysis or psychoanalytic therapy. This leads to a discussion of the psychoanalyst who is also seriously involved in meditation. The penchant for Americans to be far more open in asserting involvement in a spiritual prac-tice than are Indians is discussed in terms of profound cultural/psychological differences. For a psychoanalyst to dismiss the realm of personal destiny with its involvement in the magic-cosmic world of astrology, palmistry, psychics, the spirit world, and such is to miss a major area of every Hindu patient's men-tal life.

While the underpinning in this book for much of my understanding of Indians originally derive from American Institute for Indian Studies (AIIS) grants for psychoanalytic research in India, supplemented by further psychoan-alytic experiences with Indian patients in New York City, this last chapter, "The Psychological and the Psychosocial in Indian Organizational Relation-ships," explicitly comes from a 1991 AIIS summer grant. Hoping to update prior contacts with patients and psychoanalysts in Bombay, I fortuitously became involved both on theoretical and clinical levels with a growing ferment in Indian management theory and relationships. In small part fueled by my previous book that showed very different psychologies for India, Japan, and the United States, some management theorists such as Gupta (1991) are trying to work out an indigenous Indian management theory related to their own psy-chology, rather than the customary use of American and Japanese management theories which do not really fit.

I became involved in Indian organizations in a way I hadn't been before. I cite four case examples of problematic interactions to begin delineating some of the psychological issues involved in Indian organizational relationships. The first two examples illustrate the salience of Indian hierarchical relationships, by the qualities of the person and by the formal hierarchy, respectively, to show how dismissal of these principles by Western influences can result in highly problematic results. The second and the third case examples demonstrate the importance of envy among brothers with its resultant destructiveness in organizations, as much or more motivated by favoritism from the father than from the relationship with the mother. The fourth case example of a highly successful mid-sized company with a psychoanalytic consultant depicts the problematic interaction of a senior and two junior managers as much more involved in difficult father-son relationships. With the stress in the psychoanalytic literature on dependency relationships and mother-child ties in both India (Kakar 1978) and Japan (Doi 1973), my clinical experience in Indian organizations clearly calls for a greater psychoanalytic elaboration of relationships among brothers, and between fathers and sons, as central to men's work relationships.

The book concludes with two appendices on clinical work with Chinese and Koreans. The first appendix, "Insight-Oriented Psychotherapy and the Chinese Patient," is by Dr. May Tung, a psychoanalytically-oriented psychologist, originally from Beijing but trained and practicing for many years in the United States. Her paper first contrasts the Chinese sense of self with a North American one, and then cites case material of immigrant as well as second and third generation Chinese-Americans. From this material, Dr. Tung discusses how insight is used, the nature of the transference, and the role of the therapist with Chinese-Americans as it differs from other Americans of European origin. She also delves into bicultural issues in her case material as Chinese-Americans have to deal with two such contrasting cultural/psychological realms.

"Koreans Abroad in Therapy," the second appendix, is by Dr. Walter Slote, a psychoanalyst and a psychoanalytic anthropologist, who has worked with Koreans and is married to a Korean. Dr. Slote explores the interface between Korean families, and particularly between the second generation, and the American culture of individualism, with the resultant conflicts and dissonances in Koreans. He particularly emphasizes the conflicts between the Confucian family value-system and that of North Americans, and the difficulties for Koreans in reconciling both sides of the cultural divide.

ACKNOWLEDGEMENTS

First and foremost, I would like to acknowledge the American Institute of Indian Studies for grants that enabled me to go to India to do extensive, clinical psychoanalytic research that has formed the foundation of the Indian part of this book.

The first chapter, "How Universal is the Psychoanalytic Self?," was developed from a paper on "Psychoanalytic Universalism: The Self in India, Japan, and the United States," first presented at the Annual Meeting of the American

Philosophical Association in December 1991, and then at a scientific meeting of the National Psychological Association for Psychoanalysis in October 1994. This paper under a revised title, "How Universal is Psychoanalysis?: The Self in India, Japan, and the United States," is being published in a book, *Culture and Self: Philosophical and Religious Perspectives, East and West*, edited by D. Allen and A. Malhotra, Westview, 1996. Another paper related to the first half of Chapter One, "The Psychoanalytic Self and Western Individualism," was presented at a conference, "The Suffering Self: A Dialogue Between Psychoanalysts and Buddhists," in April 1994. Still another related paper is published as "Identity, Self, and Individualism," in *Race, Ethnicity, and Self*, edited by E. P. Salett and D. R. Koslow, National MultiCultural Institute Publications, 1994, 11–23. An earlier version of this chapter with the same title was presented to a meeting of the Rockefeller Fellows of the Asian-American Center of Queens College, and is being published in another book, *Broadening the Clinical Use of Psychoanalysis: Toward a Multicultural Perspective*, edited by R. Perez-Foster, M. Moskowitz, and R. A. Javier, Jason Aronson, 1996. This chapter has benefited from comments by Douglas Allen and Rosemarie Perez-Foster.

The second chapter, "Walking the Bicultural Tightrope: Indians in the United States," developed from a paper, "Indians in America: Adaptation and the Bicultural Self," was given as part of a year's series of presentations on the South Asian Diaspora at the South Asian Studies Program, University of Pennsylvania, in February 1991; and to an Association of Indian Psychiatrists in New York City in December 1993. One part of the paper was developed in a presentation to South Asians in the New York City Financial World, "Walking the Bicultural Tightrope: Indians in the Corporate World." A very much abbreviated version of this chapter was given as a keynote address to a conference, "Balancing Two Worlds: Indians in the United States," in November 1995, and will be published in a book of that title in 1996. Aspects of this chapter and the following one were presented to the Asia Society in 1991 and to the Institute for Asian Studies in October 1994.

The third chapter, "The Japanese and American Interface," developed from presentations at Japan Society, "The Japanese and American Self: Highlights and Contrasts," in October 1990; at the Institute for Asian Studies, "Asians in America: Walking the Bicultural Tightrope," in March 1994; and at the Educational Alliance, "Raising Children in a Cross-Cultural Environment, Parts I and II," in October and November 1993, subsequently published in *ShiSo-e* in Japanese and English, February and March 1994, volume 8, number 5, and volume 9, number 6, respectively. "The Interface of Japan and the United States in Corporations, the Arts, and Marriages," was presented at the Japan-United States Foundation in April 1995.

The fifth chapter, "Value Issues Involving American Psychoanalysts with

Asian Patients," was presented in an earlier version at the Annual Meeting of the American Academy of Psychoanalysis in December 1993, and was published in the _Journal of the American Academy of Psychoanalysis_ in 1995, 23:283–292.

The sixth chapter, "The Cultural Self, the Personal Self, and Psychological Conflict," was first given in Montreal at a conference in December 1989 on "Culture and Mental Health," and then at the Midwinter Meeting of the American Psychoanalytic Association in December 1991. An earlier version of this chapter was published by _Sante Culture Health_ in 1990, VII:185–196.

The seventh chapter on "The Influence of Culture on the Self and Selfobject Relationships: An Asian-North American Comparison," was given in an earlier version to a scientific meeting of the psychoanalytic institute for Training and Research in Self Psychology in April 1991. I am appreciative of comments on this chapter by Esther Menaker and Peter Zimmerman. A revised but still earlier version of this chapter is published in _Psychoanalytic Dialogues_ in July 1996, volume 6, with a commentary by Philip Cushman and my reply.

Aspects of Chapter Eight, "Psychoanalysis and Psychoanalytic Therapy with Indians and Japanese in the United States," was presented in a paper, "Psychoanalysis in India and Japan: Toward a Comparative Psychoanalysis," to the Austen Riggs Center, August 1988; the William Alanson White Institute, November 1988; the Annual Meeting of Division 39 (Psychoanalysis) of the American Psychological Association, April 1989; the Midwinter Meeting of the American Psychoanalytic Association, December 1989; and the Karen Horney Institute, January 1990. This paper was published in _The American Journal of Psychoanalysis_ in 1991, 51:1–10.

The ninth chapter on "Sexuality, the Indian Extended Family, and Hindu Culture," was given at the Annual Meeting of the American Academy of Psychoanalysis in San Francisco in May 1989, and published in an earlier version in the _Journal of the American Academy of Psychoanalysis_ in 1991, 19:595–605.

The tenth chapter on "The Spiritual and the Magic-Cosmic in Psychoanalysis and Psychoanalytic Therapy," was given in an earlier version as a keynote address, "The Spiritual and the Magic-Cosmic in Indian Patients in Psychoanalytic Therapy," to a conference on "Buddhism and Psychotherapy" at the Tibetan Monastery in Woodstock, New York in September 1991; and to a conference in Philadelphia on "Spirituality and Psychotherapy," in February 1992. This earlier version was published in the inaugural issue of the _Journal of the Psychology of Religion_ in 1992, 1:91–102.

The eleventh chapter, "Psychological and the Psychosocial in Indian Organizational Relationships," was presented to the New York State Association of Asian Studies in November 1992; to the MidAtlantic Association of Asian Studies in March 1993; and to a seminar at the Southern Asian Studies Department, Columbia University, in March 1995.

Appendix A, "Insight-Oriented Psychotherapy and the Chinese Patient," was published by Dr. May Tung in the *American Journal of Orthopsychiatry* in 1991, 61:186–194. Appendix B, "Koreans in Therapy Abroad," was published by Dr. Walter Slote in an earlier version as a chapter, "Koreans in Therapy Abroad: Implications for the Homeland," in *Overseas Koreans in the Global Context*, edited by K. K. Lee and W.H. Slote, Association for Studies of Koreans Abroad, Seoul National University, Seoul, Korea 1993.

I am still greatly indebted to Dr. B. K. Ramanujam who has served as a guide for my understanding of many of the subtleties of the Indian psyche and relationships. I am also thankful to Dr. May Tung for her comments on grappling with some of the same therapeutic issues as I have, but the Chinese in the United States. Finally, I am grateful to my editor, Maureen MacGrogan, for welcoming a book such as this at Routledge, not a typical work in the psychoanalytic field.

ENDNOTES

1. Before the United States Immigration Law of 1965, only very small numbers of Asians were allowed into the United States. By 1965, there were at most a million Asian-Americans; slightly more than half were Japanese and a fifth, Filipinos, who had immigrated as farmers to Hawaii and the West Coast in the first quarter of this century, and were over a quarter Chinese who had first come as workers in the middle of the nineteenth century. The earlier Chinese immigration was cut to a trickle first by the Exclusion Act of 1882, and then along with all other Asians was almost completely halted by the Immigration Act of 1924. Moreover, restrictions on bringing wives by all other Asians from the beginning until after World War II, except by the Japanese until 1924, severely inhibited the growth of their communities here, while still other restrictions resulted in the Chinese being confined to urban ghettos, the Chinatowns of various cities. It was only after World War II that Chinese families of those in the professions and sciences were allowed to immigrate to escape Communism (Uba 1994).

2. In using the designation, "American," I am specifically referring to those from the United States. I am well aware that Central Americans and South Americans can easily use the same designation as legitimately.

3. I should add we were also looking South to Central and South America as well as the Carribean countries.

Part I

A Comparative Psychoanalysis

Chapter One

How Universal
is the Psychoanalytic Self?

DIFFERENT CLINICAL VIEWS OF THE SELF

I would like to present a brief vignette to illustrate how some of our current psychoanalytic assumptions on the nature of the self and on psychological functioning are more loaded with Western cultural meanings than we realize. A Japanese psychoanalyst told the following incident that occurred early in his program of training at the National Psychological Association for Psychoanalysis in New York City. In a class on psychoanalytic technique, he presented an initial session with a Japanese patient, a young woman in her early twenties. He related to the class that the young woman was rather hesitant and cautious in telling him her problems with an American boyfriend. For his own part, he was mostly silently empathic with her, hardly asking any questions or making any comments. At the end of the session, he said to her, "now that we are working together, we shall continue in future sessions."

The instructor, an experienced analyst, was apparently astonished at his closing statement. She questioned, "how come you said 'now that *we* are working together' when there was very little if any verbal exchange or interaction between the two of you?" The Japanese student therapist became very upset since he felt he was not being understood as a Japanese.

What were the different assumptions about the self and psychological functioning that the instructor and the Japanese student were making that caused this impasse? The instructor assumed, as most of us would, that in psychoanalytic therapy there are two separate individuals speaking together with one free-associating while the other gradually clarifies the subtext of what is transpiring, each with an individualistic "I-self" and self-directedness, with more or less firm ego boundaries between each other in an "I" and "you" contractual relationship exchanging fee for time and expertise. Although the therapist is obviously thought to be more knowledgeable and therefore having a higher status, nevertheless, American egalitarianism encourages both patient and analyst to be seen as essentially equal in nature. All of these are cardinal assumptions of American individualism.

The Japanese therapist assumed a very different kind of self to be present in his patient and himself from what the instructor assumed, as well as very different ways of communicating and relating. He based his way of working on the "we-self" of Japanese, a self that is primarily experienced in relation to others, and is particularly integral to Japanese-style hierarchical relationships where subordinate and superior form a "we" relationship that is quite different from American egalitarianism. In vivid contrast to the American experiential sense of an I-self, for Japanese, a sense of "I-ness," or even of "I want or I wish," rarely exists. Rather, Japanese depend on each other to sense what the other wants. He knew from Japanese-style hierarchical relationships, and from years of psychotherapy experience in Japan, that he had to foster the development of a close "we" relationship between superior (therapist) and subordinate (patient) for any therapy to take place. In Japan, unlike for the most part in America, the superior is expected to be empathically nurturing and responsible to the subordinate.

He further knew that in a society which so stresses the correct presentation of self (*omote*) in a rigorously observed social etiquette, particularly in the formal hierarchical relationships, Japanese keep a highly private, secretive self (*ura*) in which all kinds of feelings, fantasies, and thoughts are present (Doi 1986; Roland 1988). This is a self that is to be empathically sensed and not intruded upon. Only after considerable time when a trusting relationship has been formed, and the therapy relationship has been gradually transformed from an outsider one (*soto*) to an insider one (*uchi*) will a Japanese begin to share important aspects of his or her inner life. Thus, this Japanese therapist was silently empathic with his patient, a not unusual way of communicating in Japan, where both patient and therapist, as in other hierarchical relationships, expect the other to empathically sense what each is feeling and thinking, often with a minimum of overt communication (Roland 1983). There is, after all, a saying in Japan, "Nothing important is ever to be communicated verbally."

Notwithstanding these significant differences between Japanese and Americans, it can also be said that the Japanese student therapist at this stage in his training needed to learn much more about resistance-analysis and transference-analysis, cornerstones of psychoanalytic work, which he subsequently did. But even then, resistance-analysis with most Japanese has to be far less confrontive than is characteristic of most American analysts, even when they are being tactful. As in other Japanese communication, it is often done by innuendo. This is due to a superego and ego-ideal that by American standards is highly perfectionistic, thus leaving Japanese highly vulnerable to any criticism or intimation of failure.

CULTURAL ROOTS OF WESTERN INDIVIDUALISM

It is time now to take a step back to reflect and delve more deeply into the cultural roots and philosophical assumptions of psychoanalysis. If this brief vignette can highlight such different psychological worlds—and many other cases could easily be cited—then it behooves us to examine more closely the current elaboration of psychoanalytic theory in its Western cultural context. Only then shall we be in a position to extend psychoanalysis to others from radically different cultures and develop a comparative psychoanalysis rooted in different cultural, social, and historical contexts. More specifically, we shall have to explore how psychoanalytic theory and practice is profoundly related to Northern European and North American cultural values and philosophical assumptions involving individualism. I shall try to touch upon a few of the salient issues involving individualism and psychoanalysis.

The sources of modern Western individualism began in the religious sphere of the Reformation, then spread into the secular sphere of philosophers of the Social Contract and then to ones of the Enlightenment, and later into the cultural realm of Romanticism. The Reformation transformed an earlier Christian other-worldly individualism to a this-worldly one where the onus of salvation is put squarely onto the shoulders of the individual who is in a direct, unmediated relationship to a God from whom he or she is essentially separate and tries to rejoin. In the Calvinist vision, individuals through independent, active achievement in the world, guage the degree to which they are among the elect and therefore predestined for redemption. Protestant sects have emphasized values of individualism involving taking responsibility for attending to one's conscience and making correct moral decisions, thus being self-directed, and of being self-reliant, self-sufficient, and independent. Rather than being rooted in a hierarchical social collective and cosmic order, the individual is set on his own (Dumont 1986; Kirschner 1992; Nelson 1965).

Seventeenth- and eighteenth-century philosophers such as Hobbes, Locke, and Rousseau, each in his own way, then formulated the Social Contract of essentially self-contained, atomistic individuals in interaction with each other who enter into a society with some kind of necessary authority. They were joined by the Jurists who reinterpreted Natural Law as being comprised of self-sufficient individuals made in the image of God, who are the repository of reason. Enlightenment philosophers such as Voltaire, Diderot, and Descartes, among others, laid the cultural groundwork for modern Western individualism in the social and political spheres, through formulating the basis of the modern nation state as a union of equal individuals with rights and obligations (Dumont 1986).

Individualism in the religious sphere, and then in the social and political, was followed by individualism in the economic realm. Here, Adam Smith and David Ricardo further assumed a rationally ordered economy of separate self-contained individuals with similar interests. Thus, these cultural valuations on autonomous individuals equal to each other, rather than on the social and cosmic realms as encompassing the person, have come to underlie all modern Western economic, political, legal, and cultural theories, as well as educational approaches (Allen 1996; Dumont 1986). Nineteenth-century philosophical and literary approaches in Romanticism further consolidated individualism through the ideal of the highly individuated, verbally self-expressive individual in close relationships with other highly individuated individuals.

Thus, the individual came to be considered inviolate, the supreme value in and of himself or herself, having his or her own rights and obligations, with each equal to the other. Society is considered to be essentially subordinate to the needs of individuals, who are all governed by their own self-interest in mutually consenting, contractual relationships in their political and economic strivings.

Enlightenment notions of individualism view the rational, thinking person as what is most real and valued, with analytic-deductive modes of thought that explore causal, logical relationships as primary. Rationality is considered intrinsically superior to the emotions. This rational, thinking mind is viewed as autonomous in each individual and separate from others, a universal phenomenon rather than being one that is historically or culturally constituted. All other ways of perceiving reality are discredited as superstition, or demystified such as religion, magic, and ritual. Views of the world and the cosmos became primarily secular and scientific, the latter in particular becoming supremely valued.

Reason has taken two major forms of cultural expression, dualism and universalism. Dualistic thinking became deeply ingrained in Western culture after the Reformation with the separation of spirit from matter, value from fact, and the humanities from the natural sciences. Dualism was further developed during the Enlightenment, particularly by Descartes, in the separation of mind from body, subject from object, idealism from materialism, with the separation of all of the domains of academic disciplines from each other (Marriott 1990). Similarly, Cartesian dualism pervades the work of the social sciences and psychoanalysis in their study of Western society and the individual, respectively. Thus, there is a sharp differentiation in all of the models of psychoanalysis, as well as in other Western psychological theories of personality, between what is inside oneself and what is in others.

Orignally, the focus on universals derived from monotheism and from Greek philosophers such as Plato. Universalism received particular emphasis in the Enlightenment by Diderot and other Encyclopedists in their formulation of Natural Law, and later in the ensuing pursuit in the natural and social sciences, including psychology. Universalism is such a basic philosophical assumption in Western thinking that it is rarely realized how culturally related it is. Psychoanalysts, for instance, always assume that any new formulation they make has universal validity.

INDIVIDUALISM AND PSYCHOANALYSIS

In the progression of individualism from the religious to the social and political, to the economic, and then to the philosophical-literary sphere, one can look upon psychoanalysis as the further extension of individualism to the realm of the psychological. One can easily cite psychoanalysis as the psychological theory and therapy par excellence of modern Western individualism. If individuals are set upon their own in society in a way never before done, then psychoanalysis is oriented toward enabling them to be on their own by resolving all kinds of inner conflicts and deficits. What other psychological theory and therapy is so thorough-going in its exploration of the individual psyche, or is so oriented toward individuals taking full responsibility for their lives through resolving the dictates of the unconscious?

From Freud onward there has been a continous dialogue between major psychoanalysts and the culture of individualism. Beginning with Freud, they critique some of the most important values and assumptions of individualism, while delineating psychological processes necessary to function in a culture of individualism, as well as simultaneously reflecting other values of individualism in both psychoanalytic theory and therapy.

Freud, himself, severely and successfully critiqued the Enlightenment's idea of man's inherent rationality through his formulation of the unconscious and primary process thinking. But classical psychoanalysis has always emphasized a resolution of unconscious conflicts so that rationality can once more prevail. "Where id was, ego shall be." Freud clearly carried over Kant's ideal of rational autonomy, the ability to regulate one's life by norms of one's own devising (Kirschner 1992, p. 180). There is no question that rational, secondary process thinking has always been evaluated as superior to the primary process, with the latter being seen in a pejorative way as occurring developmentally earlier in the child and in the human race. Only in recent decades has there been a shift of view as in the work of Deri (1984), Noy (1969), Roland (1972), and Rycroft (1968).

In another dimension, universal principles of conscience located within the individual were emphasized by the Reformation and later incorporated by philosophers such as Kant in his concept of the categorical imperative involving universal moral laws. Freud took this over in his view of a deeply internalized superego that functions in a principled, consistent way. It is only in very recent decades that this, too, has been challenged both from the standpoint of gender and cross-cultural studies (Bernstein 1993; Gilligan 1980; Roland 1988).

And in still another philosophical assumption of individualism, Cartesian dualism separates emotions from the rational mind. Emotions in Western philosophy have long been viewed as derived from bodily sensations. In classical psychoanalytic terms, emotions and affects are traditionally considered to be drive derivatives of sexuality and aggression, and are to be brought under the sway of secondary process rational thinking, rather than as being centered in the social world and profoundly related to cultural meanings.

From the perspective of individualism, one easily sees the self-contained individual in traditional Freudian drive and structural theory where all motivation originates within the intrapsychic drives and structures of the individual. The social surround receives scant attention except for being the aim of the drives, as gratifiers or frustrators, as the source of superego and especially ego-ideal contents through parental carriers of the culture, and as the reality principle of what an individual can or cannot do in the social world.

It is not simply that Freud veered from the issue of parental seduction to focusing exclusively on intrapsychic fantasy. From the vantage point of individualism, the problem goes much deeper. There is no place in traditional psychoanalytic theory for the impact of the psychodynamics of parents and siblings—i.e. parents and siblings in psychological depth—or even the effect of changing dynamics of the family on the patient, not to mention different family structures from other cultures.

Even the Oedipus Complex, the cornerstone of classical Freudian theory, is more of a stage setting of triangular relationships within a family than dramatis personae, each with her or his own character in depth. Or in that other triangle, that of sibling rivalry with the mother often at the apex, again the only member of the cast with any real characterization is the patient. Intrapsychic fantasy in the self-contained individual prevails in the theory.

The same holds true for the psychoanalytic process in classical analysis. The notion of the self-contained individual and the sharply delineated Cartesian dualism between self and object prevails in a setting where the personality and subjectivity of the analyst are rarely considered to have any impact on the patient. In this setting, the analyst maintains the relative anonymity of a blank screen upon which patients gradually unconsciously project and displace old images and emotions, which are then interpreted by the analyst.

This does not necessarily mean that sensitive, traditional psychoanalytic clinicians do not take the social surround into account in working with a patient, particularly childhood familial relationships and even themselves. They usually do this in the case illustration rather than the theoretical exposition, indicating that there are often two narratives in psychoanalytic writing (Schafer 1983). It is the latter narrative that delineates one or another facet of the self-contained individual; whereas it is often in the former that the clinician may detail subtle parent-child interactions that are resurfacing in the transference, and belie the paradigm of the self-contained individual.

What is true of traditional Freudian theory is equally true of the object relations theory of Melanie Klein and her followers. Similar to Freud, Klein critiques another major notion of individualism, that of the self-contained individual. She did this in part through seeing the child as more basically related to the object world of parents and other caretakers from the earliest age than in classical theory; but much more through her clinical concept of projective identification. A number of Klein's followers, starting with Paula Heimann (1950), then related projective identification to the transferential meanings of induced countertransference reactions in the analyst with analysands who have more severe psychopathology. Kleinian psychoanalysts, such as Heimann and Joseph (1985) among others, often make sensitive reconstructions of subtle psychological aspects of inner images of the parent and/or of the patient's self rooted in the child-parent relationship that are resurfacing in the transference/countertransference interaction between analysand and analyst.

In these notions of projective identification and the induced countertransference, individuals put part of their internal object world into another person, frequently evoking feelings and attitudes in others that are part and parcel of themselves. From the experience of the psychoanalyst, all kinds of feelings and attitudes are integrally related to the analysand's inner world. When this occurs, the psychoanalyst is simultaneously both a separate person and part of the patient, and the patient is both separate and part of the analyst. For both, the self-contained individual no longer exists.

A brief example of this phenomenon is in a paper by Betty Joseph (1985, pp. 62–63), where the presenting analyst in a seminar is quite dissatisfied with the work of a particular session, and in general with her analysis of a quite difficult, schizoid patient. The other members of the seminar then strive to understand more about the patient, but they, too, soon become dissatisfied with their ideas. It finally dawns on them that their very inability to comprehend what is really going on with the patient is central to the transference, and is actually a reflection of the patient's inner world. They see the patient as unconsciously evoking a self-feeling in the analyst and themselves of the patient not being able to make sense of what is going on in her relationship with a highly unempathic mother who pretends she is attuned. They also see the patient as unconsciously evoking a mother-imago in the analyst of seemingly making sense of the patient's inner world when she fundamentally cannot. In either case, the group recognized that they and the analyst's inability to comprehend was far more part of the patient's inner world than their own individual responses.

As Freud first critiqued rational man and then restored rationality and the ideal of rational autonomy through resolving unconscious conflicts, so Klein critiqued the self-contained individual in her clinical concepts and then restored a sense of the separate individual in her formulation of the depressive position. Once projective identifications are therapeutically resolved, individuals become far more aware of their own individualistic subjectivity, and are able to have concern for the subjectivity of others. Thus, Kleinian psychoanalysis also continues the main program of individualism, but in a more humane way.

In spite of Klein and her followers' critique of individualism through their notions of projective identification and the induced countertransference, much of her theory still follows the paradigm of the self-contained individual. What is introjected into the child's internal object world is primarily governed by what has been unconsciously projected onto others. These introjections are then once again projected onto others and reintrojected. In the metapsychology, as contrasted to the clinical narrative, parental figures are gratifiers or frustrators of the drives, and as in classical Freudian theory, family members are never delineated in any psychological depth. Once more in much of the theory, individualism's narrative prevails.

Turning to the highly influential ego psychology of Margaret Mahler (Mahler et al. 1965) in the United States, a psychoanalytic anthropologist, Suzanne Kirschner (1992) argues convincingly that Mahler's emphasis on autonomy, separation, and individuation strongly reflects Protestant (particularly Pietistic and Calvinist Nonconformist) values of individualism involving self-reliance and self-direction. Mahler, in effect, sets the early childhood developmental program for the secular fulfillment of Protestant values in current American individualism that earlier were essential to the Protestant religious worldview.

Kirschner further details Mahler's developmental progression from symbiosis to separation-individuation to having close relationships, while still maintaining a high degree of separateness and an individuated identity, as profoundly reflecting a high Romantic narrative of individualism. In this narrative, there is "a quasi-mystical striving towards a 'higher' reunion of subject and object in which the subject's individuated distinctiveness also is preserved ... " (Kirschner 1992, p. 187). She also sees the strong valuation that ego psychologists such as Spitz (1959) and Mahler put on verbal communication as reflecting both the high Romantic emphasis on individualistic self-expression and the Protestant values of self-reliance and separateness. Nonverbal communication is then pejoratively viewed as occurring at an earlier developmental level of merger and symbiosis.

PSYCHOANALYSIS AS CRITIQUE AND SUPPORT OF INDIVIDUALISM

Within the Freudian opus, there have been important challenges within the last few decades to the self-contained individual paradigm; while paradoxically, these same critics still reflect other of individualism's values while simultaneously delineating essential psychological processes involved in functioning in a culture of individualism. Perhaps no one stands out in this regard so much as Erik Erikson (1950, 1968). On one hand, Erikson, as much or more than any other psychoanalyst, introduced the social, cultural, and historical milieu as essential to a psychoanalytic consideration of the individual. In his psychosocial concept of self-identity, Erikson saw the individual as integrally part of this milieu rather than being self-contained, where roles, values, ideals, and norms of the community profoundly shape and are part of a personal identity.

On the other hand, Erikson, in congruence with the highly perceptive insight of Otto Rank on self-creation (Menaker 1982), framed the most central psychological dimension of American individualism: the self-creation of one's identity. His epigenetic stages of development stressing autonomy and initiative in the childhood years—in certain ways anticipating and paralleling the contributions of Mahler—lay the groundwork for the adolescent struggle to self-create an identity. Erikson's work perceptively charts the stormy seas that are more often than not encountered in this prolonged act of self-creating the identity conflicts, confusions and crises, the frequent need for a moratorium, the occasional syntheses around negative identities, and eventually, it is hoped, the resolution of a positive identity synthesis. All of this occurs within a social milieu where contemporary American culture imposes on the individual an enormous degree of autonomy in the adolescent and young adult years to choose who will be a mate or love partner, what kind of education and vocational training to get, and then what kind of work to do, what social affiliations to make, where to live, and what kind of ideology or value system to develop and become committed to. The often extremely difficult intrapsychic task of the individual adolescent and young adult in American society to integrate these adult commitments with the earlier identifications and self-images developed within the family is the crux of Erikson's elaboration of self-identity and ego-identity.

Another salient psychoanalytic critic of the self-contained individual paradigm is Winnicott in his famous statement, "There is no such thing as a baby." Winnicott (1965) challenges the prevailing norms and models of individualism by referring to the baby's profound dependence and interconnectedness with a mother or mothering person. At the same time, Winnicott's (1951) elaboration of transitional objects and transitional phenomena are essential to the individual developmentally functioning more and more autonomously, with the gradual sharp separation between inner images of self and other that is characteristic of individualism in Northern European and North American societies.

Observations of infants and children from cultures radically different from the Northern European and North American culture belt indicate that where there is a far more prolonged symbiotic mothering in more communal societies, often with multiple mothering, transitional objects are not nearly so much in evidence (Grolnick and Barkin 1978).

As a further step in delineating the psychological processes involved in individualism, Winnicott (1958) depicts the necessity for a child to internalize a comforting maternal presence in order to be comfortably alone and separate. In a similar vein, Winnicott's (1960) emphasis on the true self/false self duality can be considered a secularization of the Protestant values of self-direction where it is essential to be deeply in touch with oneself in order to know what to do morally (Kirschner 1992).

The latest psychoanalytic critique of individualism's emphasis, not only on the self-contained individual but also on secularized Protestant values of independence and self-reliance is that of self psychology and its offshoot, intersubjectivity. Kohut's (1984) emphasis on the dependent need for mirroring, idealizing, and alterego selfobject relationships throughout life for enhancing and maintaining self-esteem and self-cohesion goes completely against individualism's main paradigms and values. Even the stance of empathic inquiry versus objective, rational assessment of the analysand runs counter to Enlightenment reason and the dualism of sharply delineated boundaries between self and other. One can even assert that self psychology specifically addresses the psychopathology—involving problematic selfobject relationships with its resultant deficits in structure-building—that arises from extreme American individualism with its heightened mobility and tenuous relationships.

While these kind of deficits and problems in selfobject relationships can well be present anywhere, they are certainly not as salient in Asian cultures where empathic attunement and culturally supported figures for idealization are so emphasized (Roland 1988). There, other kinds of psychopathology predominate. Similar to self psychology, Stolorow and Atwood (1992) in their theory of intersubjectivity with philosophical roots in phenomenology, address the myth in psychoanalysis of the isolated individual mind, while stressing the interrelationship of subjectivities in all human relationships.

At the same time, in his delineation of the bipolar self, Kohut (1977) begins to spell out in self psychological terms individualism's main trajectory of individuals realizing their potential and individuality in action and relationships throughout life, a secularization of Protestant values. Ambitions are fostered in the early maternal mirroring selfobject relationship, which are then in a tension arc with the goals and ideals later developed through idealizing selfobject relationships, and carried out through skills learned through alter-ego selfobject ones. The initiative, spontaneity, and creativity of a cohesive self are further spelled out. All of this is obviously in accord with individualism's secularization in American life of individual achievement, of self-direction, of fulfilling one's inner potentials, and of expressing one's individuality in the social world.

Moreover, while Kohut takes into account the social surround involving others' selfobject functions for the individual, there is little room in his theory for others to be considered in fuller psychological depth. Thus, the emphasis still resides on the individual, although in his clinical narratives, Kohut often fleshes out the character of parental figures.

PSYCHOANALYSIS AND OTHER CULTURES

With this kind of cultural baggage of individualism, how has psychoanalysis approached persons from cultures that are significantly to radically different from the Northern European and North American culture belt? And what kinds of problems are engendered by using a theory and therapy so rooted in individualism? To answer these questions, one can do well to borrow a leaf from anthropology, which has had decades of experience in investigating different cultures. Anthropologists have interpreted other cultures in three essential ways, each with its own underlying premises: evolutionism, universalism, and relativism (Shweder and Bourne 1984). These three approaches are equally relevant to those few but increasing number of psychoanalysts and psychoanalytic anthropologists who have also worked in radically different cultures; and also, one should add, to psychoanalysts working with patients from significantly different cultures, such as Hispanic, Mediterranean, African-American or Eastern European ones. The theoretical dilemmas involved in each of these three approaches will become readily apparent in the psychoanalytic sphere, and will have to be resolved for a viable theoretical perspective to emerge. These three approaches are most readily observable in psychoanalytic work in radically different cultures such as Asian ones.

Evolutionism as applied to psychoanalysis posits definitive norms for what healthy human nature should be and how it develops in contrast to psychopathology. These norms are invariably a contemporary normative model of the Northern European and North American individualized self as formulated in current psychoanalytic theory, and are assumed to be universal and superior. Others, from cultures significantly or radically different, who do not measure up to this universal normative model are then seen as having inferior psychological development or psychopathology.

An example of the pitfalls of an evolutionist view of human nature is easily seen in Sudhir Kakar's psychoanalytic work on Indians (1978, 1982, 1989, 1991), unfortunately undermining his many perceptive observations. Kakar well recognizes that Indian psychological makeup is modally different from Westerners, but he holds to the basic premises of evolutionism that the theory

of human nature in psychoanalysis is universally normative. By thus subscrib-
ing to these norms, he invariably assesses Indian personality as modally inferior
to the individualism of Westerners. Indians thus emerge in Kakar's analysis as
having an underdeveloped ego, that is, in not having the independent, self-
reliant, self-directing ego of Western individualism; lacking in rational, logical
secondary process thinking, another hallmark value of individualism; as having
vague emotional boundaries between self and other with much less of the self-
other demarcation that is also characteristic of individualism; and as having a
weak conscience or superego because of looking to others for following highly
contextual ethical norms rather than having the categorical imperative of
Western male individualism (Kakar 1978, 105–108, 135–137). Although pro-
testing to the contrary, Kakar (1991) still fundamentally accepts the demystification and secularization of religion in psychoanalytic theory where spiritual
experiences, so valued in Indian society, are reductionistically viewed as a
regression, albeit a positive one, to the early mother-infant relationship.

The second approach toward assessing the universality and variability of the
self in different cultural settings is essentially to search for only the universals.
Differences or variability are seen as only superficially colored by culture. In
universalism, higher order generalities predominate with specific, culture-rich,
thick descriptions of human nature bleached out from consideration.

An example of psychological universalism's limitations is found in the work
of Catherine Ewing (1991), an American psychoanalytic anthropologist who has
worked in Pakistan. She avoided the pitfalls of evolutionism in Kakar's work,
with its value-laden judgments of Indians, by combining the usual cultural relativism of anthropology with the universalism of psychoanalysis—that is, that
while cultures vary enormously, everyone is essentially the same psychologically
everywhere. Ewing as anthropologist well recognized that people behave and
interact very differently in Pakistan than in the United States, attributing this
solely to their very different cultural patterns of interpersonal engagement and
interpersonal autonomy (individualism), respectively. These patterns are given
equal weight, thus avoiding the implicit superiority-inferiority norms of evolutionism. Otherwise, Ewing sees Pakistanis as being no different psychologically
from North Americans—that their self is basically alike. In this regard, her
position is similar to many other psychoanalytic anthropologists.

Ewing utilizes an ego psychology framework to focus on the differentiation
and separateness between inner representations of the self and object. However,
unlike Kakar who views Indians' degree of inner separateness of self and object
representations as less than that of Westerners and therefore inferior, Ewing
simply emphasizes the necessity for separation to occur to avoid psychopathology. She thus extends the usefulness of a psychoanalytic understanding of normality and psychopathology to an Asian culture.

But by being so completely oriented toward the universal, in this case the necessity for separation between inner images of self and object, Ewing does not attend to the different degrees of separation between inner representations of self and object in Pakistanis as contrasted to that of North Americans. She therefore does not see that Pakistanis have an experiential sense of a we-self that much more includes inner images of others of the extended family and community as part of the self than the highly individualistic, more self-contained American I-self. *Thus, modal differences in psychological makeup, or variabilities in the makeup of the self, are disregarded when the focus is on universals.* By being so wedded to psychological universalism, Ewing is unable to relate how the variability in the self in either Pakistanis or North Americans enables them to function well in their radically different cultural and interpersonal patterns, and less well in the patterns of the other.

Moreover, because of disregarding these modal differences in the self, Ewing is unable to see that the norms for psychopathology will also vary. Thus, a problem in separation between inner images of self and other that might be considered severe borderline psychopathology in North Americans might easily be along the neurotic continuum for Pakistanis. Thus, if evolutionism seems to be a sin of commission, then universalism is one of omission.

The third theoretical approach for evaluating the universality and variability of the self in diverse settings is relativism. In relativism, as applied to psychological phenomena, highly differing views of human nature in different cultures are present, but these are viewed within an entirely different framework from Western individualism, each having its own internal consistency and validity related to the indigenous culture and its social patterns. The only problem is that there are no common categories or standards for comparison or criticism across cultures.

Perhaps the best example of relativism in the psychoanalytic realm is that of Takeo Doi (1973, 1986) in his seminal psychoanalytic work in Japan on dependency relationships (*amae*) and a dual self-structure of a public and a highly private self (*omote/ura*). Doi jettisoned psychoanalytic theory because he found its norms of individualism to be too Western-centric, and its categories did not encompass central dimensions of the Japanese psyche. What he did maintain, however, was a psychoanalytic sensibility of exploring the inner world of Japanese and of probing for its developmental antecedents through exploring predominant Japanese linguistic terms. Through elaborating the various facets of Japanese dependency relationships (*amae*) and a dual-self structure (*omote/ura*), Doi was able to formulate a culturally variable psychology of Japanese in many of its important configurations that differs radically from the psychoanalytic self of Northern European and North American individualism.

Doi's basic theoretical approach differs greatly from the evolutionism of

Kakar and the universalism of Ewing in his focusing on the variabilities of the Japanese self, variabilities viewed as on a par with those of individualism. However, after elaborating this modal psychology of the Japanese, Doi searches for the universality of this kind of (*amae*) dependency in North Americans. He indeed finds it to be present, but in such diminished form due to the Northern European and North American cultural emphasis on self-reliance, that the *amae* kind of dependency relationship is only conceptualized in psychoanalytic theory in Balint's concept of passive object love. Thus, psychological variabilities hardly present in Northern European and North American psychological makeup will simply not be a salient part of psychoanalytic theory. And then the theory without this kind of category will completely either miss this variability in others or see it as inferior or psychopathological.

A profound insight of Doi's approach is to move from the exploration of psychological variabilities in a given culture (i.e. the Japanese) to formulating some of these variabilities, such as the *amae* dependency relationship, as a universal category present in all cultures, but manifesting itself in significantly different patterns and configurations from the Japanese without positing any value-laden universal norms. One can see that psychoanalysis, itself, has actually developed from the extensive investigation into the psychological variability of Northern Europeans and North Americans to a formulation of universal categories. Only Western psychoanalysts, without the comparative experience of Doi in working in different civilizations, have not realized how much of the elaboration of the contents and norms of various psychoanalytic categories, as well as the configurations of them, almost completely involve the particular variabilities of the highly individualistic Northern European and North American self.

What are the limitations of Doi's psychoanalytic relativism? Most salient is his complete jettison of psychoanalytic theory. While this was initially highly liberating to enable Doi to formulate an indigenous psychology of the Japanese, one related to Japanese cultural and social patterns, we are left with an essentially atheoretical psychoanalytic approach with almost no categories that cut across cultures.

What are the drawbacks of Doi's atheoretical psychoanalytic approach? First of all, Doi only explicitly but not implicitly puts aside psychoanalytic categories. He was not only drawing on his cross-civilizational clinical experience in Japan and the United States, but also on North American ego psychology which so emphasizes the separation-individuation process. In his elaborating the psychology of *amae*, Doi was implicitly contrasting this kind of dependency relationship with the North American psychoanalytic stress on individuation, autonomy, and inner separation. And in his elaboration of the Japanese dual-self structure, he utilized another dimension of ego psychology that explores the organization of the self. Ironically, one critique of Doi's work is that he carried over a too individualistic set from Western psychoanalysis to the understanding of *amae* dependency relationships, which are better seen in particular contextualized relationships and situations (Taketomo 1985).

In a more specific way, Doi's relativism, without the benefit of certain psychoanalytic categories and comparative work in other Asian cultures, limits some of his clinical understanding. Doi recognizes the psychopathological forms of *amae*, such as a demanding entitlement. Doi sees this primarily as a result of frustrated *amae* dependency in childhood. However, Indians, who have much of the same *amae* dependency psychology as Japanese, very rarely have any demanding entitlement, even when dependency needs are deeply frustrated in childhood.

To understand this clinical phenomena, one must take into account not only the childhood *amae* relationship, but also two other factors: a very strict conscience and the presence or absence of maternal empathic attunement with the child. I found demanding entitlement to result from childhood situations where the child has indeed been very dependent on his mother, although not always frustrated in his or her dependency needs; and has also internalized her strong expectations for very high standards of performance, but in the presence of poor maternal attunement with his inner nature. The lack of gratification was more often not from the *amae* relationship, but rather from the lack of maternal empathy.

At the point that Doi developed his theory of *amae*, self psychology had not yet been formulated with its strong emphasis on the maternal mirroring relationship. Doi, therefore, was unable to use this category since it was not yet formulated, and in my view, limited his clinical understanding. *My point is, that in the psychoanalytic relativism that Doi developed, general psychoanalytic categories and assumptions are implicitly used, misused, countered, or are conspicuous by their absence.* To the extent that these universals are not acknowledged, they enter unseen into psychoanalytic relativism for better and worse.

Thus, while Doi's work leaves us with a much fuller understanding of the variability of the self in Japanese, and with a couple of new universal categories minimally present in Westerners, we have no comprehensive theory or sets of categories to evaluate both universality and variability in human nature across cultures. This becomes particularly important as it would be highly useful, for instance, to compare the configurations of the Japanese self with those of other Asians, who are much closer to the Japanese in psychological makeup than are Northern Europeans/North Americans, or even with the self of Hispanics.

It is evident then that evolutionism, universalism, and relativism each have their own problematics and pitfalls in the dilemma of using current individualistically-oriented psychoanalytic theory across cultures. Nevertheless, variability, universals, and normality-psychopathology are essential issues in assessing the self across cultures. Therefore, it is imperative to develop newer modes of resolving these issues.

TOWARD A COMPARATIVE PSYCHOANALYSIS

To evolve a comparative psychoanalysis suitable for patients across a wide variety of cultures, a new theoretical approach is necessary. A new paradigm (Roland 1988) involves using the varied categories of the psychoanalytic theory of personality and therapy from a variety of psychoanalytic models: e.g. superego and ego-ideal, ego boundaries, developmental stages, selfobject relationships, self and object representations, self-identity, internal object world, affects and drives, transference, resistance, and dream-analysis among others. To use them, one must decontextualize them of their current Northern European and North American variability as now elaborated in psychoanalytic theory; that is, of their content and norms of normality/psychopathology as related to the culture of individualism. One then proceeds to recontextualize them from the clinical data of persons from significantly or radically different cultures, where the new contents and norms of each category are then integrated with cultural, social, and historical contexts of that culture. This approach would also add new universal categories from psychoanalytic work in radically different cultures, such as Doi has done with *amae* dependency relationships and the *omote/ura* dual self-structure.

Most importantly, to capture the true variability of human nature, a further step is taken to put these recontextualized categories into their unique configurations or organizations of the self in different cultures. Similar to a painting, whether representational or abstract, issues of values between darks and lights, color harmonies and contrasts, line, texture, compositional structure, dissonances, and such must all achieve a unique balance or configuration. Artists are well aware of this, and so must psychoanalysts be to understand the universality and variability of the self across cultures.

As a simple example of this new approach, one can take the category of ego boundaries. In a North American context, current psychoanalytic norms call for outer ego boundaries between self and object to be relatively firm so that a person can have close relationships without being involved in merger experiences, which constitute psychopathology. Whereas inner ego boundaries should be somewhat flexible so that a person is in touch with inner feelings, fantasies, and impulses, but are not flooded by them. In cultures different from those governed by individualism, such as India and Japan, one easily observes that outer ego boundaries are far more permeable and vaguer than in North Americans in the context of one's own people (Indian extended family, community, and friends) and insider relationships (*uchi*) in Japanese family, friends, and intimate group relationships. This is in keeping with Indian and Japanese close emotional enmeshment in family, group, and community—the Japanese variant having even vaguer outer boundaries than Indians. However, in their outsider relationships, both Indians and Japanese will have much firmer boundaries.

But balancing this permeable outer boundary with semi-merger experiences with others is an inner boundary of a highly private, secret self—in Japanese more secretive than in Indians—a repository of individuality that is rarely found in North Americans, where individuality is characteristically expressed in the social world.[1] The innermost ego boundary varies even more between Indians and Japanese, the former usually being far more in touch with their inner world than the latter and even somewhat more so than North Americans. This is due to cultural norms where Japanese have a far more perfectionistic ego-ideal and rigorous social etiquette than Indians and North Americans, and so are less in touch with themselves. Whereas Indian culture, while insisting on the behavioral observation of proper social etiquette in family and group hierarchical relationships, gives considerable lattitude to a wide variety of personal ideas, feelings, and fantasies. Thus, North Americans, Indians, and Japanese all have the universal category of ego boundaries; but this category has to be recontextualized for Indians and Japanese from the usual norms of psychoanalysis, adding a new category of an inner boundary involving a highly private self. Finally, outer and inner boundaries for North Americans, Indians, and Japanese have different configurations for each.

From the perspective of normality/psychopathology, norms vary considerably from one configuration of ego boundaries to another. Merger or semi-merger experiences that would be considered borderline, if not more severe psychopathology for most North Americans, are usually in the neurotic range for Japanese. By the same token, the relatively firm outer ego boundary normal for North Americans is highly maladaptive for Japanese and Indians in their emotionally enmeshed insider relationships, and is therefore neurotic.

Other categories also enter into unique balances and configurations in the overall organization of the self in a given culture area. Modes of communication such as verbal and nonverbal clearly vary with the variability of ego boundaries and the expression of individuality. The firmer the outer ego boundary, as in North Americans, the more reliance there is on verbal communication, as if to balance and bridge the separateness of autonomous individuals, as well as to implement their individuality in the social world.

Whereas, when there is a highly developed private self that is the locus of individuality and balances semi-merger experiences in longlasting family and group relationships, nonverbal empathic sensing becomes salient. And the more the private self becomes highly secretive and not to be intruded upon, as in the Japanese compared to Indians, the more finely tuned is empathic, intuitive sensing. Verbal expression is then more used to observe proper social etiquette in the hierarchical relationships. Thus, these variabilities of ego boundaries, individuality, and modes of communication enter into special balances with each other, and form unique configurations in persons from radically different cultures.

A new paradigm would also incorporate the sociohistorical experiences of persons from a given civilization as these have become internalized within the psyche. Certainly, the psychological makeup of women in contemporary North America is profoundly related to the Women's Movement and Feminism over the last thirty years, which both incorporates and critiques the values of individualism hitherto reserved for men. Whereas, both Indians and Japanese over the last century or two have become increasingly exposed to the contrasting values of Western individualism, which has had profound psychological effects. And when these values have been posited in the sociopolitical context of colonialism, which is so denigrating to indigenous cultures, the psychological effects can be devastating.

The new paradigm would also include other psychological phenomena that psychoanalysis with its Enlightenment philosophical heritage looks askance at. This would involve the realm of spiritual experiences and disciplines, which, with but the rarest of exceptions, psychoanalysts from Freud on have consistently relegated to the stage of infant-mother symbiotic, merger states, if not to other forms of psychopathology. Even more disparaged than the spiritual by psychoanalysts is the magic-cosmic world of personal destiny, which patients from a variety of cultures are involved in in a number of ways, such as astrology, palmistry, the spirit world, psychics and mediums, and rituals among others. This is anathema to most psychoanalysts. Psychoanalysts coming from a tradition of the self-contained, rational individual simply do not appreciate that patients outside of the Northern European and North American culture belt have a self that is not only far more enmeshed and embedded in an extended family/group/ community context—or what is now being referred to as sociocentric/organic societies (Markus and Kitayama 1991)—but often also in a world of invisible influences and spirits, as well as sometimes in the spiritual. To assume a denigrating attitude toward these psychological phenomena will be to miss a major portion of many of these patients' psyche.

SUMMARY

A brief vignette first illustrates the profound effects of highly varying views of the self from Western individualism and Japanese hierarchical group culture in the simplest of clinical situations. The paper then succinctly traces the historical roots of individualism in Western culture beginning with the Reformation, through the Social Contract philosophers, the Jurists, Enlightenment philosophers, economic theorists, to Romanticism. The development of psychoanalysis is then related to this progression of individualism. From Freud on, major psychoanalysts such as Klein, Erikson, Winnicott, and Kohut have entered into a dialogue and dialectic with individualism, critiquing one or another major aspect of individualism, delineating central psychological processes involved in functioning in a culture of individualism, and unreflectingly incorporating many of the other values and assumptions of individualism.

The paper then delves into the problematics of applying such a highly individualistic psychology, such as psychoanalysis, to persons from radically different cultures such as India, Pakistan, and Japan. It does this by examining the work of Sudhir Kakar, Catherine Ewing, and Takeo Doi through the theories of evolutionism, universalism, and relativism, as initially elaborated in anthropology and now adapted to psychoanalysis. In spite of the contributions of each of these cross-cultural psychoanalysts, each of their approaches has serious theoretical problems. The author then endeavors to outline a new psychoanalytic paradigm that fully takes into account issues of universality, variability, and normality/psychopathology, as well as historical change and the dimension of the spiritual and magic-cosmic.

ENDNOTE

1. One Japanese psychoanalyst, Akahisa Kondo, stated that "our individuality lies in what we do not say" (pers. com.).

Part II

The Asian and American Interface

Chapter Two

Walking the Bicultural Tightrope

Indians in the United States

INTRODUCTION

As a psychoanalyst who has worked with over twenty-five Indian patients in India and New York City for over twenty years, and who has interviewed other Indians here in psychoanalytic therapy and American life-style relationships (Roland 1988, pp. 195–206), I would like to delineate the cultural/psychological interface between Indian-Americans and Americans of European origin. I shall particularly focus on the dissonances and polarities between subtle Indian ways of social relatedness and internalized cultural values, and the American culture of individualism; and on the interface between these radically different life styles and kinds of ethos where misunderstandings from either side can easily ensue.

As Indian-Americans walk the bicultural tightrope over extended periods of time, they gradually develop a bicultural self, or an expanded identity encompassing both sides of the cultural divide.[1] Since second-generation Indian-Americans walk this tightrope in another way from their parents, they develop a significantly different bicultural self. There is also variation between genders in their reactions to American individualism, although there is frequently considerable overlap on this cross-cultural dimension.

Before delving into these areas of dissonance and potential conflict, I must stress the positives that have enabled the almost one million Indians to become the most financially successful immigrant community in the United States. There are the obvious facts that when the liberalized immigration law of 1965 opened up the United States to a much greater Asian immigration, those who came from India were for the most part the urban educated elite,[2] over two-thirds college educated (well over double the average of other Americans), most of whom speak English fluently.[3] Originally, most of those who immigrated here were engineers and scientists,[4] M.B.A.s from the Indian Institutes of Management, businessmen, and physicians, who now constitute approximately 10 percent of physicians in the United States, with over 2,500 Indian psychiatrists here, more than in India (pers. com. Prakash Desai). They are usually from the upper castes when Hindu, and from the middle- and often upper-middle classes whether Hindu, Moslem, Christian, or Zoroastrian.

Since United States immigration policy currently stresses family ties over occupation, the Indian immigration since the 1980s is much more comprised of relatives of the original immigrants, the relatives not as highly educated, or when college-educated, not having the same kind of scientific or business or medical background. They, therefore, usually end up in blue-collar jobs, such as driving taxis or working at low wages in newsstands, food stores, or gas stations, often owned by their more well-to-do relatives or others of their community. With this increased immigration, Indians have now reached sufficient numbers in the United States to have well-developed communities in the major cities or their suburbs, often with temples, mosques, and churches of their own, that are increasingly patronized by Indians from a particular region or community. They also have their own community and national organizations, as well as newspapers, magazines, and television programs. Since the Indian community in the United States has become so well developed, it is increasingly the object of studies by social scientists, many of whom are Indian.[5]

PSYCHOLOGICAL CAPACITIES FOR ADAPTATION

But beyond these considerable educational skills and a certain entreprenurial or adventuresome spirit in those originally coming to the United States, Indians bring particular psychological capacities to aid in adaptation to what is a radically different culture here. The first is a radar sensitivity to others and to the norms of a given situation. I have seen Indian friends, women and men, immediately sense what is proper in an unfamiliar situation.

One woman I interviewed, Manisha, reported that she was complimented by her American college friends for becoming so Americanized so quickly. Manisha had immediately sensed the importance of participating in a number of activities at her excellent, small, liberal arts college—in complete contrast to her college in New Delhi; but then she recuperated each month by spending all day in bed. Her immersion in college activities stemmed more from a sensing of the community's norms than from the motivation of other students to actualize their abilities and individuality in activities and in the social world, a cardinal principle of American individualism.

Another ingrained psychological orientation that enables Indians to adapt easily is an ability to contextualize situations. That is, one can follow different norms in greatly varying groups or situations without the kind of inner conflict it would generate in most other Americans, who are more oriented toward being consistent. The Indian conscience or ego-ideal for both women and men is to act properly according to the context of the time, the place, the nature of the persons involved, the hierarchical relationship, and such, and to be sensitive to the esteem of the other. This obviously relates to the Hindu concept of *dharma*, which calls for proper moral behavior to be far more oriented to varying contexts of relationships than the Western categorical imperative, which calls for universal principles of morality in all situations. *Dharma* is even more contextual than the conscience of American women, which tends to be more relational and situational than that of American men in moral behavior (Gilligan 1980).

Thus, Indian-Americans are able to adhere to extended family hierarchical norms and ways of relating at home, while acting and adapting to very different American values of individualism at work or at the university. There is far less need of a relatively consistent identity that is a central psychological dimension of American individualism. However, as they begin to internalize American norms and ways of relating, the flagrant contrasts in values and social patterns can cause considerable inner distress in the development of a bicultural self.[6]

One Indian colleague, Veena, recounted that she is a member of two private psychoanalytic seminars with radically different orientations as well as leaders, one being quite traditional, the other highly innovative. Veena feels perfectly comfortable in both groups, with no conflict whatsoever, and learns a great deal in each. No American psychoanalyst I know of, woman or man, would ever consider being a member of these two particular seminars simultaneously, because they would experience them as far too dissonant and too disruptive of a consistent inner professional identity. Since each group's members would probably disapprove of her being in the other group, Veena keeps her participation in the other group secret in a highly private self, typical of Indians and other Asians. While Veena's ego-ideal could successfully encompass these highly varying, valuable group experiences, she, nevertheless, experienced a long, difficult struggle to feel comfortable on both sides of the cultural divide of being Indian and American.

PSYCHOSOCIAL DIMENSIONS OF HIERARCHICAL RELATIONSHIPS

To understand the areas of cultural interface that can become dissonant, problematic, or conflictual, one has to appreciate the psychosocial dimensions of Indian family and group hierarchical relationships. These differ radically from American individualism with its egalitarian and contractual norms, and its ethos of the self-reliant, self-directed, autonomous individual who is verbally assertive. I shall focus on three psychosocial dimensions of hierarchy and their interactions, which I have previously delineated much more fully (Roland 1988, pp. 212–223), as they are central not only to understand the dissonant and conflictual in the cultural/psychological interface, but also central aspects of psychoanalytic therapy with Asians.

Formal Hierarchical Relationships

The most easily observable psychosocial dimension is formal hierarchical relationships based on seniority or age order and gender for all members of the extended family and other groups as well. This establishes a clear-cut hierarchy between older and younger of both sexes, and not only between brothers but also between brothers' wives based on their husband's position, and between women and men, the male gender occupying the superior social position in most of India.[7]

The difference between deeply ingrained Indian hierarchical and American egalitarian values showed up clearly in a study done by Jai Sinha (1980), a social psychologist, on Indian and American college students. A number of pairs of Indian and American students were given a task to accomplish, and at periodic intervals were asked to write down how they were working together on the task. The Indian students immediately sensed which of the pair was more knowledgeable at the task, and then formed a hierarchical relationship where the more skilled was influential over the other. This contrasted sharply with American students who clearly expressed in their interaction that neither would allow the other to have any undue influence.

Much more central psychologically in Indian hierarchy are the reciprocal expectations for attitudes and responsibilities, and for a well-delineated social etiquette in both subordinates and superiors. Whether in the extended family, or at work, or in other social settings, deference, respect, loyalty, obedience, and receptivity to the expectations of the superior are deeply ingrained in the subordinate. Whereas the superior in an emotionally involved relationship with the subordinate is to be responsible, empathically concerned, and nurturing, freely giving advice, guidance, and direction to the subordinate while being highly tactful in criticizing a subordinate's mistakes. Both subordinates and superiors enhance each other's esteem through the latter silently mirroring approval of the subordinate's proper behavior, while subordinates are always respectful of the superior. Neither is to threaten the esteem of the other, and in fact, enhancing the other's esteem is often more important than the truth of any given matter.

If these reciprocal expectations are not fulfilled by either superior or subordinate, it can occasion considerable hurt and anger in the other. The subordinate in particular, as clearly evidenced in therapy sessions, can feel deeply hurt and enraged at a nonnurturing superior while still having to observe the proper social etiquette in their relationship. Within the extended family, there is an emphasis on solidarity and cooperation, mutual affection and understanding, and maintaining harmonious relationships. Considerable efforts are made to mediate, reconcile, and resolve the inevitable problems and conflicts that do arise. Many of these familial reciprocal hierarchical expectations are then extended to others outside of the family.

What happens when these Indian expectations and ways of relating interface with North American hierarchical relationships? In the United States, hierarchical relationships are primarily governed by contractual rights and obligations, where an emotionally connected, nurturing relationship may on occasion happen, but is not particularly expected. Subordinates are often given far more leeway to do things on their own, and to question and even challenge a superior's viewpoint, especially in a university setting. At the same time, superiors are often forthrightly critical of subordinate's mistakes, the latter being expected to take it in stride.

For Indians and other Asians, forthright criticism from an American boss at work is usually felt as very hurtful to one's esteem. Indians and other Asians are simply not used to this degree of bluntness and lack of consideration for their self-regard. Indian managers in financial institutions on Wall Street have related how painful the direct criticism is to them; and a Japanese woman, Yoshiko, came for therapy because she became intensely upset over her boss's confronting her on her minimal number of mistakes (see Chapter Five).

Second, Indians and other Asians can often experience American bosses and college administrators as being unconcerned, nonnurturing, or not taking proper responsibility for them. One highly trained Pakistani man with a law degree and an M.B.A. from Ivy League universities reacted bitterly when his boss did not offer him a raise after he worked diligently and competently for a year. He learned that he had to ask for this himself; when he did, he received it. But he was aghast over his superior not taking responsibility for getting him the raise without his having to request it. In psychoanalytic therapy, I have generally worked with Indian men patients to get them to gravitate to positions where there is an interested boss with whom they can be involved, rather than being in a situation where they are left to their own devices. Unlike some other American patients who do quite well on their own, these Indian men usually do far better in an involved relationship with a superior.

In other cases, Indian-Americans in good positions within the Wall Street financial world reported that sometimes they ask advice from their boss on how to do something, even though they well know how to handle the task. They are simply trying to have their American supervisors become more nurturing toward them. But the supervisors usually react as if they believe that these Indian employees must not be very competent if they need help on such matters. They thus form a lower opinion of Indian-Americans, which makes it more difficult for them to advance.

In a number of different settings, other Americans may see Indian-Americans as being too compliant and passive, completely mistaking deference, self-effacement, and receptivity for passivity and unassertiveness. In a general way, this misunderstanding constantly happens in college classrooms. Other American professors misperceive the quietness of Indian-Americans and other Asian-Americans as being unassertive or verbally inhibited, when they are really conveying respect and deference to the instructor. They are there to learn from the instructor, not to voice their own opinions.

Within my own psychoanalytic institute, a highly competent and assertive Indian-American woman, who was the director of a large mental health clinic with considerable responsibilites, was initially not allowed to graduate from the training program because an evaluation committee misinterpreted her not speaking up in classes and seminars as pathological passivity, rather than being properly deferent. They believed she needed further psychoanalysis to work out her problem of passivity. In another instance, an Indian woman graduate student, who was apparently noted for her articulateness and assertiveness in college in Bombay, confided to me that she found it extremely difficult to question and challenge her American mentor, even when invited to do so. "We are brought up to be obedient."

Fourth, in Indian familial hierarchical relationships, children and adolescents are raised to be receptive and dependent on the direction, guidance, and advice of family elders on all kinds of matters, large and small, rather than to assert their own choices or make their own decisions. Indian women and men patients have in fact expressed considerable anger in session when they felt a family member, such as an older brother, has let them down. On the other hand, a cardinal principle of American individualism is to be self-directed and autonomously choose and make decisions on all kinds of matters, including major ones such as marriage and career, and more to be influenced by extra-familial peer groups than by parents.

Indian immigrant patients, both women and men, even when quite successful in jobs, such as an internationally recognized woman scientist, have strongly expressed in sessions that they were not brought up to be independent. That is, they often find living in America to be a considerable strain when it is incumbent upon them to make all kinds of decisions by themselves, and then to show initiative and assertiveness to get what they want. This is not to say that many Indians cannot do this. But it goes against the grain of deeply etched expectations of the extended family taking much more care of their various needs.

It is perhaps particularly in this area that Indians, women and men, gradually begin to acquire a bicultural self. They are able to become more autonomous in decision-making, and more openly assertive and display more initiative and independence than is characteristic in an Indian setting, while still retaining much of the sensitivity, emotional connectedness, and involvement in hierarchical relationships in the Indian family and groups. They move toward much greater individualization and more of a separate identity, while still maintaining various facets of a familial self. From self-reports, Indian women professionals can have an even more difficult time acquiring the necessary assertiveness, competitiveness, and verbal articulateness to function successfully in an American work environment since they were brought up to be modest and self-effacing, particularly in public. It is the varying degrees and modes of this kind of integration that I term a bicultural self (the phrase I first heard expressed by an Indian professor at a conference), which is usually developed with varying degrees of strain, anguish, and conflict.

One woman married to an American related how it took her over ten years of being in New York City to finally feel comfortable in the presence of both her Indian relatives and other American family and friends. She felt it was like having two different selves to be with Indians and other Americans, selves that were so opposite in inner feeling as to be dissonant with each other. After this prolonged period of time, she could easily switch between one self and the other.[8] While another Indian woman, living in an Indian family here but working in a career, related that for some time she had considerable stress in being able to be assertive enough in her American work setting. However, when she returned home to India for a visit, she was seen as being overly selfish and self-centered. She had become too Americanized in her family's eyes. She had thus obviously imbibed a certain degree of American individualism in developing a bicultural self.

In Indian-American marriages, there can also be considerable dissonance between Indian cultural notions of hierarchy and American egalitarianism. One Indian man married to an American woman experienced her lack of deference to him as her being quite rejecting of him, whereas Indian women married to American men have interpreted their husbands' egalitarian stance that they both negotiate decisions together as equals as his not taking proper responsibility in the relationship.

Hierarchy by Personal Qualities

The second major psychosocial dimension of Indian hierarchical relationships is hierarchy by the personal qualities of the person. Indians and other Asians make quiet inner distinctions between who is a superior in the social hierarchy, and who has truly superior qualities. Both can well be the same person, but not necessarily. A son or daughter, a younger brother, a wife, a servant, a sister-in-law married to a younger brother may well have superior qualities even though being lower in the social hierarchy. Great respect, idealization, and veneration are reserved for truly superior persons, with a wish to be as close as possible to that person. A level of complexity is created when the superior person is lower in the social hierarchy but must still be properly deferent and obedient to those in superior positions.

In one case, an Indian graduate student was appalled by the way her fellow American graduate students were denigrating some of their professors who were quite mediocre. She clearly recognized as they did that these professors were not very good. But she still felt strongly that they should be respected. In another case, some Indians on Wall Street felt very frustrated by their corporate bosses who were clearly not as intelligent or well-educated as themselves; but they still acted in a respectful, deferent way to them.

Hierarchical Intimacy Relationships

Central to understanding Indian and other Asian familial hierarchical relationships is the psychosocial dimension of emotional intimacy. These highly personalized, emotional intimacy relationships within the extended family are characterized by an intense emotional connectedness with a constant flow of affect and responsiveness between persons; by a strong mutual caring, dependence and interdependence, with a greatly heightened, reciprocal asking and giving in an emotional atmosphere usually of affection and warmth; and by a highly empathic, nonverbal sensitivity to one another's feelings and needs without the other having to verbalize them. When these intense expectations are not fulfilled, considerable hurt and anger are experienced. However, since emotional connectedness to others is always central, any disruptive feelings such as anger is usually contained or defended against through a variety of unconscious defense mechanisms in order not to disturb the relationship.

It is in this area of hierarchical intimacy relationships that Indians and other Asians develop an experiential sense of a we-self, in contrast to a more Western individualistic I-self with a sharp inner differentiation between images of I and you. Outer ego boundaries are developed that are much more permeable to others in semi-merger relationships while maintaining a highly private self, as contrasted to the more self-contained outer boundary of other Americans who have less of a private self. Indians tend to be empathically attuned to the feelings and moods, needs and wishes of the other, much more so than to one's own; but one reciprocally expects the other to be fully attuned to oneself without having to verbally express one's needs. This takes place in the context of a libidinous wishing, wanting self that feels free to be dependent on a nurturing other, while reciprocating in kind. These are some of the salient dimensions of what I have termed, a familial self (Roland 1988, pp. 223–274).

It is also in this arena of hierarchical intimacy relationships that some of the most striking differences on the cultural/ psychological interface with other Americans occur. Indians comment on the low level of concerned empathy in American-style relationships, to the relative insensitivity—at least in terms of what they expect—to each other's self-esteem. Warmly nurturing, empathic attitudes that are so central to Indian close-knit relationships are often experienced in short supply here; so much so that one Indian woman living mainly in American life-style relationships returns home to India periodically for emotional refueling. In Indians, the tremendous giving and taking or constant mutual indulgence of each other with an emotional flow back and forth of warmth and concern, and a sense of we-ness and partial merger is not easily experienced in their American relationships where the individual is much more self-contained. One Indian psychologist termed this a convenience/inconvenience continuum, with Americans much more oriented toward the convenience end of the continuum, and with Indians accepting the inconvenience in the constant giving and taking of intimacy relationships.

To give an example of the convenience/inconvenience continuum, an Indian friend related how he always had to go to JFK airport in New York City to meet any arriving relatives or friends. Even though his home was an easy twenty minutes taxi ride from the airport and he had to take an hour and a half subway ride to get there, he felt he could not ask them to take a taxi without meeting them. Most Americans would simply have given their visitors their address and told them to take a cab.

On the other side of the interface, how do Americans experience Indian asking and desires for intimacy? To understand American reactions, one must delve into a very subtle emotional exchange that goes on all the time in Indian and other Asian hierarchical relationships, as well as into the nature of insider and outsider relationships in India and the Confucian East Asian cultures— "one's own people" versus "others" in India, and *uchi* and *soto* in Japan. This kind of emotional exchange I have found is rarely understood by Westerners.

In the more intimate hierarchical relationships of family and community in India, and even of the long-time work and other groups in Japan, in what would be termed insider relationships, there is a tremendous amount of dependency of the subordinate on the superior (see Doi 1973; Kakar 1978; and Roland 1988), and a great deal of nonverbal asking of the superior to be empathic and nurturing to the subordinate—in complete contrast to predominant American ideals of independence and self-sufficiency. Psychologically speaking, dependent asking is actually a giving in, enhancing the esteem of the other by establishing the other as the hierarchical superior who can fulfill his or her ego-ideal of being the nurturing superior. This is as true of men in the hierarchy as women, as Indian and other Asian men have strong components of the maternal-feminine through long-term, closely enmeshed relationships with their mothers. Thus, there is a subtle exchange of dependency for esteem in these hierarchical relationships when all is working well, which doesn't always happen.

In outsider relationships, by Confucian norms, Japanese and other East Asians are highly restrained in their dependency needs and requests, instead being governed by whatever formal etiquette is appropriate. In considerable contrast, Indians are constantly testing the possibilities of intimacy and of emotional exchange by being dependent and making many requests in their outsider relationships. They hope to convert these to insider ones and to bring the relationship into the orbit of the extended family or one's own people (pers. com. B. K. Ramanujam).

Americans of European origin do not experience these requests as enhancing their own self-esteem. Rather, many of whom I have talked with complain of the requests as an infringement on their autonomy and privacy, and can become quite irritated, perceiving Indians as being overly aggressive or manipulative. One telling example of intercultural misunderstanding is when I referred Sunil, a close Indian friend's husband, who was looking for a corporate position to Carl, a good friend of ours who was highly placed in a large corporation. Sunil, who had just immigrated, had excellent qualifications and is an unusually fine person. And indeed, Carl upon interviewing him told us how impressed he was and how much he liked Sunil. He told Sunil he would be in touch with him as soon as any suitable position became available. But a few months later, Carl expressed considerable annoyance to us at Sunil's phoning every week. For Carl, it was an intrusion on his time and privacy. For Sunil, it was only natural to call Carl weekly since Sunil's family were close friends of ours and I had introduced Sunil to another of our friends from a family with whom we were intimate. There was obviously profound cultural misunderstandings on both their parts that contributed to an adverse reaction by Carl.

Another example similar to the one of Sunil and Carl was related to me by my wife, who is a professor of history at Pace University. A few weeks before a Christmas vacation, an Indian-American student of hers came to her office to request taking the final examination a week before she generally gives it, as he and his family were flying back to India for a visit a few days before the regular date of the exam. My wife assented to his request. The following day he returned, mentioning that he had made the same request to two of his other professors, but they had turned him down. Could she speak to these two other professors to get them to change their mind?

It is just this kind of request that other Americans find so hard to deal with. It is beyond the boundaries of what other students would ever ask. Most American instructors would simply get incensed at the request, see it as manipulative, and would usually convey their feelings about it, as well as saying, no. My wife, however, realized that he saw her as a nurturing, familial-type elder who had granted his first request, and upon whom he could now be dependent. By seeing his need for a supportive hierarchical relationship, she was able to respond in a friendly way, simply conveying that she was unable to contact the other professors.

I have learned from an informant, Christine Futia, who is a senior consultant in a corporation and is highly attuned to Indians, that this heightened asking-giving can create problems in a corporate setting. Compared to American men, Indian-American men will be tremendously generous and flowery in their promises of what they will do. For the Indian man there are implicit cultural understandings that many of these promises are not meant to be kept, but are given in a spirit of goodwill to facilitate the intimacy relationship. American businessmen do not have these implicit cultural understandings, nor are they particularly oriented to intimacy relationships in this manner, so that they react negatively to promises that are made but not kept.

Other areas of cultural misunderstandings Christine cited involve the maneuvering and bargaining for what one wants that is a usual part of Indian life, but which is looked upon askance by American corporate managers. They misinterpret this as Indian-American men being overly shrewd and sneaky. Also involved is the normal Indian attempt to openly develop a supportive personal network. Since the ethos in American corporations is for loyalty to the corporation with any personal power base being developed on the sly, other Americans look down on this. These cultural misunderstandings then result in Indian-American men having to prove themselves far more than would be the case for other Americans, Indians thus experiencing prejudice against themselves, and finding it difficult to advance up the corporate ladder.

EXPERIENTIAL SENSE OF SELF

As I have previously delineated (Roland 1988, pp. 203–204), even high achieving Indians are able to spend endless hours sitting around and being absorbed in their own thoughts, feelings, and fantasies, or to chat casually with others, or just putter around. This can be done without guilt or any urge toward a goal-oriented activity, which is so characteristic of other Americans who constantly assert and consolidate their identity through activity and work. In other words, Indians are far more content to be, without constantly striving to become an individualized entity and identity.

However, an Indian-American who has lived in this country for some time can sometimes be caught between these highly different modes of being and becoming. From out of the blue I received a phone call one day from a middle-aged, married Indian woman, Sushma, who with her husband and three children lived in Ohio. She had read my book and felt perhaps that I could help her through some phone sessions. She had actually had previous psychoanalytic therapy with an American woman psychoanalyst, who had been of considerable assistance to Sushma, enabling her to go on for a graduate degree in literature and slowly develop an academic career. Although Sushma was from an elite, highly educated South Indian family and had gone to an excellent college in India, she needed help in developing an assertive, goal-oriented side of herself in the United States. Her husband, a highly successful corporate executive, fully backed her as she worked out cultivating this side of herself.

Now, however, she was facing another conflict which she felt needed a therapist who understood more of the Indian side of herself. What she initially complained about was her husband coming home from work and just being content to be and putter around. She looked with disdain upon him when he was like that, wondered how much longer she could go on living with someone like him, and was terribly upset about the relationship. In later phone sessions, she gradually told me about her previous therapy, graduate school, and part-time career, and how satisfying it was to be successfully assertive in her work.

But what also emerged was that her mother-in-law and three older sisters-in-law, her husband's sisters, were about to return to India after a six month stay. Sushma got along extremely well with them. And when she was with them, she was quite content just to be and relate to them, chatting endlessly together without any ambition or goal in mind. In effect, Sushma was caught between her original Indian and acquired American ways of being. When she was in her American assertive, goal-oriented mode, she denigrated this Indian way of being in herself, and therefore in her husband through projective identification. As I interpreted this, and as we talked about it being quite acceptable for her as an Indian here just to be, as well as being goal-oriented when she wanted, her intense discontent with her husband dissipated. In these few phone sessions, Sushma was able to resolve a crisis in walking the bicultural tightrope over being and becoming, and therefore in her expanding, bicultural self.

BICULTURAL SELF OF SECOND GENERATION INDIAN-AMERICANS

The nature of the bicultural self in second generation Indian-Americans differs significantly, if not dramatically, from the immigrant generation. An individualized self (Roland 1988, Chapter One), congruent with the predominant ethos and social patterns of American individualism, is much more firmly anchored in the second generation. Being educated in American schools and growing up in an American social milieu, the second generation seems much more at ease in being self-directed in decision-making, in being self-assertive and competitive, in being verbally expressive, and in general, negotiating well the social ways of American life.

At the same time, the Indian side of a bicultural self is also deeply internalized from growing up in an Indian family. The second generation also has a strong sense of emotional connectedness, enmeshment, and interdependence in the family with a we-self; is very sensitive to and influenced by the expectations of their parents; and has a deep concern with family reputation and how what they do reflects upon it. While both of these sides of an expanding bicultural self are strongly present, it is often not without considerable conflict and/or confusion. It is no wonder that the second generation humorously refers to itself as ABCD, American-born confused Desai (Indian).

Conflict can frequently be generated by highly educated, well-off parents who hold on to values with which they grew up, but which are decidedly more conservative than what is now present in urban India. This is a phenomenon quite common to immigrants throughout American history, where the immigrant generation confronted with American individualism tries to hold on to an older identity, which has gradually changed in their country of origin. The traditionalism of the Indian immigrant generation can often clash with the second generation, particularly in adolescence where the latter want to have more of a say in what they do.

This often manifests itself over typical American dating behavior, especially in daughters, which may raise great consternation in immigrant Indian parents over having a suitable arranged marriage for them. Daughters, meanwhile, want much more choice in the decision-making, while still taking parental concerns into account. Some families simply set extreme curfews on their daughters, or as in one case of a college student I saw, she was beaten up for coming home ten minutes late.

But strong parental expectations can also be present with sons who might be interested in a field of study quite different from the stereotypical ones considered by Indians to be suitable for a career: medicine, engineering, science, and finance. In a more extreme case, parents threatened to withhold college tuition unless their son switched majors from literature to premed or one of the sciences. When they can, the second generation often handles this disparity between parental expectations and the autonomy that is accorded in American culture by keeping each side of their bicultural self quite separate and compartmentalized in the two milieus: when at home, they are Indian, and outside of the home they are quite American, with neither parents nor other Americans knowing too much of this other side of themselves.

Another problem, typical of immigrants from most other countries, is where the children growing up in American ways become parents to their own parents in guiding them in how to do things in the United States. This seems to be particularly true with those whose mothers who are not working. Being both child and parent can at times be confusing to the child.

Sometimes, second generation Indian-Americans may not realize the source of parental attitudes as being rooted in traditional Indian culture or in their community's (*jati*) norms. In one case, a brilliant young woman, Geeta, gained admittance to a few Ivy League colleges, but was forbidden to go to any of them by her parents. Only after considerable pressure from a high school counselor did the parents relent, but only on the condition that Geeta major in science. She had not realized until we discussed this in session how terrified her parents were that if she went to too good a college she would be unmarriageable to any of the young men from her community. The community norms were not to have the young women too well educated as very few of the young men could gain admission to highly-regarded colleges. His family would refuse to have a daughter-in-law better educated than their son.

In another case of a top high school student, Madhu, she rarely if ever received any praise for her achievements from her parents. This had impacted on her self-esteem in a negative way. It was only after we discussed this in therapy that she began to realize the cultural bases of her parents never praising her. This was rooted in avoiding the envy of other members of the extended family, and, therefore, the evil eye; in it being considered highly immodest for parents to praise their own child, for with a we-self, praising one's child is like bragging about oneself; and in distracting children from their true nature, the *atman* or spiritual self, by building up the ego of a child through praise. This, of course, runs counter to current American values of openly praising and encouraging a child to have the confidence to do things well. She later learned that her parents were indeed very proud of her.

Another value clash between second generation Indians and their immigrant parents and in-laws emerges in the handling of discord within the family. A second generation woman, Niti, was very hurt and angry when her husband's sister did not come to the first birthday party of her son, an important occasion. She felt that this and any other problems could not be brought up with her in-laws, as they would look upon her as an oddball or unhealthy person. Nor did she get any support from her own parents. They took the attitude of either minimizing any conflict or that it was simply her duty as a daughter-in-law to be cooperative with her in-laws. It became obvious that within the values of an Indian family, all conflict and discord are to be swept under the rug to maintain a semblance of harmony; whereas her more American attitudes were to openly discuss the matter and to try to resolve it. The family's side-stepping of any conflict was quite upsetting to the Americanized part of Niti's self. But all of this, I should add, took place within the context of Niti feeling that her relationships with her in-laws are tremendously important, that they be nurturing and supportive of her, and that she have close relationships with them, typical expectations of a young Indian wife.

INDIAN FAMILY RELATIONSHIPS IN THE UNITED STATES

Another area that merits discussion is the Indian marital relationship in America, and the problems and conflicts that can be engendered by the husband, wife, and children walking the bicultural tightrope. Until recent years when more relatives have been admitted into the United States, most Indian families have lived in nuclear households without the usual extended family support systems, or even without sufficient members of their own community to socialize with or have community associations. This resulted in couples being thrown back on each other much more than would ordinarily be the case in India. I have heard reports of some couples who have said that they have become far closer, much sooner than they would have in India, and have been able to make many more decisions together. Their relationship has worked out extremely wel!. But where there is strife, there have been few if any mediating extended family members to intervene.

One symptom of this strife that arises from living in the United States has been enough wife battering to merit the formation of Indian organizations in both New York City and Chicago to give support and protection to these women. They are usually from upper-middle-class, well-educated families where husbands rarely have a drinking or drug problem. From interviews with women and men psychotherapists in both Bombay and New Delhi who work with the educated middle and upper-middle classes, there seems to be less wife battering by husbands from similar backgrounds in India than in the United States.

Besides whatever personal conflicts may inevitably arise in any relationship, there are particular cultural issues for Indians living in an American social milieu that can exacerbate marital conflict. For Indian-American husbands, working long hours on the American side of the cultural divide where there is not any orientation to the reciprocal responsibilities of Indian hierarchical relationships, they often experience a lack of nurturance by their supervisors, being hurt by direct criticism, and when eventually attaining a superior position, not being given expected respect and deference. In addition, there are the frequent encounters with pejorative attitudes toward them, related to the misunderstandings I have elaborated upon above, which seriously interfere with career advancement. To recoup a modicum of self-regard, these men often fall back on their traditional hierarchical role in the family as the superior and head of the household to an even greater extent than usual to compensate for their frustrations and wounded self-esteem at work.

According to Geeta Bhatt, who has counselled a number of Indian women in the New York City area, these men's intensified hierarchical expectations then clash with their wives. Men from the original immigrant generation have married women who are well-educated themselves, not infrequently with professional degrees as part of a new dowry system that values women's earning capacity over the usual traditional gifts. As I have previously elaborated upon (Roland 1988, pp. 204–206), these women, whether in India or the United States, can usually combine a career with family with less inner conflict, anxiety, and guilt than many American women. They view career more as a family endeavor than as an expression of individualism common to American women, who are often split between being there for others in the family and for themselves in their careers (Bernstein 1993). Indian women also have an even more contextual conscience and self that varies with relationships than is typical of American women, so that they can more easily negotiate differences in norms and behavior between career and family without feeling a need for a relatively consistent, inner identity that most other Americans have.

However, educated, career-oriented women who have married and immigrated here apparently find the first couple of years a struggle in an American work environment because of having to be far more assertive and articulate than their ego-ideal of being modest and self-effacing (personal communication, Sushim Bedi). However, as they get more used to being more aggressive and expressive, and as they gain the respect and recognition that is generally possible in increased career opportunities here, together with the American emphasis on egalitarianism and the Women's Movement, these women may no longer brook traditional hierarchical roles in the family to the extent their husbands wish. Instead, they may insist on a more openly assertive, communicative, and equal relationship. It is this dynamic, according to Geeta Bhatt, that is fueling conflict in a number of Indian marriages here—even to the extent of physically abusing the wife—in a context of not having other family members to mediate, and with attitudes of still shunning professional psychological help because of the stigma attached and its possible negative reflection on family reputation.

Then there are the inevitable tensions generated by Indian children growing up in America who are exposed to completely different kinds of values, at times opposites, from their parents who have immigrated, particularly during adolescence where the cultural value systems are most dissonant. Exposed to American adolescent values which so emphasize separation from the family, autonomous decision-making, rebellion against parents, the dominance of the peer group, and dating—all preparation for the more independent, self-propelling way of American individualized functioning—Indian teenagers who have become more individualized may clash at times with their parents. This is especially so if the parents, the fathers in particular, rigidly try to reassert the old values with which they were raised, where respect for elders, receptiveness and obediance to decisions made by elders, and family interdependence were so stressed; and in reasserting these old values they may thus try to cancel out the more individualized functioning of their teenager in America.

AMERICANS IN AN INDIAN SPIRITUAL CONTEXT

If Indians and other Asians experience conflict and misunderstanding in American-style relationships, it would stand to reason that Americans of European origin could also have such dissonant experiences in Asian-style hierarchy. What happens when Americans become increasingly involved with Asian spiritual teachers, Indian swamis and gurus, as well as Buddhist monks from other countries such as Tibet, Burma, Korea, and Japan? While the teachings and practices are invaluable and have become an integral part of many Americans' lives, nevertheless, from written and verbal reports, misunderstandings and hurt feelings can easily occur here too.

It is of note that these problems rarely have a public airing. I suspect that the resistance to discuss openly these cultural/psychological differences and the problems that are engendered have a few different sources. One major factor is that it is considered to be extremely disrespectful to be even indirectly critical, especially publicly, of a superior from an Asian country. Maintaining and enhancing esteem is often far more important in Asian hierarchical relationships than openly stating an objective truth.

Another source of resistance may stem from a long colonial history in India where any discussion of differences always explicitly or implicitly conveyed a disparagement of Indians with the supposed superiority of Westerners. A third source is simply that there has rarely been any attempt to discuss these differences in terms of principles of two major civilizations, South Asian and European/North American, that are founded on profoundly different cultural and social principles, each with its own psychology, each with its strengths and weaknesses. This is often brushed aside by an emphasis on the universals of the spiritual quest.

What are the problems that may arise? Let us take the Buddhist monasteries in the United States first. While a number of Americans have become deeply involved and enriched by the teachings, there have also been some major problems. Not unexpectedly, some American disciples and sometimes the teacher-monks, themselves, whether Asian or American, have evidenced emotional problems that seriously complicated relationships in the monastery. Attitudes toward such problems tended to divide into two polarities: increased meditation would enable the person to transcend the problem, which most of the time it didn't; or seeking psychotherapy would be seen as the answer, then abandoning any meditation practice. On the other hand, a Vedanta teacher, Swami Dayananda, the American Zen Buddhist Abbot, John Daido Loorie, and a couple of swamis of the Ramakrishna Mission in America (pers. com. William Conrad) have all sent serious spiritual aspirants for psychotherapy when needed, the aspirants continuing their spiritual practices.

A more serious problem emerged when a few of the Buddhist teachers, Asian and American, became involved in alcoholism and sexual relationships with their disciples.[9] The lid blew off when one American Buddhist teacher was reported to have had AIDs, and knowing this, had sexual relationships with both women and men disciples. Why had the whistle not been blown earlier on this and other incidents by American disciples?

One possible answer relates to the profound difference in attitudes toward superiors. As mentioned above, in India and other Asian societies, subordinates make an inner distinction between who is to be deferred to as the superior in the formal hierarchy, and who is to be deeply respected and revered as a person with superior qualities. Americans, on the other hand, in their egalitarian relationships and attitudes, are not brought up with the same kind of deference toward superiors, nor to make such inner distinctions. I wonder if their judgment had become completely suspended once they entered into a deferential-reverential attitude of a disciple/spiritual teacher relationship, to which they are completely unaccustomed.

If these are some of the more dramatic problems, what are some of the day-to-day miscommunications that can arise between American disciples and Indian spiritual teachers?[10] Much of this involves the dramatic differences between American individualism and Indian hierarchical relationships. For instance, in Indian intimacy relationships it is expected that the junior person or subordinate be dependent and ask for what they want from the superior. Similarly, the swami expects his American disciples to be openly dependent, see him when they want, and ask about whatever is on their mind. This is something that many Americans are not particularly comfortable with, feeling they are imposing on the superior, and expecting the superior to take the initiative. Dependency in American adults is profoundly frowned upon.

In another vein, Americans are not used to being given the constant advice, guidance, and being told what to do, something that frequently occurs between the swamis and his American disciples. For the swami, this is fulfilling his duty (*dharma*) as a superior, and is a sign of caring; but for an American, it can easily be experienced as an infringement on his or her autonomy, a cardinal value of American individualism.

Another important area of miscommunication is when American disciples do something for the swami, who does not thank them or give any other verbal expression of appreciation. Americans then react with hurt feelings that they are not liked or that they have done something wrong, often becoming irritated as this continues. In Indian familial-style intimacy relationships, it is assumed that what you do for the elder is appreciated, and this is picked up nonverbally.

For a superior in an Indian context to express his appreciation verbally would be to demean the intimacy relationship. To thank the disciple openly would be to treat him as an outsider, since the verbal expression of social niceties is only reserved for outsider relationships. It would thus be considered insulting to those in familial-style insider relationships. Americans, on the other hand, experience an absence of verbal appreciation for what they have done as a lack of concern and involvement. This miscommunication is largely due then to certain differing cultural expectations and to a great deal more empathic sensing and nonverbal communication going on in Indian than typical American relationships.

These kinds of cultural misunderstandings seem minor in comparison to the overall spiritual endeavor. Yet, since the teachings and practices must be conveyed through a personal relationship, a greater understanding of where the American disciple and the Asian spiritual teacher come from in their attitudes and ways of relating will facilitate the teaching process and mitigate conflicts and miscommuniation.

SUMMARY

After enumerating the various factors that have enabled the Indian community to have become the most financially successful immigrant group in the United States, I delve into the areas of the cultural interface between Indian-Americans and other Americans that can become dissonant, problematic, or conflictural. I then delineate three psychosocial dimensions of Indian familial hierarchical relationships and contrast them with various aspects of North American individualism and hierarchy. I indicate how in these specific contrasts most of the misunderstandings and problems arise from both sides. And it is in negotiating these sharp contrasts that Indian-Americans walk a bicultural tightrope and develop an expanding, bicultural self, often with considerable inner distress. I then show how the tightrope is walked quite differently by second generation Indian-Americans, who develop a different kind of bicultural self. Walking the bicultural tightrope in both the immigrant and second generation has considerable effects on the Indian family in the United States. Changes and stresses from living on both sides of the cultural divide impact strongly on husbands, wives, and children, sometimes generating considerable family conflict. The chapter concludes with problems and misunderstandings experienced by Americans who are disciples in Indian or other Asian spiritual hierarchies.

ENDNOTES

1. For an excellent personal and psychoanalytic discussion within the framework of ego psychology of the development of a bicultural self in the immigrant generation, see Akhtar (1995).

2. The high numbers of Indian college-educated persons emigrating abroad are a result of two factors: the building up of an extensive Western-oriented college and university system by Jawaharlal Nehru after Indian Independence in 1947, with particularly good training in science, engineering, medicine, and management; and

of an Indian economy that until very recently has not been able to accommodate anywhere near the number of highly educated persons the university system has produced.

3. Indian English is the third largest branch of the English language, fostered in India by two centuries of colonial rule, and kept up presently in a country where North and South have two radically different kinds of indigenous languages with totally different roots. Thus, English serves as a necessary bridge.

4. Many of these come from the five Indian Institutes of Technology, the elite scientific and engineering colleges modelled after the Massachusetts Institute of Technology curriculum, where the great majority of graduates have emigrated to Western countries because of the lack of opportunities in India.

5. Some of the literature on Indians in the United States are as follows: Clarke, Colin, Peach, and Vertovec (eds.) (1990); Daniels (1990); Fisher (1980); Gonzales Jr. (1992); Jensen (1988); Kandelwal (1995); Mazumdar (1991); Sanjek (1989); van der Veer (ed.) (1995).

6. This is sensitively alluded to in Akhtar's (1995) paper.

7. As in everything in India there are always exceptions. Matriarchies predominate in some areas, such as parts of Kerala.

8. This kind of experience is confirmed by Akhtar (1995).

9. This has been documented by Sandy Boucher (1988).

10. I have learned about these issues through one of the American monks at a highly reputable Vedanta Center in the United States.

Chapter Three

The Japanese
and American Interface

INTRODUCTION

One evening after I gave a presentation at the Japan Society on "Exploring the Self: Highlights and Contrasts Between Japanese and Americans," a well-attired American man came up to me in the lobby. "Dr. Roland, I am head of Legal Services at a large Japanese trading company in New York City. We are having a lot of problems between the American support staff and the Japanese managers who run the company. I had thought that it was simply a matter of needing to improve certain lines of communication. But after hearing your talk, I am convinced that the problems go much deeper. Would you be willing to have lunch with me and the American director of Human Resources to discuss these issues?"

What he had told me was later confirmed by Margaret Haas and Kevin McBride, Japan specialists fluent in Japanese, who run a consulting firm to place Japanese and Americans in each other's corporations both here and in Japan. They have concluded that with rare exceptions Japanese and American corporate managers simply don't understand each other, that these managers feel there are huge differences they don't comprehend, and that these differences are unbridgeable, especially with such a huge language barrier.

When I gave a similar talk some months later at the Asian Institute, Rosemary Wright, then assistant dean of the Art School at Cooper Union,[1] related to me that she was most interested in the presentation as she had observed that the creative process in Japanese and American students in the art program is completely different, something further confirmed by her observations of Japanese art students in Tokyo. "Could we meet together to discuss the psychology of how Japanese and Americans create so differently?"

At still another time, I was approached by a Japanese woman, an artist, who had organized a two-day a week afterschool program at Educational Alliance[2] for elementary school age children of mixed Japanese and American marriages. "Many of our families disagree or are confused as to how to raise their children here. Some have problems between themselves as a couple. Could you conduct a couple of seminars with our group of parents about these intercultural issues?"

I have also had experience working with two Japanese men and three women in psychoanalysis and psychoanalytic therapy in New York City, all three women being married to Americans, with one of the women working in an American corporation, and one of the men doing graduate work. All of them gradually shared a great deal of their reactions to relationships with other Americans. On the other side of the interface was an American patient who was keenly aware of Japanese-American interactions through long-term, extensive negotiations with a Japanese corporation.

It is from these encounters with the corporate world, artistic creativity, Japanese-American intercultural marriages, and clinical work with Japanese and with an American with extensive contacts with the Japanese, that I would like to elaborate upon the Japanese-American interface. In certain respects, this cultural/psychological interface is quite similar to the Indian encounter with the American culture of individualism that I delineated in the previous chapter. In this sense, one can view the psychology of the Japanese as an important variant of an overall Asian psychology. But in other aspects, the interface is colored by more uniquely Japanese aspects of the self, by the nature of their family and especially work-group hierarchical relationships, and by their particular modes of communication.

PSYCHOSOCIAL DIMENSIONS OF JAPANESE HIERARCHICAL RELATIONSHIPS

In the previous chapter I delineated three major psychosocial dimensions of Indian family and group hierarchical relationships to clarify the dissonances and misunderstandings that occur when Indians encounter the North American culture of individualism. In general outline, the three psychosocial dimensions of Japanese hierarchical relationships are quite similar to those of Indians (Roland 1988, pp. 281–288), especially when compared to Northern European/ North American ones. But more specifically, each of the three dimensions can vary significantly between Japanese and Indians, and greatly affect the encounter with Americans.

Formal Hierarchical Relationships

The traditional *ie* Japanese family[3] and the work group are much more vertical and pyramidal in structure than in India, or for that matter in the United

States, with one person only at the top. These pyramids in work groups—whether in a corporation where there are a number of them, in the bureaucracy, professional associations, or various departments in a university consist of a progression of junior-senior hierarchical relationships related to seniority. These groups or factions are often highly competitive with each other in an overall institutional structure, but there is tremendous loyalty and feelings of closeness within the group (Nakane 1970). Competitiveness and self-assertion within the group are kept privately to oneself for harmonious relationships; otherwise, considerable shame is evoked over any overt display (Okano 1994). Unlike Indians, for whom the psychological locus of their emotional well-being is primarily in the extended family, Japanese men are deeply embedded in their work group. The group, itself, as well as the family, is far more closed off to outsiders than in either India or the United States. An outsider can only enter the group from the top, that is, through the person running the group.

Japanese are noted for a particularly high level of work-group functioning. The *iemoto*, or mentor-disciple relationship, is one major factor that enables the group to function so well. This follows the reciprocal expectations and responsibilities of familial hierarchical relationships that I mentioned in the previous chapter, only carried over to the work group. In a North American setting, similar to Indians, Japanese can clearly evidence disappointment and hurt over the American superior not being sufficiently nurturing and caring, and/or being directly critical of mistakes.

Decision-making is another factor, something usually done by slowly working out a consensus, with members of the group contributing their own thoughts, often by innuendo or indirection so no one stands out in his opinions,[4] with the leader withholding his own views until the various members have had their say. Once decisions are arrived at, each must abide by them without voicing any contrary view. In a corporate setting, the middle managers make the decisions by this process and then formally ask a senior manager to approve it (pers. com. Haas and McBride).

The social etiquette of formal hierarchical relationships is observed much more rigorously in Japan than in India. Whereas Indians will agree verbally to do disagreeable responsibilities and tasks but not necessarily carry them out, Japanese inevitably get them done regardless of how the person feels about it. Fulfilling social obligations (*giri*) is central in Japan. Concern and shame over what others might think of you, especially if you do things for yourself not in harmony with the group, and how this will reflect on you and your family and/or group reputation, is very powerful. The Japanese also have a complex respect language where different words are used for the same object depending on the nature of the hierarchical relationship, with different gestures also being used to mark the hierarchy.[5] Foreigners rarely master this respect language, and Japanese living abroad for some years can forget some of its nuances. Those foreigners living in Japan who partly master the respect language can be in deeper trouble socially than those who have little knowledge of it. The Japanese expect much more of them, and are therefore less forgiving of their mistakes.

Cultural ideals of perserverance, endurance, overcoming obstacles, and doing everything as perfectly as possible from tasks to observing the rigorous social etiquette are deeply internalized into the Japanese conscience. All of the Japanese patients I have seen have a far more perfectionistic ego-ideal than either Indians or most Americans I have worked with. The Japanese make an even stronger differentiation between a public and private self, *omote* and *ura*, than Indians do, with a very careful presentation of self in the formal hierarchy, and a very secretive, private self where all kinds of feelings and thoughts are contained. Beyond the family, work groups, and longstanding friendships, Japanese view outsider relationships in a highly formal way, with considerable emotional restraint, and with a need to immediately reciprocate when any favor is received.

Hierarchical Intimacy Relationships

Family and work-group relationships can be very emotionally close and interdependent where there is a we-self in semi-merger experiences, much more similar to the Indian self than the I-self and the sharply delineated I and you relationships of American individualism. Balancing these semi-merger experiences, as well as the public self in the formal hierarchy, is a degree of personal privacy that goes beyond even the Indian private self. This private self is to be sensed by others rather than expressed, so that important communication is as much nonverbal as verbal, reflecting a saying that "nothing important is ever to be communicated verbally." Instead, there is a great deal of concerned empathic sensing (*omoiyari*) of the needs and feelings of the other with less awareness of one's own, and a great deal of self-effacement of oneself while praising the other; but one expects full reciprocity in each case. Maintaining and enhancing high levels of esteem is central.

In corporate settings, Japanese are noted far more than Indians or Americans to spend considerable time together after working hours as a group in a sushi or piano bar,[6] casually socializing together. Emotional closeness is reinstated, and somewhat frayed relationships from the rigors of the day's work are repaired.

THE JAPANESE-AMERICAN CORPORATE WORLD

Problems in the interface between Japanese and Americans in the corporate world can emerge in a number of ways. One major way relates to the Japanese group being self-contained, with great loyalty and interdependence within the group, and imperviousness to outsiders. In one company, the American director of Human Resources related that the Japanese managers were supervising every last iota of what the American staff did, arousing considerable resentment in the Americans who were used to far greater autonomy in their work, and who felt the Japanese were always looking over their shoulders. He, himself, was very upset by this, seriously considering leaving the company in spite of a good position and salary.

As we discussed it further, it became clear that the Japanese managers were highly suspicious of what their American staff would do, since they felt the latter had not the kind of loyalty to the group that the Japanese have, and therefore might do something that could adversely affect the company. When I met this man again a year later, he said the situation was much improved. The company decided to have an American president of the Japanese branch in the United States, subordinate to the Japanese chairman. The American president was put in charge of the American support staff and thus did away with the Japanese over supervision.

In the Japanese trading company that I first learned about, one of the problems raised was related to the extensive renovations that had gone on for some time in the large Japanese section of their entire floor in a New York City skyscraper. At no point either during the construction or when it was finished was the American support staff allowed to see what was being done. This resulted in feelings of isolation and rejection in the American staff with a consequent drop in morale and productivity. When the director of Human Resources spoke about this to a senior Japanese manager, he agreed to invite the American staff to visit. But he and the other Japanese managers undermined this effort by remaining engrossed in their work at the time of the visit. Again, the self-containment of the Japanese work group came to the fore with little room for outsiders, and little need to understand where Americans come from. The Americans were nonplussed by these attitudes and behavior.

Haas and McBride mentioned that in Japanese companies here, Americans are not invited to go out in after-work socializing, so integral to Japanese group functioning, and so are completely out of touch with the informal news network of what is really going on, not to mention the intimacy dimension of Japanese relationships. This issue of the Japanese group being closed off to outsiders also comes out in another way. Japanese senior managers care a great deal for junior ones, helping arrange marriages, going to birth ceremonies, funerals, and such. They spend a great deal of time on human relations. Apparently, only very occasionally will they extend this to Americans working in their corporation, in part feeling that Americans won't have any long-term commitment, and in part not wanting to stand out from the other Japanese senior managers.

A second way in which problems emerge in the interface is in the decision-making process. American managers are used to a greater degree of autonomy and can feel quite frustrated when working in a Japanese company with the lengthy decision-making process of Japanese middle-managers, which then is further delayed by their having to get formal approval of a senior manager (pers. com. Haas and McBride). This also entered into the therapy of a patient, Ira, who was in lengthy negotiations with the president of a Japanese corporation to take over Ira's highly specialized, software company. The Board of Directors, investors in Ira's company, had long wanted a larger corporation to buy them out. On the advice of a Japan specialist, Ira cultivated the relationship with the president of a Japanese corporation for a few years rather than pushing to broker a deal. Ira realized that once the relationship was firmly established, everything was possible; and without it, nothing.

However, Ira's Board of Directors became impatient with the long negotiating process[7] and insisted that he deal with American firms as well. Ira, from long business experience, knew that these negotiations would entail a much more adversarial relationship. Coming from a background of childhood physical abuse, he didn't want to subject himself to "getting fucked again" by an American corporation. And indeed, when he did get involved with senior officers from a large American corporation who seemed most interested in his company, Ira walked out of negotiations once they became hard-nosed and adversarial. Ira felt much more comfortable with the relationship-centered dealings with the Japanese president, which after seven years finally came to fruition.

Another area of potential dissonance in the corporate interface is in the area of training. In a Japanese group, except for a specific task where training is usually very good, Japanese are expected to sense a great deal of what the group needs and then do it. Americans are used to far more explicit directions, and so may have a difficult time in a Japanese group. In filling certain higher level managerial positions, Japanese may put a capable man in a position where he has had very little experience expecting him to sense and learn what needs to be done, which often but not always works out. American Human Resource directors will invariably only put a person in that position who has had a good deal of experience.

Still another problem in the corporate interface, one of a subtler psychological nature, is the relationship of objective truth to relational needs of self-esteem. North Americans tend to be far more oriented toward rationality or stating the truth of a matter with less concern over how it will affect the esteem of the other. Japanese, on the other hand, are far more concerned with the relationship and the esteem or the face of the other, and will subordinate objective truth to relational needs. These very different orientations can result in discomforting problems when Americans and Japanese have to work together. Ira, a first-rate scientist in his field, constantly had to remind himself not to confront his Japanese negotiators with objective facts and truth when the nature of the relationship was much more often at stake.

On a lighter level, another American scientist, Marty, related at a meeting at the United States-Japan Foundation that one time when he was in Japan he was approached by a noted Japanese professor who held an important Chair at a highly regarded university. The professor wanted to purchase one of Marty's latest technical inventions with some modifications to use in a very specific research project that the professor had spent a number of years working on. When Marty heard what the professor's research was, he was flabbergasted as this research had scientifically been thoroughly disproven for some years. Marty became even more dumbfounded the following evening when he had dinner with a noted Japanese scientist in the same field, and told him the story. The Japanese scientist responded, "Well he is the Chair, who knows?" The Japanese scientist was unwilling to challenge the status and particularly the esteem of the professor for the sake of any objective truth.

This same issue arose as one of the unresolved, bitter problems at a Japanese trading company in New York City. An American woman on the support staff spent considerable time and effort researching and writing an article for the in-house newsletter on the long delay involved in the extensive renovations under-taken at the office. She carefully analyzed the delays as being due to the red tape of the New York City housing bureaucracy, not to any mismanagement on the part of the Japanese managers overseeing the project. Nevertheless, the Japanese head of the in-house newsletter killed the story, infuriating the writer. She had put objective truth in as tactful a manner as possible, completely absolving the Japanese of any blame. But she had not realized that just men-tioning in print publicly that long delays had occurred, even though everyone knew about them, was a threat to the self-regard of the Japanese managers. Failures, even when one is not responsible for them, are not to be publicized because of the shame involved. From a Japanese standpoint, the story should never have been written. From an American one, she had done a fine job.

What happens when a Japanese person works in an American corporation? Yoshiko, a well-educated Japanese woman with a graduate degree from an American university and married to an American, came to therapy distraught over her experiences in an American corporation. She found it very difficult to be direct and confrontational with her clients, experienced more difficulty when some clients were nasty to her, and was absolutely distraught over her supervisors forthrightly criticizing the very few mistakes she made. The differ-ences in communicative styles and in hierarchical relationships between Japan-ese and Americans made it extremely difficult for Yoshiko to be in an American corporation (see Chapter Five for a fuller discussion of Yoshiko).

ARTISTIC CREATIVITY

A young Japanese filmmaker exclaimed at lunch one day, "Being here in America is so wonderful as an artist. I can be so much freer than in Japan. But it is an emotional void." She was obviously speaking of the much greater social freedom and opportunities here as an artist as compared to living in Japan; at the same time, she felt emotional intimacy as she was used to it in Japan to be completely lacking here. This longing as an artist to be less restricted and confined socially, and to have greater opportunities, have been major factors in many of the Japanese artists living in lower Manhattan leaving Japan to immigrate to the United States. One of my Japanese patients in New York City for a year and a half, with strong interests in the arts, revelled in the greater freedom in American life from the stringencies of hierarchy.

I shall now turn more to the differences in artistic creativity in Japanese and Americans, and am indebted to Rosemary Wright for her perspectives on this. In many American art schools for a number of years, there has been a strong emphasis on risk-taking, in seeing artistic creativity as a remaking of the self, as creating one's own personal identity, and as thus being highly individualistic. Implicit in this are individuals' self-creation of their own identity through autonomously making decisions on the multiple choices and options in American life, the central psychological paradigm in American individualism. Also implicit is that the work of art, while related to one's self and identity, is essentially separate from the self in keeping with Western philosophical assumptions of dualism. Therefore, if the work fails, it is no basic reflection on oneself. Risks are therefore much easier to take, and teacher's critiques are usually very forthright and able to be assimilated.

Japanese students here apparently have trouble with the kind of risk-taking emphasized in American art schools as their psychology does not emphasize a remaking of the self, in terms of self-creating one's identity; or even that the work of art is essentially separate from oneself. Images may be done that are relatively similar, but this comes more from emulation than the highly individualistic American way of creating. Critiques with Japanese art students apparently only work when a "we" relationship has been well established between teacher and student, and communication takes place somewhat indirectly.

Japanese artistic creativity emphasizes other dimensions. One important one is the Japanese emphasis on *ma*, the space between lines and forms, such as the fog in landscapes. Another example is fireworks. Where Americans usually have a florid display, Japanese fire off one at a time, the space between the explosions being as important as the visual explosion, itself. According to Kunio Kudo, "In the West, when you fail to describe, things fail to exist. In the East, when you fail to describe, things emerge." Perhaps *ma* also relates to what the Japanese psychoanalyst, Akahisa Kondo, stated, "Individuality for us lies in what is not said" (pers. com.). It is the rich, interior private self. Thus, *ma* is not a void or emptiness in the American sense, but rather a dynamic state of being. This can obviously also be related to meditative experiences as well.

Another major emphasis in Japanese artistic creativity is the orientation to reaffirming social and cultural connectedness through the constant use of older images, even in different forms taken over from abroad. Thus, contemporary Japanese artists can still use old themes such as the four seasons; or other old content such as earth, air, fire, and water; or Zen symbols of the circle, triangle, and square. Japanese in their art constantly reassert consensus rather than to challenge it as American artists do. Therefore, American artists usually have difficulty in using symbolic content from the past since there is such a striving for individualistic expression.

INTERCULTURAL MARRIAGES

My impression of the college-educated Japanese, women and men, who have immigrated to the United States over the last few decades, is that they often experience Japanese family and group hierarchical relationships and expectations as too restrictive or oppressive. In fact, one patient was encouraged by her parents to come to the United States. They saw her as being too articulate and verbally assertive as a woman to fit into Japanese society. Nevertheless, this small immigrant community, although seeing themselves as being very different from the transient Japanese business community here or the much older Japanese-American community on the West Coast and Hawaii, still feel deeply connected to Japanese society and culture.

Unlike Indians and other South Asians who can easily go back and forth between the United States and their own countries to live in either, Japanese must either be in or out of Japanese society. A Japanese-American psychoanalyst, Nobuko Yoshizawa Meaders (1996), wrote of her own first trip back to Japan after ten years in the United States. People saw her body language as being that of a foreigner, and she, herself, had to constantly struggle to speak Japanese correctly. Thus, the educated Japanese immigrants to the United States have already chosen to live in a much more individualized society, but simultaneously can experience the American culture of individualism as being highly dissonant with their own makeup. Meaders delineates her own difficult trials and tribulations, as well as the successful resolution of her journey to attain what she terms, a transcultural self, that integrates both her Japanese and American identities. This took her a number of years to achieve, helped considerably by a personal psychoanalysis.

What then happens when such a Japanese person, usually a woman but on occasion a man, lives in American society and not infrequently marries an American? One problem frequently generated in the interface between a Japanese wife and an American husband is in the area of communication. The Japanese wife, accustomed to a culture of concerned empathic sensing (*omoiyari*) of each other's feelings, wishes, and thoughts, expects her American husband to sense what is going on in her mind, as she does with him, without having to express anything verbally. American husbands not infrequently complain of the lack of verbal communication and expressiveness from their Japanese wives. This is even more telling, since the usual complaint in American couples, when there is a lack of explicit communication of feelings and thoughts, is that it is invariably the husband. Thus, the usual pattern in American marriages becomes reversed when the wife is Japanese. One particular Japanese woman mentioned that she had to work long and hard, aided by being in psychotherapy, to communicate much more verbally and openly with her husband. On the other hand, Japanese wives of American husbands feel relieved that they do not have to give the same degree of care and attention to a husband's dependency needs that they ordinarily would have to with a Japanese husband.

There is another element often present in a Japanese-American marriage, as well as in Japanese attitudes toward other Americans in general. Japanese have extremely high standards in everything they do. Therefore, my Japanese patients have not infrequently complained about the inefficiency and relative lack of competence of their American spouses, not to mention that of many other Americans they encounter.

CHILD REARING IN INTERCULTURAL MARRIAGES

To raise a child in the United States of combined Japanese and American parents is to be involved in two radically different, almost opposite value systems and ways of relating. Perhaps this can be illustrated by an anecdote related to me in Hiroshima by a Japanese psychoanalyst about his then eight-year-old daughter. The analyst, himself, had come to New York City for training for three years with his wife and daughter when she was five. Shortly after they returned to Japan after the three years, they went out to dinner one evening. After they were sitting at the table and looking at the menu for awhile, he asked his daughter what she would like to eat. She replied, "I dunno." He waited a while longer and then asked her again. Again, she replied, "I dunno." After asking her a third time with the same result, he inquired if she was feeling all right, if anything was wrong. "No," she replied, "I am feeling perfectly fine. I am just becoming Japanese again."

What she, of course, meant was that in becoming Japanese again she expected her parents to sense what she wanted to eat without her having to express it verbally. They would simply order for her what they knew she wanted. Her parents, meanwhile, used to a more American way of relating from their three years in New York City, were expecting her to communicate openly in an American style.

The analyst, himself, mentioned that after being in New York City for a year or so, he was walking one day on Fifth Avenue when a thought spontaneously came to mind. "Totoro, what do I want, what do I wish? What is it that I want?" He then said, "This was the first time these thoughts ever occurred to me." A Japanese woman psychoanalyst told me that very often Japanese will not fully know what they want until the superior upon whom they depend does not fulfill their needs or wishes. It is only then that they become more aware of wanting something specific (pers. com. Yoshiko Idei).

In America, we put a premium on children and adults verbally expressing their wishes, wants, and needs, and often enough their dissatisfactions. Verbal expression becomes a key value in American individualism, varying from one ethnic group to another, but still remaining a predominant value. Perhaps we put such a stress on expressing oneself in words because this enables us as very separate individuals to connect to each other. Otherwise, you can hear the expression, "what am I suppose to do, read your mind?" Generally, parents here will ask their children whether they want this or that, often giving them choices and having them make up their mind. It's not that a parent will give everything a child wants. Far from it. But the open expression of these wishes is not frowned upon.

Japanese, on the other hand, from early childhood are brought up to sense what the other feels, what the other wants, and what they are thinking. The degree of concerned empathy (*omoiyari*) is central to Japanese-style relationships. I was very much struck in the psychotherapy relationship how much a Japanese therapist could pick up from the patient without the patient having to verbalize his thoughts and feelings; and how much the therapist would expect the patient to sense what the therapist was thinking. I remember also being struck upon reading Tenezake's *The Makioko Sisters* how much they were all trying to sense each other's thoughts and motives with very little being expressed. Of course, this is more traditional Japanese ways of relating and communicating, something that has changed to varying degrees.

It is not simply that there are different value systems over ways of communicating and relating. These value systems integrally relate to very different kinds of child rearing, which can introduce confusion and conflict in an intercultural marriage. It all begins in infancy. While there is great variety in various American ethnic groups, nevertheless, the predominant mode of American child rearing does not have the infant sleep next to the mother as Japanese and most other Asians do, even when there is room, which there often is not. In fact, American middle-class child rearing encourages much more separateness, with even infants having a separate crib and then bed; and if the family can afford it, for children to have a separate bedroom.

American mothers encourage their children to explore their environment, to be increasingly independent, to voice what they want and be generally self-expressive, and to be assertive—although this last may differ in attitudes toward boys and girls. American mothers maintain much more of a position of being a separate person with their young child than do Japanese mothers, as was readily evidenced in a video made of American and Japanese mothers and their 20–24 month old toddlers. Upon planned phone calls and interviews with the mothers, the Japanese did not let these interruptions interfere with a continued connectedness to their toddlers; whereas the Americans clearly asserted their separateness.[8]

All of this fosters the development of sharply separate inner images of self and other, of a sense of self that is a highly individualistic I-self, and of firm outer emotional boundaries between self and others. Too much dependency is definitely frowned upon, expressed in the pejorative phrase, "a mama's boy." This early childhood development is well conceptualized in psychoanalytic theory with Erikson's (1950) emphasis on autonomy and initiative, and with Mahler's (1965) well-delineated stage of separation-individuation.

For a Japanese mother, there is a quite different way of child rearing. Children are brought up to be highly dependent on their mothers, and there usually is a much stronger mother-child interdependency and tie than in most American ethnic groups. Traditionally, a Japanese child will sleep next to his mother until a sibling is born, and then with another member of the household, but never alone (Caudhill and Plath 1974). To place infants or very young children in a room of their own is considered dire punishment. What is developed from this is a great sense of emotional closeness, a sense of self that much more includes others in a kind of we-ness, tremendous dependency and interdependency, and this empathic sensing of others' moods, feelings, and needs. "How would the spinach feel if you don't eat it" is used instead of the American saying, "Eat your spinach and you will be strong."

In American families, as in other relationships, notions of relative equality enable children to ask questions of their parents, sometimes to criticize or challenge them, and even to become angry at them and rebel, especially as teenagers. This enables them to gradually function more and more on their own, as they gravitate to extra-familial peer groups. Anger expressed in a Japanese family by children and teenagers sometimes occurs but is usually deeply suppressed and discouraged. When there is a direct expression of intense anger at adults, it is usually by being out-of-control and therefore not fully responsible; or by being part of a group where one doesn't have to assume individual responsibility. Even asking questions of a Japanese parent, as a child of an intercultural marriage here can readily do, is sometimes experienced as an affront by the Japanese mother. Thus, how openly a child or teenager should be able to express his or her dissatisfactions, criticism, or outright anger at parents is something Japanese and Americans in intercultural marriages can easily differ upon.

In Japanese families, by and large the wife has the overwhelming responsibility in child rearing, with an extremely close mother-child tie. The father is usually seen as reticent and somewhat distant, but offers a refuge from the child being too engulfed by the mother (Taketomo 1982). While the husband is very dependent on his wife, she will defer to him when he has certain ideas on child rearing. Expectations for closeness and intimacy are generally not as strong in Japanese as in American marriages, intimacy being more fulfilled in same sex relationships and for women, with their children.

In an intercultural marriage, if the husband is Japanese and the wife American, he will generally let her make more of the decisions and take more of the responsibilities in child rearing. However, if he does have some definite ideas on how the child should be raised, he expects his wife to follow them. This can lead to considerable friction, as many American women today do not particularly defer to their husbands, but want disagreements to be discussed and negotiated.

On the other hand, if the wife is Japanese and the husband, American, the husband generally plays a larger role in child rearing. Friction is usually avoided by her deferring to his wishes. This, of course, can vary significantly depending on the actual personalities of the parents. Children, themselves, will have an early development of the self along certain cultural/psychological lines, depending on whether the mothering is Japanese or American. If Japanese, there will be maternal expectations from an early age for very high standards of doing tasks and of observing proper social etiquette, and of cultural values for endurance, perserverance, patience, receptiveness to others, and at times resignation to living out difficult situations.

It is basically from these early and later maternal expectations that Japanese children develop such high standards for themselves in both achieving and performing well socially. While it enables them to accomplish a great deal, the downside of this is experiencing considerable tension over how well they are doing, and having a vulnerability to criticism or failure of any kind.

Japanese and American parents in an intercultural marriage have to face these sharply contrasting values and ways of relating in child rearing within an American social milieu. This can be easily confusing. Bridging the gap requires a real give and take and a great deal of understanding of each other's background without assuming there is only one right way. This, of course, can get further complicated by the fact that not only are there these cultural differences, but also that each partner has her or his own particular personality.

SUMMARY

I discuss the Japanese-American interface in three major areas: corporations, artistic creativity, and Japanese-American intercultural marriages and child rearing. I do this by first outlining the psychosocial dimensions of Japanese hierarchical relationships that are similar in general to Indian ones, but in specifics vary in highly important ways. In the corporate world, I delineate problems in the interface emerging from differences in group hierarchical relationships, decision-making processes, and in the relationship of objective truth to relational needs of self-esteem. I also indicate how Japanese can have difficulties working in an American corporation.

In artistic creativity, differences center around the different psychologies of risk-taking through self-creating one's own identity in America versus reasserting the social consensus and the private self in Japanese. In intercultural marriages, I cite some of the strains due to different modes of communication and Japanese expections of high levels of competency; whereas in child rearing I highlight some of the confusions that can emerge due to radically different kinds of child rearing common to each culture.

ENDNOTES

1. Many consider the Art School at Cooper Union to be the top undergraduate art program in New York City. All students have full scholarships.

2. The Educational Alliance is one of the oldest of the settlement houses in New York City, originally started for Jewish immigrants on the lower East Side of Manhattan. The after-school program for the children of Japanese-American mixed marriages is held in its Greenwich Village branch. These children attend regular public schools during the day, but the parents thought they should also be exposed to Japanese culture and language, and so formed this after-school program. Many, but by no means all of the parents, are artists living in lower Manhattan, these immigrant Japanese wives and husbands being very different from those of the transient Japanese business community around New York City, not to mention the much older Japanese-American community on the West Coast.

3. The traditional *ie* family consisted of a main house with branch houses of older and younger sons, the oldest only inheriting, the younger ones being aided to get employment elsewhere, with a hierarchical relationship between younger and older brothers as well as with the father. While this has been dissolved legally by the post-World War II American Occupation of Japan, in practice it may still informally go on, especially if there is a family business.

4. "The nail that stands out gets hammered in" is an oft quoted statement.

5. As a simple example, a senior person will pour beer with one hand, the junior receiving it will hold his or her glass with two hands.

6. Japanese cities have much larger pleasure quarters than European, American, or Indian cities.

7. Rajesh Kumar (1993) discusses impasses in negotiations that often result between Japanese and Americans. This is usually caused by the Japanese wanting to cultivate relationships before agreements, and the Americans being oriented toward task accomplishment and contractual agreements without nearly as much attention to relationships.

8. This video was made by Drs. Calvin Settlidge and Joseph Okimoto, and was shown in the Midwinter Meeting of the American Psychoanalytic Association in New York City, December 1993.

Chapter Four

Cultural Hurdles
and Inscrutable Muddles

C hinese and Anglos[1] often have different takes on the same thing: Chinese wear white at funerals whereas Anglos prefer white for weddings; Chinese fit their routines and bedspace around a visiting guest whereas Anglos, especially Americans, expect their guest to fit into the family's routine. Sometimes, they are taken aback by their different approaches and attitudes to the same thing: Chinese traditionally reserve handholding for same-sex friends whereas Anglos habitually frown on handholding, *especially* among same-sex friends; Chinese salivate over fish eyes and tail fins whereas Anglos find them repugnant and stomach churning.

Other times, they are woefully taken in by the surface similarities of things that are actually very different. Particularly when it comes to talk conducted in the same language, they find themselves tripping over cultural hurdles that they didn't even know were there. Chinese and Anglos can come together in talk, yet unknowingly become undone by their very different takes on talk.

The trouble lies in thinking that speaking the same language means that they share the same set of values and beliefs about talk—that, indeed, they bring the same ritual routines and orientations to talk. But, in truth, the same surface linguistic code can obscure significantly different cultural assumptions and expectations about talk; culturally-specific discourse style and strategies can be deceptively dressed in the same language and go unnoticed in conversation. Interlocutors can be duped into thinking that they share common grounds for understanding and are readily able to discern and decipher each other's meanings and intentions. Engaged in talk, they unwittingly disengage interactively. Imperfect understandings can give way to impaired impressions, leaving interlocutors mired in a variety of inscrutable muddles and cross-cultural grief.

Some cross-cultural hurdles lend themselves to easy resolution and ready explanation. Consider, for instance, a British woman's recollection of her initial consternation when asked by a stiffly circumspect Chinese bank clerk whether she'd had lunch yet. New to Chinese ways and unaware at the time that "Have you eaten?" is a common Chinese greeting, she wrote: "In British culture, his question would be regarded as an indirect invitation to lunch and between unmarried young people, it indicates the young man's interest in dating the girl. Since he was a complete stranger, I was quite taken aback" (Oatey 1988, 48).

Other cross-cultural hurdles can be harder to identify and neutralize; familiar words can take on unfamiliar forms and feel. To illustrate, let us consider at greater length the following discourse example from a simulated, taped budget meeting among English-speaking Chinese businessmen. All were employees of various British-based, multinational corporations in Hong Kong. Of the five participants assembled, one assumed the role of chairman whereas the other four played section heads. The meeting began with the chairman announcing a budget surplus of 180,000 pounds and asked how it should be distributed. Each of the section heads argued for a portion of the money. Each, moreover, structured his argument in a particular way, using what I call, for convenience, the because . . . so . . . . constructions.[2]

Chairman: Uh, Mr. Lincoln do you think the new machinery that you just mentioned that will cost us sixty thousand pounds will cater for the the ( ) the new model, that is, the portable TV set that was just mentioned by Mr. Jeffrey?

Alpha: I think this new machine will certainly reduce the production cost. And, uh, *AS* WE HAVE AN EXTRA BUDGET OF ABOUT ONE HUNDRED EIGHTY THOUSAND POUNDS STERLING AND WE JUST SPENT ABOUT ONE THIRD OF THE TOTAL AMOUNT BUYING THIS NEW MACHINE AND AS THE SALES OF IT INCREASING THE PRODUCTION OF HOURS, *therefore I think it is very worthwhile at minimal to invest in this new machine by buying a sixty thousand pounds sterling new machine.*

            I have also one thing to say, *BECAUSE* THE PERSONNEL MANAGER, HE MENTIONED A FEW DAYS AGO THAT UH THERE ARE SOME DIFFICULTIES IN THE EQUIPPING MORE NEW WORKERS AND ASK THE EXISTING WORKERS TO WORK OVERTIME BY PAYING THEM SOME EXTRA MONEY, AND *therefore I think that we have no alternative but to buy a new machine or otherwise incur a lot of cost by using the existing one.*

What leaps out immediately is the presentation's unusual rhetorical pattern; the argument unfolds in a direction different from what Anglos would expect. The Chinese speaker begins with the reasons or justifications for his request before arriving at his request; that is, he seems to be setting up the situational framework before proceeding to his request. In contrast, a native English speaker would typically start more straightforwardly with his or her position and then back it up with subsequent subpoints. Note also that "because/as" seems to initiate the discussion whereas "so/therefore" seems to signify new information; that is, they seem to function as discourse markers with "because/as" signalling orienting, supporting information and "so/therefore" signalling upcoming main information. Note further that the speaker twice organizes his thoughts in the same way; I have divided his utterances into two separate paragraphs for the reader's convenience. That all the participants structured their discourse in like manner suggests that this is not an isolated example nor an idiosyncratic personal habit. In addition, the fact that the meeting proceeded smoothly seems to indicate implicit agreement and understanding about the orderly progression of ideas packed in a because . . . so . . . format.

Nonetheless, English-speaking Anglos asked to listen to the budget meeting in its entirety faced numerous difficulties. As they explained, the opening lines of the discourse gave them little indication about the argument's main point; they were initially disoriented and led astray. As a matter of fact, the point at which the Chinese began was so far from the point of the argument that it seemed almost irrelevant to the English-speaking Anglos. Another major stumbling block was the organization of ideas; the discourse was messy with reasons or justifications appearing in a loosely-related listing. In short, the English-speaker's ability to establish a coherent interpretation was jeopardized. All in all, they found the Chinese arguments lacking in focus and force; their persuasive powers were compromised. Worse yet, the lack of precision and the failure to directly address the point made the Chinese appear passive, indirect, and unaccountably reluctant.

However, subsequent inquiries with a number of native Chinese speakers revealed that they found the Chinese businessmen's arguments appropriate to the task and situation. Indeed, when asked to role-play a similar budget meeting themselves, they all began by outlining the reasons for the request before proceeding to the request itself, just like the discourse example above.

Judging from these responses, it appears that the Anglos' distress has less to do with an irresolute weakness or feeble effort on the part of Chinese and more to do with a fledgling understanding of the underlying aims and ends of Chinese discourse on the part of Anglos. In other words, it might be more appropriate to say that the Anglos were challenged by cultural hurdles they did not know existed. Let us now turn to a closer look at these cultural hurdles in light of our discourse example.

One cultural hurdle has to do with unrecognized differences in the features and requirements of grammar and language structure. For one thing, Chinese is a language that puts the "because" part of an utterance before the "so" part. Exceptions and alternatives abound but, on the whole, a Chinese speaker is more obliged to say "Because the tide was low, (so) the shark got trapped inside the reef" rather than the other way around. An English speaker, by contrast, can switch between "The shark got trapped inside the reef because the tide was low" or "Because the tide was low, the shark got trapped inside the reef," generally favoring the former over the latter.

Because . . . so . . . in fact is a fixed construction in Chinese. It falls into that group of complex constructions where subordinate information must precede main information. Sometimes, either "because" or "so" can be optionally omitted in discourse; other times, both can be dropped and the speaker then relies on inference—that is, contextual or real world knowledge. Whatever the case, the appearance of "because" and "so" follows a definite sequence in Chinese, whether on the sentence level or the discourse level. In using this construction, a Chinese speaker can pull together a mass of backgrounding or contextualizing statements before proceeding to his or her assertion. That is, in the case of because . . . so . . . , a mass of explanatory information can be crowded in betweeen "because" and "so." This makes the discourse appear indirect. At the same time, crowding a mass of information between "because" and "so" forces a listener to attend to the circumstances and explanation rather than the speaker's assertion. In this event, situation is foregrounded and assertion is backgrounded.

Chinese is also a language that features the topic-comment construction (or topic-prominence) in contrast to the subject-predicate construction (or subject prominence) more dominant in English. Unlike English's subject-prominence where an utterance can be self-contained with all its parts of speech intact and exact, topic-prominent languages like Chinese can dispense with verbalizing the topic in subsequent utterances once it has been established. The topic will, in other words, be understood. This means, however, that subsequent utterances are linked together into a sort of gigantic sentence and rely on one another more intimately for meaning. This also means that subject (or, more accurately, topic) pronouns like "I", "you" or "(s)he"—and, I will add, the Chinese English speaker's "It"—can be dropped in discourse. The last two utterances of actress Tracy Ullman's caricature of an English-speaking Chinese donut shop owner neatly captures this Chinese discourse characteristic: "Romance like donut. Everybody hungry for donut. Everybody hungry for romance. But when romance over, you not feel so good. Maybe vomit. Same with donut" (*People Magazine*, January 29, 1996, page 80).

Looked at from a certain perspective, dropping topic pronouns can have two other effects. In the first place, the distinction between a "you" and an "I" can be muted in discourse. In addition, a series of dropped "I"'s in discourse can effectively background agency. We catch a glimpse of the latter in a movie snippet from the Billy Crystal-Meg Ryan runaway hit, *When Harry Met Sally*, in which an elderly Chinese gentleman is reminiscing about his arranged marriage and his attempt to sneak a look at his betrothed: "So I sneak into her village. Hid behind a tree. Watched her washing the clothes . . ."

Yet another cultural hurdle has to do with differences in worldview and the rituals and strategies of engagement. Person, self, and ritual for Chinese assume different parameters and affect than for Anglos. Along with that come very different views about deference and decorum, obligation and cooperation.[3] As Chinese see it, persons are embedded in enduring networks of multiple loyalties and reciprocal obligations; one's personal identity is not found deep within oneself but, rather, derived from one's intimate links and bonds with others. Chinese persons are more meaningfully understood in their interrelatedness rather than in their isolation, much like many Chinese utterances can be better understood as relying on one another more intimately for meaning. Correspondingly, Chinese selves are more fully developed in interconnection and interdependence with others; boundaries become diffuse, letting others involve themselves in one's affairs and life choices and vice versa. In a way, it might even be said that they share a collective conscience; they have a personal stake in each other's well-being and doings. Their fates are intertwined and, in fact, in ancient times, the words for "I" and "we" were not distinguished; the same character was used for both. We can better appreciate this sense of self if we remember that in Imperial China, a son, younger brother, or grandfather of someone convicted of a crime, even in a capital case, could assume the punishment of the offender.

If we reach back to Confucius's thinking, we note that ritual plays a prominent role in developing one's self or, as Confucius emphasizes, one's humanity. For Confucius, ritual is hardly a matter of social nicety or polite form, unfelt and empty. Rather, in his thinking, self or one's humanity develops and flourishes through ritual interaction; ritual is the means by which one's humanity is expressed and cultivated. More specifically, one's humanity—that is, one's maturity or growth is revealed and refined through ritual or the ceremonial harmony of civilized intercourse. A mature person knows and shows that he or she has cultivated the ability to constrain personal or selfish desires and to move towards harmonious integration with others. A mature person, in short, knows how to cooperate with and to defer to others, to surrender and sacrifice for the greater good and, in fact, the Chinese word for ritual carries the meaning of "sacrifice."

Ritual lets people come together in interaction; people become integrated through the ceremonies and rites of social intercourse. But ritual also sets people apart; the Chinese ethos of harmony and hierarchy requires respectful distance and careful regard of another's superiority and status. Even when the interactants share equal status, each will take active steps to elevate the other while humbling one's self. As part of the ritual requirements and strategies of facework, a well-mannered Chinese will aggressively try to defer to the other. An uninformed Anglo might therefore be astonished upon witnessing senior and junior Chinese alike scrambling to the rear and pushing others to the front at a formal group photo session; this is just one polite ritual expression of the cultural imperative to willingly efface oneself so as to greatly enhance others.

But the point is not simply that one is lower or higher than the other. Rather, the idea is that one humbles oneself *in relation* to another. What matters to Chinese is the relationship—its constant nurturance and respectful acknowledgement—between persons. This emphasis on relationships and its respectful acknowledgement goes far back into ancient times. Since the third century B.C., for instance, using "you" in direct speech was considered crude except among intimates; instead, Chinese preferred kin or other honorific relationship terms (Hong 1985). Conversely, instead of "I", one might have referred to oneself as "unfilial child" before one's parents or "worthless one" before one's teacher. And even among workmates and chums, *xiao* "young(er)" or *lao* "old(er)" are still affectionately prefixed to surnames to indicate who is younger or older (and so more senior and, sometimes, more studied). More practically, given the bonds and burdens of reciprocal obligations in Chinese thinking, one might artfully opt for the ritually lower or courtesy position in order to manipulate a situation to one's advantage. By emphasizing the other's superiority and power, and, correspondingly, one's inferiority and weakness, one can adroitly appeal for assistance or consideration.

In their ritual routines of everyday talk, Chinese put far greater stress on personal acts that generate social cooperation and harmony rather than public expressions of individual needs or wants. And even though Chinese businessmen are justly famed for their zealous pursuit of competitive advantage, they still take great care in their face-to-face communications to downplay any sign of personal advantage or assertion and to refrain from words or acts that would set themselves apart from others. Instead, they try to start off on a strong footing by seeking out areas of common agreement or relevance or, at least, a mutually accepted direction. Among those that count, they construct their discourse in such a way as to emphasize mutual consideration or a negotiable flexibility; they strive to cultivate an image of responsiveness, all the while steering others their way. In their search for harmonious attunement, they aim for a discourse style that is inclusive and interactive with a great deal of adjusting and accommodating to come. In this regard, harmony is never at a standstill in Chinese thinking; rather, it depends on joint effort and ultimately gets co-constructed in dialogue. Put differently, harmony is never a temple in which to worship but, rather, a journey one negotiates and achieves with others.

Returning to our discourse example, then, we might say that foregrounding background information makes people aware of the circumstances behind one's request; it allows a listener to become gradually oriented to the reasonableness of a speaker's position. Moreover, structuring information this way ensures that shared bonds of understanding will emerge; the listener gets drawn into the reasoning process as a joint enterprise. The roles between speaker and listener—between I and you, self and other—start to blur. In addition, clarifying the circumstances behind one's request not only forestalls premature interruption and face-threatening opposition, it also wards off undue charges of a demanding egotistical self-assertion that ultimately threatens the interconnectiveness and interdependency undergirding Chinese social existence. As for the notes of reluctance and passivity, they signal deferential intent and negotiable flexibility, or, at least, an unwillingness to impose. Taken together, they show respect for one's listener and open the possibility of one and all participating in the mutual adjusting and accommodating necessary to develop a consensual agreement and to achieve the cultural ideal of a harmonious integration.

This cultural sense of harmonic integration and interdependency—a sort of dynamic unity in diversity—ramifies throughout Chinese thinking and exerts a strong influence in their methods and goals of personal engagement. Start with the ever-moving, interlocking yin-yang figure: its dark and light parts are different, yet each contains a smaller patch of the other. Similarly, Chinese assume an intimate and robust dependency in their constant cultivation and conscientious conduct of personal relations where there is a "me inside of you" and "a you inside of me" (Yang 1994: 192). Even their busy pursuit of *quanxi* relations, those useful—and sometimes crucial (see Yang 1994)—social connections replenished or deepened by the immediate or staggered exchange of gifts and favors, are shot through with warm personal feelings of *renqing*, rendered colloquially by some as "human emotional debt." That is, when someone does you a good turn, one "receives a human emotion" whereupon one becomes obliged to return the benevolence two-or-more-fold, materially or spiritually, in due time (Chang and Holt 1995). There is, in other words, no free lunch for the interlocked participants involved in *quanxi's* giving and getting.

Speaking of food, we find that Chinese not only pair tastes and textures—e.g., hot and sour, warm and cold, soft and crisp, delicate and spicy—for ultimate culinary delight, but according to the late Shanghai-born, British-based gourmand, diplomat, and Chinese renaissance man, Kenneth Lo, Chinese combine their meats and vegetables "to impregnate flavor into each other" (Lo 1958, 13). Continuing with food, we can see the same sense of harmonic integration and interdependency extending not only to dish selection and pairings but also to their very eating. Unlike Western restaurant dining, where each diner chooses a dish according to one's palate or allergies, Chinese pair dishes, one with the other, with an eye to combining and complementing flavors, textures, colors, and cooking techniques. And since Chinese dining is nearly always a communal affair with dishes brought out simultaneously on common plates, each diner selects a bit of this and a bit of that in between bites of rice from their individual bowls.

It is a style of dining that many Anglos can easily step into and partake with relish; culture presents few barriers to the pleasures of communal dining and the rhythms of consumption from common plates. Yet, it gets trickier when moving from dining to talking; the rhythms of cross-cultural talking are harder to negotiate than the rhythms of mixed communal dining. Sharing a common language can just make things worse as people become lulled into falsely believing they share common grounds for understanding. More likely instead, their conversations run aground as missed understandings slip into misunderstandings. Efforts to socially connect unexpectedly turn into fundamental disconnects. Instead of interlocking in talk, interlocutors can find themselves locked into inscrutable muddles from which they cannot easily extract themselves. The cross-cultural hurdles can be formidable, particularly when we consider that one culture's two most commonly used words, "I" and "you," respectively, can be conveniently omitted in the other culture's discourse and when we consider how one culture's valuation of "getting straight to the point" meets its match in the other culture's belief that "evil spirits travel in straight lines."

It is often said that England and America are two cultures divided by a common language. The differences and difficulties compound exponentially in the Sino-Anglo crosstalk. Chinese in the know might describe the situation as akin to a chicken talking to a duck. Or better yet, a chicken mistaking a duck for a chicken. A duck's "quack" may sound like a sick "cluck," and sometimes it is, but, more often than not, a "cluck" is a "cluck" is a "cluck," just as a "quack" is a "quack" is a "quack," and wiser are those whose ears are attuned to the difference.

ENDNOTES

1. By "Chinese", I refer to speakers of Putonghua, Taiwanese, and Cantonese (as well as some of their English-speaking descendants). These Chinese dialects are mutually unintelligible, yet they all share a core grammar and feature the because . . . so . . . construction. Just as pertinent, the speakers of these various dialects are readily able to identify the businessmen's underlying intentions and strategies. By "Anglo," I refer to the English-speaking natives and descendants of people from dominantly Western countries who share a middle-class, mainstream orientation.

2. Some readers may find this passage confusing because I have transcribed it word for

word and deliberately left in stammers, ungrammatical elements and so on to provide a piece of authentic speech. (The empty parenthesis indicates unintelligible words; this adds to the difficulty.) The reader is advised, however, to attend to the discourse structure which I have tried to mark out using a series of capital letters and italics. In addition, the Chinese businessmen assumed the role of Westerners, which accounts for their English surnames in the data. Please see my book, *Crosstalk*, pages 32–34, for the other Chinese discourse examples from the budget meeting.

3. My book, *Crosstalk*, gives a fuller account of these differences; see, for instance, pages 41–42, 44–46, 108–112, 137–167.

Part III

Clinical Issues

Chapter Five

Value Issues Involving American Psychoanalysts with Asian Patients

VALUES AND NORMALITY/PSYCHOPATHOLOGY

In our psychoanalytic work, it is only when we are confronted with a patient from a radically different culture that we realize we are constantly guaging patients' associations and ways of relating to us and others against a backdrop of what is appropriate or not on a normality/psychopathology continuum. We base these evaluations on our implicit understanding of what goes or doesn't go within our own culture. More specifically, we are constantly evaluating how a patient talks, what the emotional tone is, the kinds of relationships he or she has, how the person relates to the analyst, and such along a normality/psychopathology continuum with which we are familiar. Since psychoanalysts are constantly working with persons from a relatively similar background, analysts almost never reflect on this process. We simply go about making our evaluations automatically without any great problem.

Even with someone from our own culture but from a different ethnic and/or regional background, we simply take into account certain obvious differences. Thus, a New York City analyst would not necessarily consider that a person from a Midwestern Protestant background speaking in session with a relatively flat emotional tone—at least compared to those from many New York City ethnic groups—is emotionally detached. Unless there were evidence to the contrary, the analyst would consider this within the normal range for someone of that background.

When an American psychoanalyst from European roots works with a patient from a radically different culture, such as from any of the Asian societies, one is faced with the realization that our implicit understandings and judgments might not work. Analysts then might find themselves at sea, not knowing what is or isn't normal or skewed. That is, unless one falls back on American cultural norms of individualism that are integral to psychoanalysis today as a universal yardstick. In this case, what I would term colonial attitudes toward Asians may very subtly surface in the analyst. These attitudes view Asian norms of dependency and interdependence, deference to superiors, and communication by innuendo as inferior to American psychoanalytic norms involved in separation-individuation, autonomy, self-assertiveness, and verbal articulateness. We often do not reflect that our norms are profoundly related to the modern Western culture of individualism in its American variant.

It is only when we are involved in an experience with persons from vastly different cultures that we begin to ask more questions of ourselves. What is this person talking about? Where is my assumed background from which I can make judgments and evaluations? What is normal? What is abnormal? Where is development skewed? Where does the problem actually lie? It is not that our usual psychoanalytic work precludes these questions. They just beset the analyst with more urgency and anxiety in these intercultural encounters.

Psychoanalysts who do not have these comparative experiences are usually blithely unaware of the enormous variations in the human psyche that challenge the very basis of our work. They often respond, "Oh yes, I encounter that all of the time in my practice," oblivious to the possibility of an experience very different from anything they've ever encountered. Asians, however, are very aware of the differences. A Chinese-American graduate student in clinical psychology confirmed how unaware the rest of the students and faculty were to her own unique background.

It wasn't a surprise when a group of Japanese, Korean, and Chinese students in a major social work program in New York City invited me to educate the faculty about Asian psychology since all the readings and lectures were oriented to predominant American psychological makeup and development and not to Asian. These students wanted something taught about human development in their own East Asian societies where infants and toddlers usually sleep next to their mothers, and then with someone else; and where close interdependencies are fostered rather than the American emphasis on separation, independence, self-reliance, and self-directedness, as well as a host of other practices that result in very different developmental emphases.

For the practicing psychoanalyst, recognizing that there is a different normality/psychopathology continuum is a sine quae non for working with persons from these other cultures. To become acquainted with this different continuum requires a degree of openness, inquiry, and not knowing that goes well beyond the attitudes that a psychoanalyst ordinarily needs to cultivate. It is therefore a constant challenge to develop new understandings of what goes or doesn't go in patients from Asian cultures.

But recognizing a different continuum is only the starting point for a psychoanalyst. The even greater challenge is to find out where the particular problems a patient has lie on this continuum. That is, where there is skewed development, problematic family relationships, and psychopathology within this other cultural/psychological continuum. Even such basic things as transference displacement to the psychoanalyst may be misread if the kind of affect expression varies significantly. Although I have worked for some years with Indian and Japanese patients, this still constitutes an ongoing struggle.

To facilitate this understanding, it becomes incumbent on the therapist to be sufficiently aware of radical cultural differences that enter upon the psychological stage. To do this may mean reading up on that person's culture or consulting with a knowledgeable colleague, or more frequently to use the patient as a resource to explain characteristic values and social patterns. This enables the therapist to differentiate the characteristic from the skewed.

I would like to give a few brief case examples to illustrate these points. The first one is Mrs. Kakkar, an Indian woman in her mid-forties, who came for psychoanalytic therapy to resolve intensely distraught feelings about her mother who had died a couple of years before the patient saw me. She and her mother had become bitterly alienated in her mother's last years after a lifetime of extreme closeness, companionship, and mutual support. While there is much that is of interest from a cultural standpoint in this case, I shall focus in this chapter only on points relevant to value issues.

From my work with a number of Indians (Roland 1988), I was quite used to Indians expecting a greater degree of emotional relatedness and care from a psychoanalyst than the usual American patient. Indians feel freer to be much more dependent. Mrs. K. was no exception. Mrs. K., a highly educated and cultured woman, would sometimes come late, held up after being in her responsible job at a publishing house. Any inquiry into her lateness was usually brushed aside with an apology. Sometimes, because of responsibilities toward her teenage daughter, who had become quite ill, she would have to reschedule or miss a session. She would expect that this either be made up, or if there were a few sessions in a row that she missed, that she not be responsible for them. Sometimes, payment would be late, always with an apology and a clear-cut reason. From a value standpoint, I sensed that a usual rigorous inquiry and analysis of resistance, or a firm setting of the structure of sessions, would so alienate her as an Indian that I would no longer have her in therapy.

Nevertheless, I also sensed that while Mrs. K.'s departures from some of the structures of the psychoanalytic session and fees were cultural in manner, there seemed more to them. I gradually felt after a long period of time that I was being subtly intruded upon. But then my experience of working in Bombay was of feeling intruded upon all the time by any number of persons, and in fact, feeling swallowed up by them. One's normal American ego boundaries between self and others can easily disappear in an Indian setting. Or was there some deeper problem being communicated in the transference? It is just this kind of tantalizing problem of appreciating what is different in an Asian patient, but then struggling to see what, if any, psychopathology is involved that becomes so much of a challenge.

After a period of over two years of twice a week psychoanalytic therapy, when we began probing much deeper into her relationship with her mother, it emerged that Mrs. K.'s mother had frequently come to her bedroom when she was a child, confided all kinds of feelings and thoughts to her, and not infrequently slept in the same bed with her rather than with her husband. Here, I knew that while children and their parents may well sleep together for a number of years in an Indian family, it is unusual for a mother to depart from her husband's to her child's bed, especially in another room. I further knew from other patients I had worked with, that while Indian mothers and daughters can at times be unusually close, at least from an American perspective, somehow this constant confiding to her daughter seemed out of the normal range for an Indian mother.

With this awareness, I began working on the transference with Mrs. K., how she subtly and unconsciously reenacted the role of her mother with me and put me in the role of herself. As we talked about this, it emerged that one of her greatest problems with her two daughters was her tremendous vulnerability to their demands on her. She simply could not say "no" to either of them, as she couldn't with her mother. Discussing and interpreting all of this obviously began to help her. But the key element was pinpointing the psychopathology from an early problematic familial relationship embedded in a cultural pattern of intimate interdependent relatedness that differs significantly from the prevailing American ethos.

VALUES AND THE MAGIC-COSMIC

There were other aspects of the therapy that could easily challenge the usual value orientation of an American psychoanalyst. Similar to every Hindu patient with whom I have worked, Mrs. K. was at times oriented to the magic-cosmic world of personal destiny, as well as to the spiritual. This, I may add, is equally true of Hindu psychoanalysts, especially to the magic-cosmic world. The magic-cosmic is an area that Indian patients will keep secret to themselves if they sense a Western psychoanalyst has denigrating attitudes of rationalism toward astrology, palmistry, the spirit world, and psychics, all of which are used for learning about one's destiny. Asians are extremely sensitive to what a therapist will or won't be receptive, and are quite capable of keeping secrets in a highly private self throughout therapy.

Sensing that I was open to these realms and not caught up in the mode of Western rationalism that so abhors these areas, Mrs. K. matter-of-factly related one day that her teenage daughter had told her she was having out-of-body experiences. Her daughter's experiences seemed to come from long periods of meditation which she had learned from a baby-sitter and secretly practiced for years. Mrs. K. was taken aback by this revelation from her daughter, but handled it in a quite practical way. She simply brought her daughter to a highly respected teacher of meditation whom Mrs. K. knew. The teacher told her daughter that she was over-meditating for someone her age, and then gave her instructions for what was suitable. To have suggested that her daughter needed to see a therapist because of these seemingly psychotic experiences would have totally alienated Mrs. K. Her daughter actually did see a therapist, but for completely different reasons.

Mrs. K. also commented on this daughter's psychic ability that seemed telepathic at times, and felt that she was quite possibly a reincarnation of a younger sister of Mrs. K. who tragically died at an early age. Both were afflicted with a serious illness very difficult to diagnose. Again, to dismiss or treat these attitudes as psychopathological would have been to impose a rationalist Western value system on an Indian patient.

This is not to say, however, that some Indian patients might not use this predominant cultural form in a problematic way. One Indian patient, Asok, who was extremely self-defeating through lengthy periods of an analysis, frequently consulted astrologers and psychics for advice and guidance, as he was constantly conflicted over what to do with his life. This seemed overdetermined. In one aspect, he turned to them as a repetition of earlier familial relationships in which older brothers and sisters constantly gave him advice and made major decisions in his life, which he often only reluctantly followed if at all. Similarly, after seeking the advice of the astrologers and psychics, he frequently ignored it, instead later railing at them in session as he increasingly did about his siblings. In another aspect, Asok unconsciously turned to these conveyors of the magic-cosmic world as a manifestation of a highly passive orientation to life that was filled with hidden self-destructive willfullness and inhibited rage, as well as loaded with transference meaning to defeat the therapist and the therapy. Once the rage fully emerged in the transference with me over a prolonged period of time, consultations with astrologers and psychics ceased, although it was still a fundamental part of Asok's world view.

VALUES AND GUIDANCE

Still another aspect of the psychoanalytic therapy with Mrs. K. embodies a different value orientation. Most Indian patients approach an analyst with the expectation that the analyst will give advice and guidance, very similar to what is common with parents and other family elders, not to mention gurus. Indians are brought up with an attitude of being receptive to such advice and guidance as they expect a caring, concerned, and nurturing attitude that goes along with the advice in their familial hierarchical relationships. It enables them to traverse the complex, highly involved hierarchical relationships of the extended family and other groups.

Mrs. K. similarly came to sessions with an expectation I would guide her about what to talk about. Here, I find it incumbent on an American psychoanalyst not to treat this as a problematic resistance, but rather to educate the patient into expressing whatever is on her mind as freely as possible, as a way of getting to the bottom of her problems and issues. And indeed, Mrs. K. gradually became much freer in expressing her thoughts and feelings, but still began sessions in a respectful manner that there might be something I wanted her to talk about.

Again, a culturally normal mode of relating, such as expecting an analyst to give advice and guidance, can be unconsciously used in the service of a problematic transference. Asok, whom I mentioned above, would seek counsel from astrologers and psychics as he was used to receiving from family members, also constantly and persistently asked and expected me to give him guidance and make decisions for him. He repeated this pattern in group sessions as well. He even experienced ordinary interpretations or questions as some form of guidance for making decisions.

It gradually became clear that he negated any direction that group members suggested, or anything that he took for guidance from me; moreover, he later incriminated either myself or other group members for giving him bad advice. All of this turned out to be the unconscious repetition of a family situation in which his father had to leave India when Asok was in his early teens, which resulted in older brothers and sisters making major educational and vocational decisions for Asok, which he long resented as being antithetical to his own interests and wishes. Since he was so dependent on all of them, it was impossible to assert his own desires.

MALE CHAUVINISM AND WE-SELF ESTEEM

I would like to briefly share the case of a young Indian man, Gopal, whose attitudes so enraged a quite competent American woman psychoanalyst because of her own values that she referred him to me as someone who might understand Indians better. What angered her was his seriously considering divorcing his American wife for no seeming cause. The relationship seemed quite good. The analyst could not understand such an attitude, which she felt was completely narcissistic and male chauvinist.

The story quickly unfolded that Gopal had come to America because he was not able to find a job in India after graduating college, and felt he was a failure in his family's eyes. The only way he could remain in the United States was to work for relatives in New York City who thoroughly exploited his trapped situation with them. And the only way he could escape this entrapment without returning to India was to marry an American woman. This he did, a divorced woman with a child, with whom he got along very well.

Gaining free entry here, he quickly left his relatives and established his own business, worked very hard, became successful, and sent back considerable monies to his family in India. One must appreciate that a great deal of Indians' and other Asians' self-esteem is tied up with the reputation of their family, how they reflect on the family, and the respect the family gives them. It is actually more accurate to describe this as we-self esteem than as our individualistic self-esteem. Gopal had now become a success, enhancing his family's reputation and earning great respect from them. This was all-important to him as it enhanced his we-self esteem.

But he had also married a divorced woman, moreover one with a child from a previous marriage. This was an enormous blot on his upper-caste family's reputation. On one hand, marrying her enabled him to enhance his family's reputation and his own we-self esteem through his being able to go into business for himself and become successful; while simultaneously, it negatively affected his family reputation and his esteem. He was quite attached to his wife, but living the rest of his life with her was like having a scarlet letter. This was his dilemma, one I could clarify for him, but unfortunately not resolve.

VALUES AND NORMALITY/PSYCHOPATHOLOGY IN JAPANESE

I shall now turn to a Japanese patient seen in four times a week psychoanalysis to illustrate further the difficulties in separating out tremendous differences in value orientation from psychopathology. Keigo came to the United States to do graduate work in comparative literature. A college counselor wisely advised him to be in psychoanalysis as it would be very helpful to him for doing his doctorate. His parents were financing him for this several year period of graduate work in a New York City university from an old successful, family business. Before starting the analysis he had asked me to give him the lowest possible fee as the cost of his schooling and living in New York City was considerable, even considering the higher value of the yen. I quoted him a fee that was my very lowest.

After a year's time, as is my customary practice with patients who can seem to manage it, I brought up that I generally raise my fee $5 a session. Since he had been recently awarded an assistantship in the graduate school program, this seemed equitable to me. But not to him. He asserted that in Japan once a fee is agreed to, it is set forever, even in the case of a five-year psychoanalysis.

He mildly upbraided me that with my background about the Japanese I should know that Japanese need to express *amae*, or be highly dependent and nurtured in their important hierarchical relationships, which would obviously include the psychoanalytic one. Further, he felt deprived living in New York City, and this would be a further deprivation paying a higher fee.

Once we got past the initial phase of the analysis, he had a great yearning to be dependent and be taken care of by me (to *amaeru*) in the closer, more symbiotic mode of the Japanese with an intimate superior. It emerged that he had been deeply frustrated in his dependency needs by a mother who was all too preoccupied with the family business. He clearly wanted me to make up for this as a much older female cousin had partially done, with whom he spent considerable time throughout his childhood. And one way of satisfying his *amae* dependency cravings was to keep the fee the same.

What made the situation even more complicated was Keigo saying that if I wanted to raise the fee, I certainly could and he would have to go along with it. Another face to Japanese hierarchical relationships is that the superior can easily dictate what is to happen, and the subordinate loyally obeys, keeping all kinds of angry feelings secret within a highly private self. I felt caught between the two poles of Japanese hierarchy: that of being the nurturing superior fulfilling Keigo's dependency needs as his older cousin had done; or of being the authoritative superior who simply makes decisions regardless of the subordinate. If I chose the latter course of simply raising the fee, as I easily could have done, it would not have clarified any underlying transference meanings; displaced negative reactions might simply be kept secret. I decided for some period to keep the fee the same.

Gradually I realized that money, itself, was a highly charged topic for him because of the way his family in general, and his mother in particular, used money to manipulate others. When I sensed almost two years into the analysis that his insistence that the fee stay the same was not only an expression of Japanese cultural values, but also a resistance against the transference experience of having me as the money-preoccupied mother, I interpreted this to him. I told him it was important for the analysis that the fee be raised, even if it were just 25 cents a session. He could see the point although he was not happy about it.

When the fee was raised, and he indeed experienced me as the greedy, manipulative mother always preoccupied with money, he became increasingly enraged at me. This enabled us to analyze this highly problematic relationship with his mother, together with his strong obsessive-compulsive defenses against the rage. It was a key turning point in the analysis.

In effect, in this case, I had to see where an unconscious resistance against experiencing a highly problematic transference was supported by normal Japanese cultural attitudes. If I had known these particular Japanese values of keeping the fee the same, I would have undoubtedly discussed the whole matter of fee increases in the beginning. But this would not have addressed the intertwining of cultural values and personal psychopathology that became so difficult for me as an American psychoanalyst to untangle.

One value issue that Yasuhiko Taketomo (1989) has written about is that the male analyst is always experienced as a mentor by a Japanese male patient not only through the analysis but also for the rest of their lives. Even during the most intense expressions of anger in the negative transference, Keigo still experienced me as a mentor. This kind of idealization is more a deeply internalized cultural attitude intrinsic to Japanese hierarchical relationships than a defensive one, as an object-relations psychoanalyst might see it, or a reparative experience as a self psychological analyst would understand it. To have analyzed Keigo's seeing me as a mentor would only have brought grief to the analysis, unless I perceived that it was also being used in a psychopathological way.

I should also add that the kind of nurturing Keigo expected from me and his need to be dependent and have an *amae* relationship with me went well beyond the usual boundaries of an American-style psychoanalytic relationship, but not an Indian one. Keigo, for instance, fully expected me to give him guidance on handling many of the complexities and intricacies of dealing with American-style situations and relationships, including those in graduate school. But more of the time, it was a subtle, unspoken quality of comfort in his feeling that I would take care of him in a nurturing, empathic way.

Indians, too convey this same quality of being very much at home in their dependency on me. One Indian woman, who had not yet become Americanized, simply walked into my consulting room and sat down if she arrived before I did. To have analyzed this normal mode of Indian relating would have only brought grief to the therapy. Whereas when one American patient did the same thing, it quickly became apparent that his entering the consulting room before I had come was loaded with transference meanings.

More particularly Japanese was Keigo bowing to me before and after each session as a sign of deference and respect, even when he was enraged at me. As he resolved the intense negative transference around his mother and became a much less obsessive-compulsive person, the bowing continued but seemingly in a more perfunctory way.

THE JAPANESE CONSCIENCE

There are two other significant differences in value orientation that have to be taken into account in working with a Japanese patient. The first is that every Japanese patient I have worked with or supervised a therapist on has a deeply entrenched ego-ideal of having to do everything perfectly, both socially and in tasks. This has profound implications for psychoanalytic work because Japanese are extremely sensitive to failure and criticism. Thus, an analyst has to be more than ordinarily tactful in interpeting. A direct, confrontive approach that some American psychoanalysts pride themselves on can be fraught with problems in working with a Japanese.

As an example of this perfectionistic conscience, Keigo worked extremely long hours in his graduate school studies, on an assistantship, at another job to earn extra monies, and on his dissertation, all at the same time. Moreover, everything had to be done extremely well. He both marvelled at the inefficiency of Americans and became very annoyed at it, such as when his furniture was delivered an hour and a half late with a mistake in the bill. He frequently made derogatory comments on how Americans function. They obviously unconsciously represented a repudiated part of himself that was not allowed to ease up in any way because of his strict values.

Another Japanese patient, Akahisa, had become the only eldest son since the twelfth century not to become a Buddhist priest in his family, an inherited position. Instead, he left the rural area where his family lived and became an educator, though still being very much interested in Buddhism. Much of our twice a week psychoanalytic therapy over a year's time was to clarify why he had made such a far-reaching decision, and to alleviate obvious guilt about it. Certainly, one of the most important motives, if not the most important, was his reactions to his mother's expectations that he would become a great Buddhist priest such as her grandfather and uncle had been. Her expectations were simply too much for Akahisa to live with for the rest of his life. They were so strong that he felt it left little room for being himself. It seemed to be an extreme version of the normal cultural mode of Japanese mothers having high expectations for their children. Instead, he became a kind of maverick in Japan, more individualistic than most, still coping with his guilt over opting out of his family role, and unlike Keigo, revelling in the freedom of American life where one is far more able to do what one wants.

JAPANESE COMMUNICATION

The second difference in value orientation is that Japanese traditionally expect a great deal of communication to take place by concerned empathic sensing (*omoiyari*) rather than by verbal expression. The Japanese saying that nothing important is ever to be communicated verbally goes directly against a cardinal value of American psychoanalysis and culture to express all kinds of feelings and thoughts verbally. Therefore, an American analyst working with a Japanese patient should be attuned to the possibility that a great deal may be going on by innuendo, more so at an earlier stage than with an American.

This Japanese mode of communication surfaces in other relationships with Americans. Two Japanese women married to Americans both expressed in sessions that they expected their husbands to sense what they were thinking and feeling without expressing it verbally, and became quite angry when they didn't. For an American analyst to consider this as some kind of malfunctioning rather than as a differing cultural mode of communication would short-circuit an empathic understanding of what was creating the problem in the marital relationship, and thus make it more difficult to resolve.

VALUE DISSONANCES OF ASIANS IN AMERICAN RELATIONSHIPS

Another highly important value issue for an American psychoanalyst working with an Asian patient in the United States is that these patients may enter psychoanalysis or psychoanalytic therapy intensely distraught over the extremely difficult time they are experiencing in American social and work relationships. I should emphasize that it is usually very helpful and sometimes necessary to clarify the radical differences, at times opposites, in values in social functioning and development between their culture and the predominant American one. For the analyst to delve immediately into their personal psychopathology and biography without dealing with this existential, intercultural stress may result in the patient leaving treatment.

An empathic stance over the enormous differences in social values and ways of relating will not only enable Asian patients to delve more easily into their personal problems, but will also enable them to begin sorting out just how much they want to take on new ways of social relatedness, how much to remain in indigenous values and patterns, and how to put the two together in a bicultural self. It is a decision, or rather series of decisions that they have to work out themselves.

As an example, an Indian woman who is an internationally recognized scientist living in America complained of having to make her own decisions all of the time. "We weren't brought up to be independent." This echoed other Indian patients I have worked with.

This kind of value dissonance surfaced in psychoanalytic couple's therapy in a much more pervasive way in the relationship between Meena and George, a Hindu woman married to an American. Meena complained bitterly that George never stuck to his word, neither as her boss and mentor, nor as her husband. "He says one thing one day, and then changes his mind the next. It drives me crazy. I can't trust him." George, on the other hand, complained that Meena wanted everything cast in concrete. "I see nothing wrong in renegotiating agreements when circumstances change."

It took some time to see that whatever personal problems they were bringing to the relationship, there were strong cultural assumptions on both their parts that contributed to the strife. Meena viewed her marital as well as work relationship with George essentially as an emotionally enmeshed hierarchical one. Quite similar to other Indian women, she looked up to George as the superior who makes the decisions in their marriage, usually in full consultation with her; and once made, she goes along with them. Thus, his decisions were the orienting point of a compass from which she took her direction. For him to change his mind meant to her an abdication of his responsibility as the superior. George, on the other hand, coming from a culture of individualism, assumed their marriage to be an equal one between two separate individuals, where decisions would be made by talking things over, and easily changed through further negotiation. It was only as these cultural assumptions came to the fore in therapy sessions, that they could begin to accommodate each other.

But the value dissonances that Meena experienced were not only in her marriage. They also surfaced in her work as manager of the most important department in the firm of which George was the director. George constantly challenged Meena to be much more assertive, direct, and articulate American-style with those under her; otherwise, she could not be a successful manager. There was apparently little room for accommodating Meena's Indian-style notions of being the nurturing superior who expected deference and loyalty from her subordinates. Meena gradually incorporated American-style modes of managerial leadership into a bicultural self through courses in assertiveness training and her own individual therapy. She eventually became a fully competent manager within this American firm as she took on American ways of relating.

These kinds of value dissonances that Meena experienced in the workplace can also be experienced by Japanese as well. In Chapter Six I shall focus on the distressing situation of Yoshiko, who was also called to function in an American corporation in certain ways totally antithetical to her indigenous modes of relating.

SUMMARY

American and other Western psychoanalysts operating from a value system rooted in the culture of individualism must be aware that Asian patients have an entirely different world view. By realizing the cultural context of one's own values, a psychoanalyst can then be more open to other orientations cited in the case material above: Indians' familial source of self-esteem, or their involvement with spiritual pursuits and the realm of personal destiny with its concomittant use of astrology, palmistry, psychics, and such; or the Japanese ego-ideal of doing everything perfectly and communicating a great deal nonverbally or by innuendo. An analyst's cultural self-awareness will also make it easier to recognize different patterns of functioning, particularly in dependency relationships that have significantly different norms than North American ones; and then to make the difficult evaluations as to what went askew for a patient within this different continuum of normality-psychopathology. Finally, this self-awareness will enable an American analyst to empathize with the conflict and anguish many Asians have in adapting to such a different life style and values in the United States, many diametrically opposite to their own.

Chapter Six

The Cultural Self, the Personal Self, and Psychological Conflict

CONCEPTUALIZING THE CULTURAL SELF

I would like to speak from the vantage point of a psychoanalyst who has worked with a wide variety of American patients from different ethnic groups, social classes, and regions of the United States, as well as with Indians and Japanese in their own countries and in New York City. Over the years I have become increasingly struck with having to consider social and cultural factors with all of these patients in order to understand and resolve their inner conflicts. I find that cultural values, social patterns, and sociohistorical change enter into the human psyche in a more important way than is often appreciated, and sometimes can result in intense, emotional conflicts. Thus, sociocultural patterns and social change are not simply out there to be studied by the social scientist, humanist, and historian; they are deeply embedded within the self and certainly enter the domain of the psychoanalyst who is attuned to them.

The issue is how to conceptualize the role of sociocultural and historical factors in psychological conflict and psychopathology. Freud (1923, 1930) partially addressed this issue in his structural model when he postulated that conflict is inherent in the human condition because of the demands and strictures of social living which he deemed civilization. These strictures, mediated from the larger culture through parental figures and then internalized into the superego and ego-ideal, inevitably result in inner conflict with an individual's drives and wishes.

Within the Freudian opus, Erikson (1963, 1968) made the most far-reaching formulations of the effects of sociocultural and sociohistorical factors on personality development and psychopathology. Locating individuals within the mores and world views of their communities, Erikson (1946) explored the effects on their identity, particularly on identity conflicts and resolutions. While Erikson studied radically different cultures such as India, his clinical work was confined to persons from various European and American cultures.

As psychoanalysis expands to working with persons from a far greater range of cultures, a much more detailed consideration of social, cultural, and historical factors within a psychoanalytic framework of the self is clearly needed. I would characterize my notion of the personal self as constituting the various characteristics of the self in both its normal development and psychopathology as currently delineated in psychoanalysis: in ego psychology, the experiences with familial figures in terms of self and object representations, and the overall organization of the self; in object relations theory, the internal object world as well as the true and false self; and in self psychology, self-cohesion versus self-fragmentation, self-esteem, and selfobject relationships.

But we also need to posit a cultural self that is profoundly linked on all levels of self-experience, developmental stages, earlier and later object and selfobject relationships, inner structures, and normality/psychopathology to the sociocultural milieu(s) within which a person has grown up, as well as to experiences in a particular sociohistorical era and the changes that have taken place. What complicates this further are possibly different sociocultural milieus and sociohistorical experiences of parental and other familial figures. In other words, the cultural self of parents may differ significantly from each other and have varying effects on the child.

On a theoretical level, aspects of a cultural self must give new shape and texture to accepted descriptions of the self derived from current psychoanalytic theories, especially when a person comes from a radically different culture. It is important theoretically to posit and emphasize a cultural self because psychoanalysis, originating and developing within the Northern European/North American culture of individualism, largely ignores the influence of the cultural world without realizing how much psychoanalysis, itself, is related to it.

On the personal level of self experience, sociocultural factors are very much experienced as an integral part of a personal self. In fact, one might term them the most invisible part of the self. Because these factors are so much a part of the basic fabric of the self, a person is rarely aware of them. They almost only become conscious if persons through circumstance or choice, live in a significantly different culture from their own. A comparative living experience glaringly highlights aspects of our self that we take for granted.

To discuss the clinical issues of a cultural self in a North American setting, it is helpful to formulate a continuum. At one extreme on the continuum are persons from radically different cultures, such as Asians, Middle Easterners, and Africans, who can experience considerable emotional conflict and even anguish in a North American milieu. In the middle of the continuum are persons originally from Mediterranean and Latino societies, as well as African-Americans who have lived in America for some generations. Their internalized sociocultural patterns may also differ significantly from the predominant North American life style, but not as much as Asian patterns do. At the other end of the continuum are those with Northern European roots, or others who have more or less acclimatized themselves to this ethos. With patients from this background, where their culture is highly congruent with the predominant North American one, sociocultural factors can still play a role in their psychopathology, occasionally in a major way. Regardless of which part of the continuum a person is on, sociohistorical, regional, and class factors in a particular culture can also play an important role in inner conflicts.

AN INTERCULTURAL ENCOUNTER

To illustrate various aspects of my perspective, I shall present some case material. The first example involves the interface between the cultural self of a Japanese woman and predominant North American business relationships. I saw a young Japanese woman, Yoshiko, in psychoanalytic therapy for approximately a year. Although working at a good job in New York City and happily married to an American, she came for therapy because of very disturbing emotional problems at work. These were of two kinds. The first involved difficulties phoning people and bargaining assertively with them for a product the company needed. She found this very hard to do, and then would become even more disturbed when the other person would sometimes be nasty to her. All of this was exacerbated when her supervisor took her to task for not being assertive enough. The second problem involved her reaction to criticism for occasional minor mistakes in her reports. She apparently made far fewer mistakes than her coworkers, but suffered emotionally far more than they when her boss took her to task in what she perceived was a harsh manner.

In this case, I immediately sensed that it was essential to deal with both problems as part of Yoshiko's cultural self and the conflicts it engendered as she had to function in an American environment. From my experience of supervising therapists in Japan, I appreciated that Japanese are not used to confrontation or self-assertion in the predominant American mode. In Japan, communication is always indirect and polite. I was able to acknowledge with Yoshiko how difficult it must be for her to have to function in a way so drastically different from what she was used to. Somehow, acknowledging this conflict of her cultural self in the American social milieu enabled her to feel less disturbed and somewhat more assertive. We also talked about how sensitive Japanese are to any criticism because they have internalized extremely high standards of performance, and are constantly sensitive to any failures. She felt that if her superior would only very gently indicate any mistake she had made, she would feel sufficiently chagrined to strive toward perfect performance—unlike the other workers who seemed to let the supervisor's carping roll off their backs like water off a duck.

As we worked on these conflicts of her cultural self in its adaptation to American relationships, she began to reveal a more personal, idiosyncratic relationship that made criticism or nastiness from others so intensely upsetting. She had a powerful, assertive paternal grandmother who had ruled the roost of her samurai family. Unlike other grandmothers, who generally spoiled their grandchildren in contrast to the mother who would have strict expectations, this grandmother had extremely high standards and could be constantly critical. Even in public life, she participated in an articulate, assertive manner rare for Japanese women.

On the one hand, my patient internalized her grandmother's high expectations and standards: she went to one of the foremost colleges in Japan, where the ratio of women students to men was one in a hundred, got a graduate school degree, and had both a career and a family—an extremely unusual combination for educated Japanese women at that time. On the other hand, Yoshiko found her grandmother's criticisms so grating that these affected her reactions at work as well as in other relationships. In her adolescence, her ambivalence toward her grandmother was so intense that after she won a nationwide Haiku poetry contest—which the grandmother said was natural since she, herself, wrote Haiku—Yoshiko never wrote another verse. Thus, once we moved beyond issues of the cultural self in this Japanese woman, the more usual types of emotional conflict could be explored and resolved as is typical in psychoanalytic work.

Yoshiko's psychoanalytic therapy illustrates how helpful it usually is, in working with Asians, to clarify the radical differences in social functioning and development between their culture and the predominant North American one. This empathic stance often enables them to begin sorting out just how much to take on new ways of social relatedness, or how much to remain rooted in indigenous patterns, and how to put the two together in a bicultural self. This is a decision, or series of decisions, that they have to work out themselves. Paradoxically, this enables them to delve more deeply into problems stemming from their own idiosyncratic family background.

DIFFERENTIATING CONFLICTS

The more familiar a psychoanalyst is with the particular sociocultural patterns a patient comes from, the easier it is to differentiate when a given conflict or problematic behavior stems from internalized cultural values, or when it relates to a difficult family relationship. I would like to describe the case of Narayan to illustrate how these two sources of conflict must be differentiated. At one point in sessions Narayan began complaining frequently about his newly married American wife: as a musician she wasn't earning very much money, and further, she sloppily left things lying around the house. My sense of their relationship was that it was a good one, and certainly one that he freely entered into, rejecting family pressures for an arranged marriage. Narayan had in fact come on his own to the United States to escape constant parental pressures and expectations. Upon delving into his critical attitudes toward his wife, I found two very different sources.

I learned during the therapy that as an extremely bright Indian man from a middle caste, middle-class South Indian background, Narayan had graduated from an elite engineering college in India, and now held a good job in one of the top research centers in the United States. He had been one of the only ones from his community at that time to go to college. At one point when he was complaining about his wife earning so little, I inquired about his parents' attitudes toward an arranged marriage. He then told me that since he had always been a star in school, his parents had frequently expressed that Narayan's future wife would bring a very large dowry, either in jewels and property, or more likely, in its modern-day equivalent of her being a physician or having an M.B.A., so that her earning power would be considerable. His parents' attitudes were, he explained, normal expectations from his particular caste background, ones which he had apparently fully incorporated. Narayan was blithely unaware just how much these incorporated expectations fed his discontent with his wife's earning power, especially since he had always known that as a musician she would never earn very much. Once the connection was made in session between his current criticisms and his older internalized attitudes, his complaints greatly subsided.

On the other hand, Narayan's criticism of his wife's leaving things lying around the apartment was actually a projective identification of his own tendency toward sloppiness. His father, an army sergeant, was always severely critical of any sloppiness whatsoever on Narayan's part. He ran his family, and particularly his son, with all of the rigor of an army barracks.

Thus, to Narayan his wife's leaving things lying around unconsciously represented a forbidden part of himself, that part which previously came under severe paternal criticism. Through my interpretations of his projective identification with his wife and his identification with his father's criticisms, Narayan's complaints about his wife's sloppiness eased considerably. It was thus essential to differentiate Narayan's litany of complaints about his wife into their different psychological sources in order for them to be resolved: one involving internalized cultural values around marriage, the other a disciplinarian father criticizing any disorder at home. In each instance, Narayan had been unaware of the earlier sources of his complaints.

THE CULTURAL SELF IN THE TRANSFERENCE

Inner conflicts that profoundly involve cultural factors and sociohistorical change can also surface in the transference. Prakash, an Indian man who had immigrated from New Delhi to New York City, was in combined individual and group psychoanalysis. He complained in group session one evening that most of the group members, including myself as the therapist, were pressuring him to become more American and independent, and to abandon his close, dependent ties to his Indian family who had also come here. At the same time, he experienced a couple of other group members as sanctioning his Indian way of intense involvement in family relationships.

On the surface it looked like a simple example of being caught between two worlds, with one group of us encouraging him to become more Americanized, the other upholding his right to his Indianness, all of this reflecting a conflict within himself over how American he would become. On closer examination, however, Prakash's reaction stemmed from a much earlier drama of dissonant cultural encounters right within his own family, and basically within his self. While his parents originally came from the same small town Gujerati culture where they had an arranged marriage, his father, with an entreprenurial spirit, moved the family to New Delhi. There, he more and more identified with British cultural and colonial values of getting ahead in the world; whereas his mother remained rooted in indigenous Indian culture with its emphasis on extended family ties. This split was not at all uncommon in upper-caste, urban Indian families of that era.

Prakash's father insisted on his six sons and daughters being educated in the elite British-style convent schools and then in the elite colleges of New Delhi, and afterward to emigrate to the United States to become financial successes. This is exactly what the two older brothers did, one becoming president of an American corporation, the other a vice president of a firm, each marrying an American woman. The change in this family from rural India to corporate America in one generation was astounding!

But it was not without its price for Prakash. His mother had wanted all of the sons to remain in India deeply attached to her and the family, married to women of her own choosing who could get along well with her. Within an Indian context, this is an insurance policy for aging parents, having sons and daughters-in-law who will gradually take care of them. When the two much older sons left for America and then married American women, she turned to Prakash as her last hope.

Thus, a conflict that originated with his parents identifying with two disso-nant cultural attitudes and ways of life, in good part fostered by the effects of British colonialism in urban India, generated an intense conflict within Prakash that was now being played out in the totally different cultural arena of adapting to American life. All of us in the group represented the attitudes of one or the other of his parents as they were at odds with each other within him-self. At that point in the analysis, the transference was one in which Prakash mainly sided with maternal attitudes of maintaining family ties, railing against those of us who represented his father's attitudes of being independent.

A few years later in the analysis, the transference changed dramatically. As Prakash became more and more in touch with his mother denigrating his father and trying to keep Prakash totally to herself, he became increasingly enraged at me for making any kind of interpretation or remark that smacked of any criticism of his father, and for trying to manipulate Prakash to be depen-dent on me. As he became more and more involved in this negative maternal transference, for the first time in his life Prakash was able to get into a field of work that he was interested in.

It is apparent in this case that a psychoanalyst has to take into account both cultural and sociohistoric factors that have become internalized into the self to understand the transference. While these factors are obviously mediated through the personalities of the parents and other family members, in this case it was important to appreciate the tugs between indigenous Indian and Western values that still beset so many of the urban, upper caste Hindus. To state it another way, it is not only necessary to know the indigenous cultural background of Asians in America, but also the dissonances and conflicts within their own culture and how it affected them through family relationships before immigrating.

THE MIDDLE RANGE OF THE CONTINUUM

From my work with Indians and Japanese, originally abroad and then in New York City, I was forced to be constantly sensitive to sociocultural and sociohis-torical issues different from my own background in order to understand my patients. This prolonged and systematic exercise in being attentive to these issues then had a reverberating effect in my own practice in New York City. I gradually found that important cultural and social issues are inevitably present in all of our patients. Every one of us comes from a specific sociocultural back-ground, and has been affected by specific sociohistorical factors of change. Some-times these play a very subsidiary role in our work with a patient; at other times such factors play a major part in our patients' psychological make-up and psy-chodynamics, regardless of their background. I discovered, or more accurately rediscovered, what Erik Erikson (1946) earlier had emphasized in his clinical thinking.

I have further found from supervision with advanced candidates and newly graduated analysts, as well as listening to case presentations of other analysts, that an exploration of a patient's sociocultural background and the historical circumstances of their family is all too rarely done. I have had to train myself to go into the specifics of the family's background at appropriate times, and then to train others to do the same. It is usually not enough to learn that the patient or analysand is from a Jewish, Italian, or Midwestern Protestant family. One needs a more detailed investigation. What can be easily left out from case reports in conferences or in the literature so as not to identify the patient, is often data that is integral to the patient's inner conflicts.

Turning to the middle range of the continuum are frequently those from a Mediterranean, Latino, or African-American background, where sociocultural factors may also play a highly significant role in analysis. An example is Graziella, a woman from a blue collar Sicilian family and community, who through educational opportunities had become a highly functioning professional person with a graduate school degree. She had entered into psychoanalysis to resolve certain issues in her love relationships. From her family origins in Brooklyn, she had moved into her own apartment in Manhattan but still seemed overly emotionally tied to her mother, whose daily phone calls sometimes evoked considerable annoyance. But what bothered Graziella much more was her compulsively bringing her laundry home every week for her mother to do, sometimes at great inconvenience to herself.

Psychologically sophisticated through her graduate school counseling psychology program, Graziella looked upon this laundry compulsion as her inability to separate sufficiently from her mother, something I tended to agree with. After all, her father had died when she was quite young, and she grew up very close to her mother. We were both oriented toward cardinal psychological values of American individualism, that of the basic importance of emotional separation and individual autonomy. The problem was that approaching this compulsion from the standpoint of insufficient separation and individuation produced no change whatsoever. Nor did one or another interpretive approaches that I used.

Finally, sensing that there could be cultural factors here that I didn't understand, I asked her one day, "what is the meaning of doing laundry in your Sicilian community?" She immediately exclaimed that it is of great importance, that the women hang out the clean laundry to dry on lines in the back for all the neighbors to see. The subtext seems to be one of a public display of conscientious cleanliness and purity.

Graziella then related that on those extremely rare occasions that she went by necessity to a laundromat in her own neighborhood, she felt intensely ashamed, that everyone's eyes were on her for not doing her laundry in a way that the neighbors could see. It was as if metaphorically she was hiding her dirty laundry. Thus, it was not a psychological issue of separation, but rather one of internalized cultural values. But there was more to her conflict.

A further important motive involving the laundry compulsion emerged, a highly subtle one that I had only gradually become familiar with in my work with Asians, but which is apparently present with Sicilians as well. Asking is a form of giving. It runs completely counter to pervasive American values of self-reliance and independence. In this other mode of relating, by asking and being dependent on another, you enhance the other's self-esteem by establishing the other as a superior who is able to give; and with this subtle exchange, there is a greater sharing and emotional intimacy. Moreover, Graziella felt special by her mother going to the trouble of doing her laundry. Thus, Graziella's compulsive need to bring her laundry home to her mother each week was not only to avoid the shame of doing her laundry in an essentially private way, but was also a way of enhancing each other's esteem and the intimacy they shared. As Graziella and I discussed this in terms of these Sicilian values and ways of relating, she was then able for the first time to either bring her laundry to her mother or do it on her own, whichever way suited her best.

Our work together on her laundry compulsion was of course but one among many elements in the analysis, and one that did not involve complex transference/countertransference interactions. The latter were very much in evidence in the analysis as she resolved inner conflicts that centered a great deal on her relationship with her mother, on a father who was killed by the mob when Graziella was a young child, and on her mother's depression after her father's death. Thus, even these transference/countertransferences were strongly colored by the sociocultural patterns of her working class Sicilian background with its Mafia influences.

ETHNIC LAYERING OF THE SELF

Cultural factors surfaced in another important way in Graziella's analysis, one that I find not uncommon in second or even third generation Americans from this middle range of the continuum. On one level of the self, Graziella was very Sicilian in her emotional life, as we have just seen. However, on a much later level of the self, Graziella also began identifying with the values of her graduate school courses, particularly those in ego psychology, which so emphasize the separation-individuation process in childhood and adolescence.

Graziella sometimes chastised herself in sessions that she should be more independent rather than being constantly involved in a large social network reminiscent of her Sicilian extended family that actively took care of her after her father's death. She further felt critical of herself that her late night roller-skating in rinks was somehow not fitting with the decorum expected in her professional work. What would her fellow professionals think of her if they knew she roller-skated to the wee hours of the morning? It was very helpful for her to discuss these dissonances between her blue collar Sicilian and more mainstream American professional values and social patterns. It enabled her to be more comfortably herself rather than to be critical of her Sicilian self.

A similar layering of the self occurred in Albert, a second-generation Albanian-American, who grew up in a tightly knit Albanian community in New Jersey. Albert came for therapy because of increasing dissatisfaction and frustration in his position in a classy "white shoe" design firm that renovated and decorated office interiors in the various skyscrapers of Manhattan. He complained of not being appreciated and not advancing in his firm in the way he felt he should be. He felt both slighted and insulted.

Albert felt particularly uneasy because his superiors looked askance at his style of relating to his clients. The ethos of the firm was that the designer knows best. He should be self-sufficient and authoritative in directing the client as to what should be done, and never to get too close to the client. Albert, on the other hand, formed close relationships with his clients, consulted with them frequently, and sought their input at each stage of the work. Of all the designers, Albert actually came closest to meeting deadlines with the least cost over-runs. Nevertheless, he strongly believed he was not doing things the right way, and became severely self-critical when his bosses conveyed he should be conducting himself more their way.

We gradually discussed his style of working with clients versus the firm's ethos as stemming from two different cultural worlds. His was that of an Albanian emphasis on relationship and interdependence in working together, which he had experienced growing up in his Albanian community. His firm's was more oriented toward Anglo-American WASP values of individualism, where the designer-client relationship is more authoritative and distant. As we discussed his approach in these cultural terms, Albert became much more self-assured in his way of working, and was therefore more confident and assertive with his superiors. He became increasingly valued as a member of the firm in spite of his different approach, and was given the promotion he had long sought.

There were, of course, the more usual transference issues in our psychoanalytic work together. They were far more related to a highly problematic relationship with his mother, which years previously had greatly interfered with his functioning in college and graduate school. He had seen a therapist at that time who had helped him considerably. But this more typical psychoanalytic work does not preclude the presence of this layering of the self whereby the later incorporation of values of individualism result in a great deal of self-criticism and inner consternation around an earlier ethnic cultural self.

ETHNIC ENCOUNTERS WITHIN THE SELF

Still further divisions within a cultural self may be generated from having parents from sharply different cultures. Here it is not so much a case of a layering of the self as that of a deeply embedded conflict from childhood around cultural attitudes located in the specific family cultures of each parent, and therefore their own cultural selves.

Frank came from a professional family where his father was of Germanic background, strict, frugal, authoritative, and distant; whereas his mother was from one of the poorer South American countries, although from an educated family where she was far more emotional and nurturing. Throughout much of a long-term analysis that dealt primarily with family trauma, Frank was beset, and at times upset, by a book-buying compulsion. Every week, in spite of his very limited resources, he made the rounds of a number of the Manhattan second-hand bookstores to buy books on sale that were related to architecture, his field of study. While they were clearly relevant to his studies, and later to his practice as an architect, his purchases went far beyond the usual, occasioning considerable strain with his wife for his trespassing on the family budget. He, himself, was bewildered, upset, and ashamed of this compulsion, although very proud of his growing library.

While many much more severe problems were gradually resolved in the analysis, this compulsion seemed singularly immune from anything I said. I interpreted it from one angle, then another, not the least of which were obvious competitive feelings with me and my library in the office. He readily acknowledged his wish to outdo me and his fear of my retaliation, but nothing really changed. This is a not so uncommon happening in psychoanalytic work where a great deal is resolved but a given symptom remains stubbornly resistant.

After a number of years, one day I decided to ask Frank in detail about his mother's South American family background. For the first time, he described his maternal grandparents, uncles, aunts, and cousins not simply as an educated family, but one in which a surprising number of them were important poets, playwrights, novelists, intellectuals and professionals, a few with major international reputations. His mother's family were obviously among the intellectual elite of their country, and moreover, were descended from Spanish nobility with a couple of illustrious forebears.

It was now easy to surmise that in the buried past of a childhood, before his family collapsed during his adolescence, Frank's mother had strong expectations that he, too, would be of the same ilk as these illustrious intellectuals of her family. Whereas his father with his distant, strict attitudes often put Frank down as as he got older for getting too big for his britches. This resulted in a suppression and even denigration of his early identity as a nascent intellectual that was so tied in to his mother's familial cultural values and expectations.

Nevertheless, Frank did not fully abandon this early part of his identity. His book-buying compulsion was unconsciously related to his mother's desire and his own that he make a major intellectual contribution.[1] As we discussed these maternal roots, as well as his suppression of them through his father's attitudes, we were able to make much more sense of the competitive Oedipal transference with me and his fear of my retaliation. All of this enabled Frank not only to moderate his book purchases considerably, but also to become much freer in writing the articles and gaining the recognition he had always dreamed of.

He was now more openly striving to excel through writing, not simply through his practice as an architect. Since it is possible to be a recognized architect without having to publish, Frank's becoming an intellectual in his field became even more striking as a fulfillment of these childhood expectations. Through this detailed inquiry into his cultural roots, we were able to resolve a highly conflictual, ethnic intercultural encounter right within himself, one that had become part of an Oedipal conflict.

Another brief case vignette illustrates that it is possible to have parents from the same ethnic group who identify with two very different cultural traditions within that group, thus occasioning considerable conflict within a patient. A supervisee of mine was treating a middle-aged Jewish woman who was living with a man whom she constantly denigrated as being inferior to herself. My supervisee was well aware that this woman's mother had also denigrated her father and that the patient was identified with her own mother. This had, indeed, helped the patient to some extent, but something was still missing.

Further light was shed on the background of this conflict when I asked the supervisee about the patient's cultural background. She said the patient was Jewish. I then asked, "what kind of Jewish background?" Coming from a Christian background, the therapist hadn't thought herself of asking any further. She then inquired and found that the patient's mother was from a German Jewish family that was well-educated and had earlier held positions of importance and some wealth before fleeing Nazi Germany. Her mother then married a Jewish man of Eastern European origins, who was always considered inferior by her mother's family as well as by her mother, in spite of his being a professional—a not uncommon attitude of German Jews toward Eastern European ones. Thus, her mother's denigration of her father was rooted in pervasive cultural attitudes within the European Jewish communities. As these internalized cultural attitudes were clarified in therapy, the patient's attitudes toward her boyfriend gradually changed.

SOCIOHISTORICAL TRAUMA

It is now recognized that any psychoanalytic treatment with a holocaust survivor or with children of holocaust survivors must take into account this sociohistorical trauma. Individuals, themselves, may not necessarily have had to go through the trauma. The effects of it can be passed down through parents or even grandparents. An example of this is a third generation American Jewish woman, Marilyn, who was quite assimilated into the American mainstream. She came to see me in her middle twenties for psychoanalytic therapy because she felt so socially isolated, lacked friends, and deeply distrusted others.

Marilyn had an enigmatic, anxious obsession of being convinced that she would die young. Every time she would come down with a cold, or have a headache, or even some muscle strain from exercise, she would be absolutely convinced that her life would soon end. This obsession seemed quite unrelated to her tremendous sense of social isolation. Over the years we addressed many aspects of her inner life and her earlier family relationships, resulting in considerable improvement in her emotional and social well-being, and in her own sense of self. But delving as I could into the obsession from a variety of vantage points was to no avail. It remained untouched.

One day in session, as Marilyn with a cold was once again expressing this conviction of dying young in an anxious, almost whiny voice, I spontaneously exclaimed, "It sounds as if the Cossacks are coming!" I had unreflectedly drawn upon my own Eastern European Jewish roots with its intimations of impending doom. As a child, I had heard stories of the pogroms in almost the same tone of voice as Marilyn's from older members of the family. The anxiety and fear of those past traumas had lived on from one generation to another.

Marilyn instantly associated that the Cossacks had indeed come. They had buried her grandmother's father and brother alive after forcing them to dig their own grave. Her grandmother's mother (Marilyn's great grandmother) became ill soon after and died in her middle thirties, undoubtedly in reaction to the trauma. Marilyn's grandmother had come to America just before the pogrom to live with relatives, her family soon to follow. Her grandmother was suddenly orphaned at age 14, a trauma that was overwhelming.

We already knew from several years of work that Marilyn's grandmother was an important, almost overwhelming figure in her early childhood. She and her parents had lived in the grandparent's home until Marilyn was four, and the grandmother had apparently taken over the raising of Marilyn from Marilyn's own mother, the grandmother's daughter. More than once in session, Marilyn would inadventently call her grandmother, "mother."

Marilyn's further associations in this session were even more telling. When Marilyn was a very young child, her grandmother repeatedly told her the story of the family tragedy, and would repeatedly call Marilyn, "my mother." And in fact, Marilyn's Jewish name, different from her regular American one, was the same as her great grandmother, the grandmother's mother. Her grandmother clearly related to Marilyn as her own deceased mother for whom she had never stopped grieving. Marilyn had thus taken on within herself the identity of her great grandmother, who had died so young after her husband and son were killed.

All of this I should state was completely within Marilyn's memory. None of this had to be recovered or reconstructed. What was repressed was the connection between her anxious obsession with dying young and her identity as her great grandmother so fostered by her grieving grandmother. Once this connection was made, the obsession subsided considerably. This insight also clarified Marilyn's conscious choice of a husband who wasn't Jewish, and her dressing and carrying herself in a way that could easily pass in the American Christian world. The vulnerability of appearing Jewish in public was much too great for her, although in private she valued her Jewishness. Thus, a sociohistorical trauma within a deeply rooted family relationship was central to an extremely painful obsession and strong character attitudes.

Andrew, similar to Marilyn, was also named after a deceased elder of the family, in his case a maternal grandfather who was killed in the holocaust. His mother and grandmother, who had survived in hiding, had come to the United States and looked to Andrew as a remembrance of his deceased grandfather. The effects on him were powerful and varied.

A few months after Andrew had begun psychoanalytic therapy, he came to session quite depressed, which was generally out of character for him. His birthday was in a few days. He mentioned that he always became depressed on his birthday. When I asked what came to his mind about this, he conveyed that his birthday was profoundly associated with his grandfather, whom his mother and grandmother still deeply mourned. Rather than being a cause for celebration, his birthday brought back grim memories. This simple connection enabled him to be much happier on future birthdays.

This related to another problem that we worked on in therapy over extended periods of time. Andrew felt completely vulnerable to a woman's suffering, either his wife's or occasionally a female colleague's. He found it extremely difficult to assert any of his own needs or to dissent from his wife or colleague if he experienced them as suffering. This was clearly related to the inner suffering he perceived in both his mother and grandmother, which came from the holocaust tragedy. Even when this connection was made, it took some time for Andrew to gradually become more appropriately assertive.

But being the child of holocaust survivors had another, quite different effect on Andrew. Unlike Marilyn who hid her Jewish identity and vulnerability in public, Andrew drew upon this family and ethnic trauma as the leitmotif in his photography. Internationally recognized, Andrew's work not only directly deals with the holocaust, but also with other places of terror, victimization, and trauma, all reminiscent of the holocaust and unfortunately all too common in today's world. Thus, he has been able to draw upon this profound identity theme within himself to give great emotional power to his art.

A REGIONAL CULTURAL SELF

It would be almost impossible to appreciate Lucille's way of being in the world without taking into account her Southern background. Entering the upper echelons of New York City's cultural and political world through her husband, a noted public figure, she easily held her own through her Southern charm, wit, graciousness, and intelligence. In another age and place, she could well have conducted her own salon. Lucille had come from a well-to-do Protestant family from Georgia, one in which there were distinct class differences, her mother originally coming from a sharecropper family. But it was a dynamic, paternal grandmother, who adoringly raised Lucille in her infancy when her mother suffered a prolonged post-partum depression, that resulted in Lucille having a far better sense of herself and her place in the world than her younger siblings, who were only brought up by her mother.

Over the course of a long analysis, it became apparent that one of the traumatic turning points of Lucille's life was around age ten when the first of her younger siblings was born, a sister. The trauma did not simply involve her mother's preoccupation with the new baby, which indeed occurred and had its own effects of Lucille feeling greatly neglected. Even worse was her father inexplicably turning on her. From a fondly remembered earlier loving relationship in which she was the apple of his eye, he became harsh, punitive, and violent with her from age ten until she went away to college. Through considerable work in the transference/countertransference relationship in the individual analysis, and in her interactions in group analysis, we were able to understand and resolve her adult sado-masochistic relationships in which she replicated the abuse she received from her father.

Nevertheless, we remained baffled as to why he suddenly had turned on her. It was only many years later in the analysis that this skewed father-daughter relationship was finally clarified when Lucille had to confront a crisis in her own marriage. Her husband had a brief affair with another woman, and this forced Lucille to confront skeletons in her family closet she had never shared with anyone, including me. The answer to her earlier relationship with her father very much involved the ethos and attitudes of a Southern woman's cultural self.

What had happened at age ten that Lucille had kept so secret out of intense feelings of shame was that her father became openly involved with another woman, making something of a public display of the affair. For a family of high social status in this Georgian town, this was an overwhelming humiliation to her mother. What led him to do this remained unclear, although he apparently evidenced at the time a deep disappointment over the birth of another daughter.

Lucille's mother apparently responded to her humiliation in the ways typical of Southern women of her class—whom Lucille referred to as "iron butterflies." Her mother stayed in the marriage but wreaked vengeance on her husband. Behind his back, she constantly denigrated him to Lucille and others, treated him with great aloofness and disdain, and withdrew into her own shell, shunning others and any social life altogether. Lucille's father reacted with rage to his wife; but unable to express it directly to her because of his own guilt, and in collusion with her, he took it out on Lucille. Thus, the dynamics of the family radically changed due to the affair. Deeply ingrained cultural attitudes prevented Lucille from relating this material in the therapy as it was too loaded with the shame and humiliation that she had incorporated from her mother.

It is obvious that many of these cultural attitudes are not only present in the South. But they attained a particular coloring, flavor, and power that made it extremely difficult for Lucille even to mention this family humiliation to anyone. Lucille then had to differentiate herself from her mother's Southern ways of reacting so that she could handle the acute problems in her own marriage in a more direct and constructive way, rather than simply to wreak vengeance.

WOMEN AND SOCIAL CHANGE

There was still another major issue that entered into Lucille's therapy, one of profound social change relevant to all of the women patients I have worked with in New York City. They all have or are considering serious careers, when possible combining them with marriage, and not infrequently with having children. In a remarkable period of three decades, the possibilities and options open to educated American women have changed dramatically with the Women's Movement and a Feminist world view. This groundswell of change has not only altered the social landscape in America, but also introduced new struggles and conflicts in the inner world of women.

Lucille, herself, greatly influenced in her adult years by Feminist values, remained in psychoanalytic therapy to work out issues around developing a career. In a past era, most women in her position would be content to remain in the shadow of a wealthy, prominent public figure, mainly attaining visibility herself in frequently hosting other luminaries and in actively participating in social causes her husband had espoused. Instead, Lucille gradually chose to develop her own career interests.

Similar to many other women, Lucille had to struggle to resolve problems around a layering of the self, where her earlier self was far more rooted in traditional women's roles and values, in contrast to her current Feminist ideals. In Lucille's case, two major factors made it emotionally difficult for her to proceed. Her own mother, who came from a sharecropper background of hard manual labor, was more than content to be the lady of the house once she married

Lucille's father, a successful businessman. Lucille's childhood identification with her was thus totally dissonant with her adult aspirations. Compounding this was Lucille's father, who in her teenage years, became increasingly abusive over any display of independence on Lucille's part. The furtiveness with which Lucille proceeded to develop her career training and interests was a marked part of the transference that had to be interpreted. Only on rare occasions would Lucille let slip that a major museum had contacted her to consult with them on one of their collections.

Most of my women patients today, similar to Lucille, struggle over what to keep and what to repudiate in their old identifications with their mothers as an integral part of the psychoanalytic work. And when there is an unsupporting father, or in Lucille's case an abusive one, their striving to fulfill aspirations and options not open to their mothers and grandmothers can become even more of an inner conflict.

The layering of the self in women today attained a different structure and coloration in Dolores's case. She came for psychoanalytic therapy in her forties after having already worked out an important career as a senior editor at a major publishing house. Some years previously, she left a long, unfulfilling marriage to develop her career, helped by another therapist. Nevertheless, Dolores was discontent with her current life on two counts: she really wanted to be a writer much more than an editor who occasionally wrote; and she wanted a love relationship with a man who more fully shared her artistic and intellectual interests than her current devoted boyfriend.

A major turning point came in the therapy with the exploration of Dolores's childhood relationship with her maternal grandmother, with whom she had spent considerable time before her family moved away when she was ten. Her grandmother turned out to be a highly educated woman with a doctorate in her field of study. Attaining this education before the era of the Women's Movement in the 1960s, her grandmother's options were confined to having an academic career and probably not getting married; or of marrying and having a family, but giving up a career. Her grandmother chose the latter, confining her scholarly interests to part-time research and writing papers. Dolores's mother, on the other hand, was devoted to being a housewife and mother, and it was with her that Dolores seemed mainly identified.

As we talked about this childhood relationship, it became apparent what a momentous influence her grandmother had been on Dolores's early intellectual and artistic interests. It was this earlier childhood self, deeply identified with and in part shaped by her cultured grandmother, that increasingly emerged in the therapy. As Dolores consolidated a much more assured sense of self devoted to her cultural interests, she first broke off the relationship with her boyfriend, and then left the publishing house to become a full-time freelance writer. She was not only able to earn a living by her writing, but also became seriously involved with and eventually married an artist who was much more on her intellectual wavelength than her previous boyfriend.

Unlike Lucille, Dolores had an earlier suppressed self around a highly supportive and cultured grandmother, whose values and interests were far more congruent with Dolores's adult ideals. Once this self fully emerged, it assumed a predominant position over other aspects of her self more identified with the role of her mother as housewife, as well as with her father's more traditional expectations. This enabled Dolores to work out a much more fulfilling life both in her career and love relationship.

SUMMARY

I have endeavored to show the oft-neglected importance of sociocultural and sociohistorical factors in the psychological makeup and inner conflicts of patients in psychoanalysis and psychoanalytic therapy in a number of ways. To do this, I have conceptualized a cultural self and its relationship to the usual personal self described by a variety of models in contemporary psychoanalysis. For clinical work with patients in the United States, I have posited a continuum of persons from radically different cultures to those from significantly different ethnic groups to those from mainstream American culture. Sociocultural and historical factors enter into inner conflicts of those all along the continuum, but with variations from one end to another. A layering of the self, sometimes conflictual, is also part of most educated American women today due to momentous social change.

ENDNOTE

1. See Litchtenstein (1977) on identity thema and Kohut (1977) on maternal mirroring and ambitions for a fuller understanding of this dynamic.

Chapter Seven

The Influence of Culture on the Self and Selfobject Relationships

An Asian-North American Comparison

SELF PSYCHOLOGY FROM A CROSS-CULTURAL PERSPECTIVE

I would like to explore what I have increasingly come to see as a highly complex relationship of culture to self psychology in North Americans and Asians. I shall first endeavor to situate the very need for the development of self psychology within the culture of North American individualism where it was initially formulated. I shall then turn to Asians to delve into marked variabilities in their selfobject relationships and self from North Americans, and to delineate how these are related to Asian sociocultural patterns.

From a cross-cultural perspective, the very formulation of selfobject relationships —individuals' needs throughout life for others to be empathically attuned, idealizeable, and to share in the comraderie of skills for the maintenance and enhancement of self-esteem and a cohesive self—is a trenchant critique of the Northern European/North American culture of individualism that so stresses the self-contained, self-reliant individual (Dumont 1986, Kirschner 1992). In contrast to traditional psychoanalysis, which Mitchell (1988) refers to as a one-body psychology and Stolorow and Atwood (1992) as the myth of the isolated individual mind, self psychology delineates essential dependencies and interdependencies with others throughout life. Where these selfobject relationships are deficient, individuals have poor self-esteem and develop defenses against any wounds and slights to their self-esteem to which they are so vulnerable, resulting in highly problematic relationships and a limited work capacity. In more extreme cases, their self becomes fragmented.

It is perhaps no accident that Kohut (1971, 1977, 1984) formulated self psychology, with its central emphasis on selfobject relationships and its psychopathology resulting from deficiencies in these relationships, in the midwestern United States where the sociocultural patterns of individualism are at their strongest. America is noted by many commentators to have the most radical individualism of Western societies, with unusual physical and social mobility, an extreme emphasis on self-directedness and self-reliance, and a resultant fragility of relationships. Confronting a number of patients with poor self-esteem and self-fragmentation resulting from deficient selfobject relationships, Kohut gradually conceptualized a new psychology of the self that after considerable controversy has now become one of the major paradigms of contemporary Freudian psychoanalysis.

When a different kind of psychopathology becomes salient in patients in a given society and historical era, a need arises to formulate new psychological processes and a new view of the relationship of normality to psychopathology. Thus, particular kinds of disfunction are central to the need for another conceptualization, not only for describing the psychodynamics of the psychopathology, but equally important, for highlighting aspects and processes of normality that have been taken for granted. With the elaboration of the psychology of the self, self psychologists then extended their understanding to the presence of selfobjects in the psychoanalytic relationship with all patients, sometimes as central to their work, at other times as a background element to the more usual transferences (Lachmann and Beebe 1995).

As much as self psychology critiques North American radical individualism, it also delineates what is necessary to function psychologically in a culture of individualism that so stresses the development and social actualization of individual potentials and of individuality, itself. And in this process, self psychology also incorporates various other views of individualism. For Kohut, as Erikson before him, has not been immune from taking basic cultural assumptions for granted, which then enter unreflectedly into his theory. Thus, Kohut delineated the centrality of individuals developing a center of initiative and agency in fulfilling socially an intrinsic design of their self. This is done through a tension arc of ambitions deriving from early maternal mirroring selfobject relationships, to ideals and goals from later idealizing ones, implemented by skills developed through alterego relationships. This process is essential to functioning well in a culture of individualism; otherwise, deficiencies in these selfobject relationships can render individuals especially disfunctional in a society where they are put so much on their own.

Perhaps I can put self psychology in a broader cultural/psychological perspective by citing an incident with Japanese psychoanalysts during a two-day seminar I gave on self psychology in Hiroshima in 1982. I was asked by my Japanese psychoanalytic hosts who were trained in the United States, "why has self psychology become so important in America?" They had read Kohut's work, they felt they understood much of it, but they couldn't see its relevance since the concepts of empathic attunement and having others who can be idealized are so integral a part of Japanese social relationships. I was puzzled for a moment by the question, but then spontaneously replied, "Have you seen any of the paintings of Edward Hopper or Andrew Wyeth's 'Christina's World?'"

The leader of the group, Mikihachiro Tatara, while in training at the William Alanson White Institute in New York City had taken slides of both a Hopper and Wyeth exhibit. After lunch, he showed "Christina's World" and a number of Hopper's paintings. They clearly expressed the feelings of isolation and loneliness which are so much part of the American emotional landscape, with Hopper's people being quite unrelated to each other. The Japanese then easily understood the need for a psychology of selfobject relationships in the United States.

CENTRALITY OF ESTEEM IN ASIAN RELATIONSHIPS

What happens when we delve into the self of Asians and the nature of their selfobject relationships? What immediately strikes the psychoanalytic observer is the cultural and psychological *salience* of selfobject relationships and the dominant place that self-esteem occupies in their relationships. Whereas it took psychoanalysis three quarters of a century to frame a psychology of the self, Asian cultures basically assume that this is the core of human relationships. The Dalai Lama, for instance, at a conference on "Buddhism and Psychotherapy" apparently reacted with disbelief that Americans can have a problem with low self-esteem. He found it difficult to understand the whole notion of poor self-esteem.

The centrality of self-esteem in Asians—more accurately *we-self esteem* as the self of Asians is much more experientially a we-self from the prolonged symbiotic mothering and emotional enmeshment within the family—is related to four major selfobject kinds of relationships. The first is the extraordinary, to the Westerner, development of high levels of empathic attunement which are universally emphasized in all Asian societies, if not always fulfilled. Asians live in very close, long lasting family and group intimacy relationships that depend on enormous interpersonal sensitivity. In Japan, this is referred to as *omoiyari* or concerned empathy, that is central to relationships on all levels in the society.

In the pervasive hierarchical relationships of Asians, there is a constant reciprocity in which subordinates are empathically attuned to the needs of superiors, displaying deference, respect, and loyalty to enhance the esteem of the superior; while in turn, superiors are expected to be attuned to the needs of subordinates, including offering direction and criticism in a tactful way that enables them to maintain their own esteem. The cultural/psychological norm is to be constantly sensitive to the needs of the other, or to those of the family or group, itself, rather than to one's own; but then to fully expect that the other(s) will be attuned to one's own needs without having to voice them. Within this overall norm, important variations occur with gender, between different Asian societies, and between the Westernized/modernized and traditional segments of a given Asian country.

Communication is another major factor in maintaining and enhancing high levels of esteem in Asian hierarchical relationships. The indirect communication, the strong tendency to avoid all "no's," and other aspects of Asian communication that Westerners find so puzzling and even exasperating, are all ways of either enhancing, or at minimum not challenging the esteem of the other, while protecting one's own by not putting oneself too much on the line (Young 1994). In Japan, all kinds of nonverbal gestures, such as the frequency and deepness of bows, are in good part related toward maintaining esteem within hierarchical relationships. An interesting example of this in Chinese communication emerged from an informal dinner conversation with professor Ben Lee, a second generation Chinese-American anthropologist. He told of negotiating a relationship between his own social science research center in Chicago and one in mainland China with three older Chinese professors. As negotiations drew to a successful close, the oldest Chinese professor asked Ben who should be director of the China branch. To his own amazement, Ben became suddenly silent, looking down for some time at his shoes or his watch, behavior that was completely anamolous with his usual talkative manner. Finally, the Chinese professor suggested who should be the director, and then asked Ben for his concurrence. When Ben told the story to his father, a former Chinese diplomat to the United States, his father replied, "you are Chinese after all." Ben had automatically drawn upon his Chinese background to act and communicate properly in a Chinese hierarchical relationship that honored the superior status and esteem of his counterpart. For Ben to have initially stated his choice of director, even though being asked for it, would have been an affront to the Chinese professor.

I have observed in psychoanalytic conferences in India and Japan that a large percentage of those present may have little interest in the subject, but are there to give support to the esteem of the speaker with whom they have some relationship. Challenging questions or comments are rarely raised so as not to threaten the speaker's self-regard. The issue of maintaining each other's esteem is always more important than hashing out the truth of a matter. *Maintaining esteem always has precedence over objective truth in Asian relationships, whether in the family, academia, or business.*

Another way of enhancing esteem in hierarchical intimacy relationships is through dependency, an exchange very difficult for most Americans to understand, although present in the case of Graziella, a Sicilian, in Chapter Six.

Depending on and asking of another (expectations of being able to be dependent and being given to are much more intense and pervasive in Asian than typical North American relationships [Doi 1973]) is actually a way of enhancing the esteem of the other. It establishes the other as the superior in the hierarchical relationship, and evokes an ego-ideal response of being able to be the nurturing superior who can fulfill the subordinate's dependency needs. Thus, subordinates use superiors to get their dependency needs fulfilled, while subordinates become selfobjects for superiors in enhancing the latters' esteem. Asking is a giving where dependency and esteem are so subtly exchanged.

IDEALIZATION IN ASIAN HIERARCHICAL RELATIONSHIPS

The second major selfobject relationship that so enhances esteem in an Asian context is the cultural emphasis on idealization. This manifests itself in two subtly different kinds of idealized relationships. The first includes idealization of the elders of the family and/or group or community, which includes older siblings. In Japan, esteem-enhancing idealizations are played out by Japanese men who assume a position of humility while lavishly praising others; but they expect full reciprocity (pers. com. Dr. Miyamoto). It is of note that Japanese baseball players, in contrast to some well-known American ones, usually lead exemplary lives in public. They are expected to as objects of idealization by youth.

In a more subtle and intense idealization, Asians quietly distinguish those who have superior personal qualities from those who occupy a superior position in the social hierarchy and are to be respected. The superior person may well be the superior in the social hierarchy but not necessarily. It may be a younger brother, a wife, or a servant. But it is this person—the mature, the wise, or the spiritual—who is truly venerated, imitated, and closely identified with.

Indians may attribute mythic status to certain elders, gurus, and others in intensely idealizing selfobject relationships, or may indeed identify with idealized mythic figures or with the gods or goddesses, themselves. In a metonymic way of thinking in India, the idealized elder or an idol may be considered a partial manifestation of a god or goddess rather than simply a symbolic representation of it as in Western dualism. Traditional first names all have transcendent meaning, or parents may identify a child with a mythic figure. Anthropological work has described Indian women's identification with attributes of the goddesses in important idealizing selfobject relationships (Wadley 1980).

The psychology of this kind of idealization differs from that of self psychology. Asian psychologies also have notions of an intrinsic design of the self, the *hara* of the Japanese, *gunas* and *samskaras* of Indians. However, the goal is not to realize this self in the social and work world as is the case in American individualism where there are far more social options and autonomy of choice. Rather, it is to become involved in self-transformation to becoming a better or more mature person, and ultimately a spiritual being. *Darshan*, or sharing in the presence of a spiritual person or object, is an example of this kind of psychology.

FAMILY REPUTATION AS A SELFOBJECT

Another major selfobject for enhanced feelings of esteem in Asians is the reputation of the family and/or community (India) or work group (Japan) of which one is a member. How one reflects on the family, and how one's contributions and behavior are or are not valued by other family members, as well as the very reputation of the family, itself, becomes central to we-self esteem. Shame plays a major role in this process (Okano 1994). This was clearly evidenced in the case of Gopal in Chapter Five when his self-regard was greatly enhanced by sending monies home to his family; but was seriously impaired when he married a divorced woman with a child. Each had primarily to do with how he was impacting on family reputation: well in the first instance, with shame in the second. Another patient's whole sense of herself as an internationally recognized scientist was tied in to her being an offspring of an illustrious Indian family whose women were college educated since the mid-nineteenth century, with some of her forebears being famous names of their times. She spent more than one session describing this extended family, and how her sense of self, purpose in life, and achievements were related to them.

The interdependence of esteem and family reputation is particularly true of the Indian father-son relationship, where each expects the other to reflect well on one another continuously, and where the son even as an adult strives to gain the respect of his father, even after the latter's death. Three of my patients went considerably against their own inclinations or endured real hardships to reflect well on their fathers. Whereas another, Ashis, experienced a serious decline in we-self regard when his father committed suicide, even though he was nineteen at the time. He kept his father's suicide secret from the most intimate of friends because of how it would reflect on himself; and quickly terminated therapy with me when I first saw him as soon as this secret surfaced through a dream (see Roland 1988, 25–47).

In a few of my cases and in other Indian men I have known socially, I have found that when fathers have not treated sons as the latter felt they should be, the sons never became involved in any open rebellion to strive to do what they wanted as is common in North America. Rather, they did poorly at what the fathers insisted they do, thus getting back at their fathers by reflecting badly on them. This dynamic had been central to a highly negative father transference of an Indian man in long-term psychoanalysis with me, where during one period his intense self-destructive behavior was to reflect badly on me as the supposed expert psychoanalyst on Indians.

RECIPROCITY OF SELFOBJECT RELATIONSHIPS

I would like to digress from delineating esteem in Asian selfobject relationships to reflect on two theoretical issues relevant to self psychology. The first is the issue of reciprocal selfobject relationships. In Asian cultures, reciprocity is culturally emphasized as integral to their pervasive hierarchical relationships. Their selfobject relationships are also highly reciprocal where concerned empathy is expected from subordinate and superior, and there is idealization of the superior who in turn empathically nurtures the subordinate. This contrasts with the assumption of contractual relationships in North American hierarchies with their rights and obligations.

Self psychologists have rarely dwelt on the need for reciprocal selfobjects in human relationships. The stress is usually on the need for the selfobject from an individual standpoint, and particularly how problems in self-esteem and fragmentation can be resolved through selfobject transferences in the psychoanalytic relationship. The need for a psychology of reciprocal selfobject relationships has been partially, but by no means completely addressed by intersubjectivity (Atwood and Stolorow 1984; Stolorow and Atwood 1992). One dimension of such a psychology must include the ability of the parental figure to be able to function as a mature selfobject for those with developmentally earlier selfobject needs, but where the latter, too, stand as selfobjects to enhance the esteem of the parent (Hagman 1996).

While North American culture does not stress the reciprocity of selfobject relationships, it is noticeably present in the long-term student-teacher relationship in music in a way that echoes Asian hierarchical relationships. Students' self-regard is intimately tied to the reputation of their noted teachers; but it is also clear that their teachers' esteem depends a great deal on how their students progress and perform.

The second theoretical issue involves the cultural patterning of selfobject relationships. Self psychologists tend to dismiss this as simply an involvement in social psychology, not psychoanalysis. Since self psychologists have gone to such pains to delineate the selfobject *function* of the other to the individual, making it psychoanalytically relevant, they have shied away from considering other aspects of social relatedness, or even the individual nature of the person who is serving a selfobject function. The whole thrust of this chapter, however, is to show that once a psychoanalyst begins working with patients from radically different cultures than one's own, such as Asians, it is essential to be aware of the cultural patterning of selfobject relationships and how this impacts on issues of esteem and the self. Ignoring the influence of culture and social patterns on the inner world is a luxury that has been affordable to psychoanalysts while working with a relatively homogeneous group of patients from various Western societies. In a global age it will be less feasible.

MODES OF EMPATHIC ATTUNEMENT

I shall now turn to other significant differences in Asian selfobject relationships from North American ones. The very mode and content of empathic attunement can vary considerably across cultures. In contrast to the American emphasis on verbal articulateness and expression, Asians often convey their empathic awareness nonverbally. In Korea, it is called "heart-to-heart" communication. Within close intimacy relationships, it is considered impolite, if not insulting, to verbalize one's thanks or other marks of appreciation. To actually say it in words to the other implies that you are not so intimate, and are more like outsiders or strangers to each other. This is often very difficult for Americans to understand. Even more foreign to North American modes of communication is that Asian women in particular have dozens of different kinds of silences by which they communicate to each other, especially in the family.[1] This takes considerable empathic attunement on the part of the other, as psychoanalysts well know from the different kinds of silences in sessions.

In a discussion of this kind of silent communication, May Ng, a Chinese psychoanalytic psychologist, related how a teenage Chinese boy from Chinatown in New York City became so enraged at her in a therapy session that he threw a chair against the wall. She asserted that his rage was not over the content of an interpretation she had just given him. Rather, it was over her mistake in verbalizing to him something he had already realized that she knew about him. To put it into words was a gross insult to him and deeply humiliating, as if he were not capable of sensing what she knew about him. In retrospect, she was communicating to him more in an American mode, while he expected to be related to as a Chinese.

Japanese psychoanalysts working with patients from the more traditional sectors of their society are expected by their patients to empathically sense a great deal about them with a minimum of verbal communication; and in turn, analysts expect their patients to pick up what the analyst is thinking without this being verbally articulated (Roland 1988, pp 186–194). When Japanese conduct Rogerian psychotherapy, introduced to Japan during the American Occupation, the empathic reflections are always made *nonverbally*. Similarly, as previously discussed, Japanese women in psychoanalytic therapy with me in New York City have not infrequently complained that their American husbands are unable to understand what they want without their saying it. For an American psychoanalyst to see this as a regressed form of communicative demand rather than as a deeply ingrained cultural way of relating is to be empathically out of touch with such patients.

This same issue has occurred in a highly reputable American ashram where American monks experience feelings of hurt and irritation when the swami never voices his thanks or appreciation for anything they have done. As previously discussed, they don't realize that within the intimacy relationships in which they are living to voice such thanks would be experienced by the swami as being insulting to them. From an Indian standpoint, it would demean the intimacy relationship; from a North American viewpoint, where appreciation is always to be expressed verbally, it shows a lack of concern and involvement.

CONTENTS OF EMPATHIC ATTUNEMENT

If the mode of empathic attunement can vary so radically across vastly different cultures, so does the content of what is empathized with and valued. A video shown at the American Psychoanalytic Association Midwinter Meeting in December 1993, based on a study of American and Japanese mothers and their 20–23 month old toddlers by Drs. Calvin Settlidge and Joseph Okimoto, visibly demonstrated significant differences in what is empathized with and encouraged. The American toddlers evidenced far more initiative and exploration of their play environment, something obviously valued by their mothers. On the other hand, when there were planned phone calls and face-to-face interviews with the mothers, the Japanese mothers maintained total eye contact and nonverbal communication with their child, and easily accepted the child wanting to be much closer to the mother once the interruption occurred. American mothers, on the other hand, became much more involved in the phone conversation and interview, tending to discourage their child from being too dependent on them. In the American mode, some mother-toddler separation was assumed; but not in the Japanese dyad.

Self psychologists and intersubjective analysts have critiqued Mahler's (1975) developmental theory of separation-individuation as ignoring the fundamental selfobject tie and needs of the toddler to the mother. This study, although originally conceived and conceptually based on Mahler's theory, shows that the separation-individuation of the American toddler takes place within the context of a culturally specific kind of selfobject relationship. This selfobject relationship is one that actively encourages a certain degree of separation between mother and toddler, and for the toddler to explore his or her environment gradually using a number of the child's abilities. This contrasts sharply with a more Japanese symbiotic kind of selfobject tie where constant empathic attunement and the fulfillment of dependency needs are emphasized.

What was not shown on the video but delineated in other studies (White 1987) is the Japanese mother's understanding of her child's nature to encourage and value high levels of skill both in tasks and interpersonal behavior. On the other hand, from my own observations, educated North American mothers empathize with and encourage the individual inclinations of their children far more than educated Indian and Japanese mothers. In North American child rearing, a much more individualized sense of identity is fostered.[2]

I would like to cite a clinical example to illustrate just how much the contents of empathic attunement can vary so radically from what is current in educated North American circles today. Lakshmi, a second generation Indian-American woman of college educated parents, complained in session that she was rarely appreciated by her parents, particularly by her mother. In spite of Lakshmi doing brilliantly in elementary and high school, and then getting admitted to various Ivy League colleges, there was never a word of praise for her achievements over the years.

I indicated that this lack of overt valuing could well be due to characteristic Indian attitudes of never praising one's child. A leading Indian child development psychologist, Anandalakshmi, had explained to me that parents do not verbally praise their child for three reasons: 1) it is considered highly immodest, like praising yourself, because of the sense of a we-self; 2) it can incur the evil eye, or the envy of other women of the extended family; and 3) it encourages egoism which detracts from one's true nature, the spiritual self (*atman*). And indeed, after a couple of years of psychoanalytic therapy when her relationship and communication with her parents had improved substantially, she learned that they were always immensely proud of her. But with characteristic Indian attitudes, they felt constrained about conveying this openly to her or to any relatives or friends. For an American psychoanalyst to view this lack of praise as part of a deficient selfobject relationship would be to seriously misjudge the situation.

PROBLEMS IN ASIAN WE-SELF ESTEEM

This is not to say that there cannot be real problems in Asians with inner feelings of esteem. In a general way, threats to their esteem stem much more from the need to maintain high levels of it, such as "maintaining face," than from previously deficient selfobjects as is more the case among North Americans. They expect very high levels of selfobject functioning from others in current-day relationships.

When there are the inevitable slights or disappointments or untactful criticism, there are indeed experiences of hurt and anger. What makes this decidedly more difficult in an Asian context is that there is usually no exit from problematic relationships. Any anger must then be contained, especially by the subordinate, frequently resulting in somatic symptoms.

In North American-style relationships, the Asian need for caring, empathic selfobjects can easily be frustrated, resulting at times in considerable hurt and anguish. The case of Yoshiko in Chapter Six well illustrates this where she was extremely upset by the direct criticism from her boss. As previously discussed,

I have heard the same upsetness from both Indian and Japanese patients concerning the lack of involvement of college administrators and bosses.

Besides the inevitable slights and disappointments of everyday life in any society, the consequences of real selfobject failure can be graver in some Asian societies than in North American ones. In Japan, where extremely high levels of nonverbal, empathic sensing are required for everyday functioning, if the senior person is relating more in terms of unconscious projections than empathy, the relationship can become very destructive for the subordinate who cannot leave. It can result in considerable anxiety over not being understood (Okano 1994). In any Asian country, where the superior is to be deferred to and obeyed, caring and empathic attitudes make relationships work. But if the superior is sadistic, uncaring, or unattuned, highly problematic relationships result.

In Japanese child rearing where maternal expectations for high levels of performance from an early age are extremely strong, if empathic attunement to the child's nature is present, development goes well. However, if the mother is unempathic, then with the strict demands she makes on the dependent child, the latter develops a false self. As Mrs. K. put it, "My mother does not have her own thoughts and feelings; instead she does what she should . . . So far I use mother's response as the major criteria to evaluate myself; therefore, unfortunately, I do not even know what kind of person I am." (See the case of Mrs. K. in Roland 1988, pp 186–194.) Feelings of a demanding entitlement to be taken care of also results. It is as if the person is saying, "I am entitled to be taken care of because you are to blame for my failure (with Mrs. K. it was her childlessnes) because of your high expectaions of me and lack of empathy (Roland 1988, 274–281).

CLASSICAL SELF PSYCHOLOGICAL PROBLEMS IN ASIANS

Asian patients, similar to North American ones, can also have severely deficient selfobject relationships that deeply affect their sense of self. When I supervised a couple of Indian women psychoanalysts in Bombay during the summer of 1991, the only patients with whom they felt stymied were just those with intense selfobject transferences. They weren't the usual kind of patient that these analysts were used to working with. I would like to illustrate these selfobject problems and transferences from my own patients, also showing how the texture of Asian cultures impact on them.

Udayan, the youngest of nine children from a Hindu family, spent the first two to three years in his analysis in a mirroring transference to solicit my involvement with him. His associations had much of the same wildly imaginative and fantastic quality of Salmon Rushdie's *Midnight's Children*. I asked myself more than once what was it about his associations that were so different from any other American patient.

I gradually was able to pinpoint two different modes. The first was Udayan's penchant for metaphorizing everything, which only subsided after a year and a half of the analysis. As an example, one day he cited that his family's empty flat in Ahmedabad is like a tomb. From that time on, whenever he referred to the flat, he simply said the tomb. "I had a dream about the tomb the other night;" or "when I visited Ahmedabad a couple of years ago, I stayed in the tomb." This use of metaphors for concrete objects strongly animated his everyday world and lent a fantastic quality to his associations.

The other mode which lasted for over three years in the analysis was to refer to everyone significant to him—and the cast of family and other characters was a very large one—in terms of their relationship to him or some other descriptive term, but never by their individual name. "My California brother" or "my California brother's wife" refers to his oldest brother and his wife who live in California. Then the next to his oldest brother is "my Shearson Lehman brother" with "my Shearson Lehman brother's wife," referring to where this brother worked. For years I did not know any of their names. Sa'ida, his most important former girlfriend who was still on the scene during the early years of his analysis, was referred to as "my ex-girlfriend"; and another woman, Meena, with whom he was seriously involved for a while as "my new girlfriend". His older sisters were likewise referred to in various ways, but never by their names.[3]

While this manner of communication is obviously overdetermined, nevertheless, during the early stages of the analysis it had a strong component of soliciting my interest and involvement. Who would not be taken with such an imaginative, lively patient? I did not analyze this, but delved into other aspects of his problems. I gradually realized that in the highly dysfunctional family in which Udayan grew up, in spite of the large number of family members, he could often be easily ignored or simply used for others' needs. And when his parents separated from each other in his early adolescence, Udayan was left with no one to serve a selfobject function for him. I was also the object of considerable idealization in those early years to make up for an absent father. As Udayan developed a better sense of self through these selfobject transferences, he could begin to express more negative feelings both at family members and myself.

Manoj is a North Indian man whose early relationship with me in the analysis was characterized by a very strong idealization. In good part, this selfobject transference was to make up for a relationship with his father with whom he had never been able to be close; in part, it was also a reflection of an idealized relationship with three much older brothers whom he was taught to revere as gods. It was only after several years of the analysis that I realized that the highly problematic relationship with his father was in good part caused by his mother, who in her frequent fights with his father kept denigrating him to Manoj. It took some six years of the analysis for Manoj's intense rage to emerge full force in the transference over his experiencing me as putting his father down, similar to what his mother had done. Since Manoj had been so profoundly dependent on his mother, as he was on me for some years—he had slept by her side until he was eleven—being in touch with this rage earlier was far too threatening. This dynamic of the idealized selfobject being seriously interfered with by one parent denigrating the other to the child, in Manoj's case the mother denigrating the father, happens frequently in a North American context of divorce.

MULTIPLE MOTHERING

In Asian extended families, there is usually multiple mothering. While the anthropologist, Stanley Kurtz (1993) has advanced the thesis that all those participating in the mothering are of equal importance to the child, this has not been my psychoanalytic experience with Asian patients. There is no question that the mother is the more important figure, although aunts, grandmothers, older sisters, and servants can also play a very major role. As a partial exception, I would like to discuss a case of an Indian woman where another mothering figure, an aunt, was highly prominent to this patient because the mother, herself, was deficient in her selfobject functioning to the child. I could also cite a Japanese man I analyzed, whose aunt played this same role because of his mother's poor selfobject functioning.

Alka, a graduate psychology student who came to the United States when she was four, felt intensely left out of various graduate school and other social relationships. She experienced herself as always being on the outside, that something was wrong with her. Yet, at other times in her high school and college experiences, she had extremely close relationships with some of her teachers who thought very highly of her, and in college was at the very center of a great deal of community-oriented organizational work. On the surface, her disturbed feelings could easily be related to her feelings of being an outsider as an Indian-American.

On a deeper level, she was the first grandchild born into a large, extended family in India where she was the center of everyone's attention, and where over fifty different names of endearment were used for her by various members of the family. I interpreted to her that being taken away at age four from such a loving, attentive family to live with her own parents alone in the United States must have been quite traumatic. Seriously compounding this was her early bonding to an aunt whom she always felt was far more in tune with her than her own mother. The latter was much more inclined toward running the complicated affairs of the extended family than being close to her daughter. This loss of her aunt and the extended family to live with a mother in America who was unempathic with her was behind much of her feelings of being on the outside. She had mistakenly thought that her feelings as an outsider were primarily due to cultural issues of her being Indian in an American social environment. At other times, during her school and college years she strove to be the adored child of the extended family and aunt.

The poignancy of her feeling left out was evoked in me when one day she came to session mentioning that she was considering psychoanalytic training at an institute where I would not have been accepted as a training analyst. This was the turning point in the therapy when I realized how she must feel, and have felt for years over being excluded from the important relationships with the extended family and her aunt. I could well work from these induced countertransference reactions to explore the trauma of leaving India and being separated from important selfobjects as a very young child.[4]

However, other problems that Alka experienced as personal turned out to be more cultural. When Alka was dealing with her toddler, she felt she must have some deep-rooted emotional problems as a mother. She found it extremely difficult to set limits and to say "no," normal child rearing practices in North America which Alka learned in her developmental course in the graduate psychology program. I pointed out that the more usual Indian mode is to distract toddlers with something else when you don't want them to do something, rather than to set limits. Alka immediately felt greatly relieved, remembering that this was the way she was brought up as a young child in the extended family, and particularly by her aunt. Alka felt far more comfortable distracting her toddler than entering into a struggle to set limits.[5]

Alka then began discussing her clinical work with patients in a psychotherapy practicum. Even as an inexperienced therapist, she naturally responded much more in an empathic, concerned way than her classically-oriented psychoanalytic supervisors wanted her to do. Initially, she had experienced this, too, as one of her emotional problems, until she was able to see this difference as being rooted in very different cultural realms.

I should also comment that Alka's having developed a self from early childhood in relation to another maternal selfobject than her mother, and then living after age four with her mother and father alone, is something I have observed with two American patients, Marilyn and Lucille (see Chapter Six). Though of very different backgrounds, these women had grandmothers who were dominant in the early formation of their self, and mothers who were empathically unattuned, with whom these women lived with from around age four on. This issue of these women having two different selves, one with a distinctly different texture from an early childhood relationship with a grandmother, the other developed later with a more unempathic mother, and the problems resulting from this, is something that needs further exploration in the self psychology literature.

SUMMARY

I first delineate the formulation of self psychology within the North American culture of individualism, and how self psychology both critiques this culture and incorporates some of its basic assumptions. I then cite the centrality of self-esteem in Asians and their four major kinds of selfobject relationships: the extraordinary empathic sensing with its nonverbal and indirect verbal communication, and the exchange of dependency for esteem; idealizing selfobject relationships in the formal social hierarchy; idealizing selfobject relationships in hierarchy by the qualities of the person, with its ultimate goal of self-transformation into a spiritual being; and family reputation. I then discuss two theoretical issues: reciprocal selfobjects in social relatedness and the cultural patterning of selfobject relationships. Two other significant differences between Asian and North American selfobject relationships are delineated: modes of empathic attunement and contents of empathic attunement. Problems in Asian esteem are delved into, first in a general way and then in a more clinical way illustrated by three patients.

ENDNOTES

1. May Tung sees this communication by silence in Chinese as not only related to a heightening of interpersonal sensitivity or empathy in complex familial relationships; but also to knowing what others are feeling and how they are behaving out of a longstanding, shared cultural tradition of well-defined "shoulds" (pers. com.).

2. Peter Zimmerman, an American self psychologist originally from Switzerland, sees different transformations of narcissism from a cross-cultural perspective: Americans mirror the grandiose or expansive self of the child; central and northern Europeans tend to shame the expansive self, instead mirroring self-control; while Asians exchange an idealizing merger with the superior for empathic attunement (pers. com.).

3. In Hindu families, each member of the extended family is referred to by their exact familial position to oneself, not by their given name, nor by a more general designation such as cousin or aunt. Which cousin or which aunt or uncle is specified. The same is apparently true in Chinese families (pers. com. May Tung).

4. Self psychology and intersubjectivity have unfortunately not yet been able to incorporate the use of induced countertransference reactions to empathically understand patients. This major contribution of British object relations and American interpersonal and paradigmatic schools of psychoanalysis was once highly controversial in traditional Freudian circles; now, it is increasingly accepted. Sooner or later, self psychology and intersubjectivity will have to incorporate such reactions for an expanded use of empathy.

5. This reminded me of a conversation overheard at a party of Columbia University

South Asian scholars, American and Indian. An older American woman, a grand-mother, asserted to a younger Indian mother, "How can you not tell your young child what to do! Suppose he was about to run out into the street with cars com-ing!" The Indian woman retorted, "But I am a mother! How can I tell him not to do something!" What she neglected to say was that she would have found some-thing to distract her son from the dangerous situation.

Chapter Eight

Psychoanalysis and Psychoanalytic Therapy with Indians and Japanese in the United States

THE PSYCHOANALYTIC RELATIONSHIP

In the history of cross-cultural psychoanalytic work, considerable attention has been paid to the psychological nature of the other, and to psychoanalysts from one culture working with analysands from a significantly different culture or race. More recently, Cabaniss, Oquendo, and Singer (1994) have shown that psychoanalysis, itself, embodies many values from the culture of individualism which can be at complete variance with those of patients from radically different cultures. This can result in impasses in the analytic work unless the analyst recognizes these value dissonances.[1]

For understanding the psychoanalytic relationship with Asians, there are important additional factors beyond the different values of American psychoanalysts and Asian patients (see Chapter Five), and the value orientation of psychoanalysis, itself (see Chapter One), although both of these are of considerable importance. I shall particularly emphasize the very different emotional patterning of relationships, with its underlying psychological attitudes and needs, in Asian and North American societies as they are manifested in the psychoanalytic relationship.

As I briefly stated in the first chapter, the North American psychoanalytic relationship is based on a clear assumption of two separate individuals with an individualistic I-self and subjectivity, with relatively firm ego boundaries between each other in an "I" and "you" contractual relationship, exchanging fee for time and expertise, where the patient gradually free-associates while the analyst, who remains relatively anonymous and nonjudgmental, gradually clarifies the subtext of what is transpiring, especially in the transference, in an empathic, forthright way. Only later in the analysis there may sometimes be a relative blurring of the separateness of analyst and patient when projective identifications occur and the induced countertransference is noted and used by the analyst for understanding the transference.

Self psychologists have gradually realized that the psychoanalyst serves a selfobject function to patients even when the major transferences are not necessarily selfobject ones (Lachmann and Beebe 1995). At times, the selfobject function of the analyst is integrally related to a selfobject transference; but at other times, these empathic, idealizing, and alter ego selfobject functions serve as a background to the figure of more usual transference displacements and projections, and in cases of more severe psychopathology, projective identifications and defensive idealizations. I shall here detail how this generalized selfobject function of the analyst is manifested in Asian selfobject ways of relating that significantly affect the psychoanalytic relationship.

The Asian variation on the psychoanalytic relationship is perhaps best understood within the framework of the three psychosocial dimensions of familial/group hierarchical relationships that I partially delineated in Chapters Two and Three, and more fully in my previous book (Roland 1988, pages 212–223, 282–288). In the formal psychosocial dimension of hierarchical relationships with its distinct social etiquette and reciprocal responsibilities, both Indian and Japanese patients perceive the psychoanalyst as the superior to whom they will defer and be receptive; and in turn, they will expect the analyst to be a nurturing, concerned person, who will give advice and guidance, and take care of them. Asians are usually highly attuned to what the superior wants or expects from them, and this is true of the psychoanalytic relationship as well. Thus, if they sense the analyst to be more interested in one train of association than another, they will subtly switch to that. They are also highly sensitive to what the analyst as superior may or may not be receptive. I have found Indians and Japanese to be very capable of keeping either meaningful interests or conflictual material completely out of their associations if they sense the analyst might be judgmental, unattuned, or simply not particularly interested. Secrets are easily kept within a private self in relationships with superiors.

It was only when an American psychoanalyst realized through her reading about Indians that Hindus may be deeply involved in religious rituals and spiritual practices, that she asked her patient if he was indeed involved in these. He had never once mentioned such interests in session. But upon her concerned questioning, he revealed that he was indeed seriously involved on a daily basis, and that this played a large role in his sense of self and meaning in life (pers. com. Monica Rawn). He had probably assumed that she would have no interest or understanding of his practices; or even worse, might have considered them to be superstitions.

As another aspect of the hierarchically structured psychoanalytic relationship, Asians will always idealize the analyst regardless of whether or not there have been deficient idealized selfobjects from the past, or defensive idealizations related to more borderline psychopathology. In other words, idealization will more distinctly and overtly occur in Asian patients, regardless of psychopathology, than in North American patients. For a Japanese man with a male analyst, either Japanese or American, the analyst will be idealized as a mentor or teacher for life, as this is a normal part of Japanese extra-familial, male hierarchical relationships (Taketomo 1989). Indians, too, will continue an idealized relationship with their therapist throughout life (Ramanujam 1989). This, of course, will take on a particular coloration in each individual depending on idiosyncratic familial experiences with idealizing selfobjects.

Idealizations will become even more intense, again regardless of psychopathology, to the extent that the patient actually experiences the analyst as a really caring, mature, empathic, insightful, and psychologically helpful person. In another psychosocial dimension of Asian hierarchical relationships, that of hierarchy by the qualities of the person, idealization intensifies in the presence of a superior person. In these cases, the subordinate, or patient, may try to be as close as possible to the analyst. There are strong values in Asian cultures to imbibe the qualities of a superior person, such as a holy man, to become a better person oneself. This can be best done through effecting a close bond to the former. This kind of psychology tends to be foreign to North American relationships, where the emphasis on egalitarianism, an important value in individualism, militates against it. Psychoanalytic work only really progresses when the analyst is gradually perceived as having some superior qualities versus simply being the formal superior.

Turning to the intimacy dimension of hierarchical relationships, Indians and Japanese will expect much more of an emotionally connected we-relationship between patient and analyst than is typical of North American patients. This might well start from the very beginning with Indian patients, who can pour forth a great deal of their inner feelings, thoughts, and fantasies from early on if they find the analyst to be receptive, empathic and concerned, and preserves confidentiality. Japanese patients, on the other hand, will relate initially more in the mode of meeting the expectations and etiquette of the formal hierarchy, since the psychoanalytic relationship is experienced initially as an outside one (*soto*). It may take a number of sessions for the relationship to gradually move into an insider one (*uchi*), where the intimacy dimension is very strong.

Indians often experience the analyst as a parental or an extended family elder with whom they have felt intimate, and in India, will try to draw the analyst into the extended family as is done with any signficant, extra-familial relationship. Whereas for Japanese men, the analyst is an extra-familial mentor based on the model of the mentor-disciple relationship (Taketomo 1989). For Chinese, according to May Tung (see Appendix A), the therapist is viewed more as a teacher, but quite emotionally peripheral to the patient as the therapist is perceived neither as a family elder nor a mentor.

In one aspect of the intimacy dimension of the psychoanalytic relationship, Indians and Japanese assume there will be a great degree of caring and concerned empathy from the analyst. In psychoanalytic therapy with a traditional Japanese patient (Roland 1988, 186–194), the Japanese analyst is expected to empathically sense what is not at all being openly expressed by the patient; and in turn, the Japanese analyst expects the patient to sense interpretations that are again not being openly expressed by the analyst. This kind of concerned empathic sensing (*omoiyari*) of the innuendos of communication by Japanese is mind-boggling to most Americans who are so verbally oriented. They can easily view it as almost telepathic. I find Japanese patients make allowances and try to be more verbally expressive when with a North American psychoanalyst. With Indians, the analyst is expected to be empathic with a complex interplay of highly verbal communication, that in itself can sometimes be quite ambiguous, with nonverbal facial expressions, gestures, moods, and behavior. The analyst is expected to read Indian intent on all of these levels, which might or might not be congruent with each other.

In another aspect of the intimacy relationship, Asians will feel entirely comfortable in being very dependent on the analyst, subtly and unspokenly exchanging dependency for enhancing the esteem of the analyst as a superior who is capable of taking care of them. Again, Indians can manifest this very quickly as they try to convert any relationship to a familial, insider one; whereas Japanese will take considerably longer. If North American psychoanalysts are not aware of this subtle exchange of dependency for esteem in Asian hierarchical relationships, an exchange that is foreign to North American psychology, they can easily experience this asking and depending on as psychopathological, or as a manifestation of deficits, or even as an infringment on their own autonomy, and can therefore react unempathically or judgmentally. On the other hand, by recognizing this different degree of dependency, judgments will then have to be made as to whether or not it is excessive for even one or another Asian culture (see the discussion of Mrs. Kakkar in Chapter Five), or when it shades over into a demanding entitlement as with Japanese patients.

RESISTANCES

As I have previously mentioned (Roland 1988, pages 67–69), psychoanalysis primarily depicts resistances as relating idiosyncratically in different individuals to their particular anxieties, unconscious defensive structure, superego strictures, and rejecting internalized objects; whereas other resistances are far more tied to various cultural norms incorporated into a patient's ego-ideal and to predominant modes of relating in a given society. Thus, patients influenced by certain traditional values of individualism, such as being self-reliant and keeping feelings to oneself, may find it quite difficult to become involved in a dependent, psychoanalytic relationship where one is to express oneself freely. Psychoanalysts handle these culturally related resistances all of the time. In an Asian context, there are other sociocultural values and ways of relating that can bring up considerable resistance to the psychoanalytic process.

First and foremost, most persons from any of the Asian societies are highly reluctant to see a psychoanalyst, or any psychotherapist for that matter, because of feelings of shame of how this will reflect on themselves and family reputation. Being emotionally disturbed is not an individual matter, and may have to be addressed at the very beginning of therapy. For Japanese, seeing a therapist is often an admission of failure in the context of internalized standards for very high levels of functioning.

Another general resistance results from Asians having a far more private self, with the capability of keeping all kinds of secrets to themselves throughout therapy, especially if they perceive that the therapist will not be sufficiently receptive to some aspect of themselves. As part of the secretive, private self, there are strong cultural values over not divulging any skeletons in the family closet. This is to preserve family reputation, but can obviously serve as a hindrance to the open exploration needed in psychoanalytic work. And as the therapy progresses, Asians will be extremely reluctant to convey any dissatisfaction directly to the analyst. If they feel discontent enough, they will simply leave treatment without any discussion as to why.

As Cabaniss, Oquendo, and Singer (1994) showed with a Korean woman patient, Confucian cultures such as Korean and Japanese may value silence and nonverbal communication more than verbal expression, and in fact, may put a negative value on talking too much. This can result in a very strong reluctance to free-associate, a mainstay of psychoanalysis. An analyst working with such patients may not only have to address the value dissonance, but also to become more empathically attuned and intuitive to establish communication with such patients.

Indian patients will actively seek and expect advice and guidance to be given in their role of subordinate, as in the extended family. For a therapist to assume the usual cultural role of superior in giving guidance and direction, as some Indian psychotherapists are wont to do, is to preclude a great deal of productive psychoanalytic work. One Bombay psychoanalyst handles these expectations in the very beginning by telling a new patient that he is not there to help him in his life, but simply to have him understand himself better (pers. com. Udayan

Patel). I usually work with these expectations by telling the patient that he or she has apparently received a great deal of advice and guidance from others, but the problem still remains. Obviously, there are hidden roots to the problem that no one so far understands. Perhaps by working together we can gradually get to the sources of the difficulties.

TRANSFERENCE

Some non-Western psychoanalysts have expressed a view that culture only enters into psychoanalytic work with non-Western analysands in the initial phases of the therapy; but once the transferences are developed and established, these analysands are no different than those from Western societies.[2] This is not my experience with Indian and Japanese analysands. I find that culture must absolutely be taken into account in working with their intense transferences and the transference neurosis.

One possible explanation for the difference between my own experience and their view is that Indian and Japanese patients may be more significantly different from European/North American ones than are their patients from Turkey and Egypt. But another possible explanation, a more subtle one, comes from observations and conversations about the general adaptation of non-Western psychoanalysts into European and North American psychoanalytic societies, an obviously touchy subject. My impression is that their indigenous cultural self is often insufficiently attended to either in their own psychoanalyses by their Western analysts and/or by their colleagues. This can lead them to suppress or downplay their indigenous self and any cultural/psychological differences between themselves and the majority members of their psychoanalytic societies. Thus, to seek parity and acceptance they adopt mainstream psychoanalytic attitudes, such as ones that generally dismiss cultural issues in psychoanalysis.

There is sometimes another dynamic as well. Coming from societies that European/North American ones have historically regarded as inferior, and having internalized some of these colonial-type attitudes as they became Western-educated, feeling vulnerable, they can be motivated even more toward assimilating completely into the culture of their European and North American psychoanalytic societies. Obviously, these dynamics can vary considerably from one Asian or Middle Eastern psychoanalyst to another.

What is most striking in two long-term psychoanalyses with an Indian and a Japanese man, and confirmed by an informal conversation with a noted Chinese-American social scientist from his own psychoanalysis, is the difficulty all of them had in expressing any anger, criticism, or ambivalence directly to the analyst for a very long period of time. My two analysands, as well as other Indian and Japanese patients, men and women, in psychoanalytic therapy have been easily able to complain and rage from almost the beginning at all kinds of authority figures in their life whom they felt had treated them badly or let them down. But these two analysands each took well over a year to express the slightest criticism of me, the Chinese-American taking two years into his analysis to express any anger at his analyst.

And when all of them did, they all came to the following session in an anxiety state that had to be interpreted as being related to the criticism or anger from the previous session. This enabled my two analysands to become slightly more bold in their criticism of me in one of the following sessions, again followed in the next session by another anxiety attack. Again this was interpreted as being connected to the criticism of me, and again each of these analysands became increasingly bolder in a future session in complaining about me. After a number of these repetitions of criticizing me, anxiety attacks, and interpretations, a full-fledged negative transference developed with both of these patients, eventuating in a transference neurosis. All of this contrasts with most of my American patients who at a very early stage are usually able to criticize me or bring up some dissatisfaction, although obviously they also have some anxiety attached to this.

What are the cultural factors involved in this transference progression? There are two major ones. For men and women in all of the Asian societies, there are strong cultural strictures against voicing any criticism or anger directly to a superior, whether a parent, elder, in-law, teacher, or boss. This is deeply internalized into a powerful superego. The other factor is that in the subordinate-superior relationship, and the psychoanalytic one is subsumed under this, there is a tremendous expectation in the subordinate of being taken care of by the superior, and in the superior of being honored, obeyed, and depended upon. The subordinate, or analysand, therefore will have intense anxiety if anything occurs that could undermine this important, nurturing relationship. And the anticipation is that any criticism or anger voiced by the analysand to the analyst will cause the latter to retaliate by becoming far less nurturing.

In both of these cases, the negative transference could only become fully established with considerable anger, and at times rage, at me when it was clear that the nurturing hierarchical relationship would not be shaken. My impression is that none of this intense anger had ever been expressed earlier toward the primary parental figure, in each case their mothers.[3] What is also striking is their acting out behavior. It was as if there was a great need to get even or hurt the mother in the transference. The Indian patient, Manoj, acted out by failing in his work and getting fired, eating the wrong foods and becoming ill, and generally doing himself in in a number of ways. It gradually became evident that he was getting even with me by being a failure, with the direct implication of reflecting very poorly on me as a psychoanalyst supposedly knowledgeable about Indians. He would be my living failure.

It was only when Manoj became able to express his rage directly and unrelentingly at me that he began to pull his life together and set out to do more what he wanted to do, rather than what his extended family had directed him to do. The content of his rage in the transference also had cultural elements as well as sociohistorical ones. While initially his anger was directed at me as a father, who at times had been both sadistic and seemingly rejecting of him, it more and more focused in a maternal transference. In a family where his Western-oriented father encouraged his sons and daughters to become highly Western-educated, and for his older sons to go abroad to the United States and marry Americans, his mother turned to him as the youngest of her sons to take care of her in her old age. This went against the cultural custom of the older sons and their wives bearing the major responsibility for aging parents; but the older sons with the father's encouragement had already opted out.

His mother kept Manoj to herself by being unusually pampering and gratifying, well beyond the normal highly gratifying Indian child rearing patterns, and by constant negative remarks about his father. His rage at me in the transference was over my being highly manipulative of him, making him very dependent on me, and my putting his father down through remarks I had made much earlier in the analysis when he, himself, portrayed his father in a very negative light. It took almost two years of constantly venting his rage at me in the maternal transference before he could establish a relationship with me as a reliable father-figure. As he resolved this maternal transference, he could juxtapose images of the divine family of Shiva, Durga, and their son, Ganesh, much closer together in his apartment. In the meantime, he made considerable strides in his new career, one where he eventually began blending positive aspects from both of his parents.

The Japanese patient, Keigo, acted out by starting an affair with another woman some time after he had become seriously involved with an American woman he had met in graduate school here, had moved in with, and was planning to marry. This came at a point in the analysis when he had become increasingly angry at me as the money-hungry mother who wasn't taking sufficient care of him. He would punish both me and his fiancée by starting this affair, which was transferentially connected to his often being taken care of in his childhood by a much older, favorite female cousin with whom he would have preferred to live. The cultural part was his expectation and strong feelings of entitlement that his dependency needs should have been much better fulfilled by his mother, rather than her being so involved in the family business. I have found a strong sense of this kind of entitlement in Japanese patients, which seems related to having to fulfill very high maternal expectations for doing everything extremely well. It is as if the person were saying, "I have to constantly strive to fulfill your high expectations of me; therefore, I am entitled to be better taken care of by you." Interestingly enough, my induced counter-transference reactions often encompassed an unusual preoccupation with my finances during his sessions, quite reminiscent of his mother who dwelt so much on money.

PSYCHOANALYTIC THERAPY AND THE INDIAN ENCOUNTER
WITH AMERICAN LIFE

Cultural issues with Indian and Japanese patients in psychoanalytic therapy in the United States not only encompasses their indigenous self and the sociohistorical changes that have taken place in their own countries before immigrating, but also their encounter with the American culture of individualism, both with the value dissonances and the newer opportunities. While both Indian and Japanese immigrants go through a difficult inner struggle in balancing their two worlds, my impression is that those who cannot make a reasonable adaptation are usually burdened with difficult inner conflicts and/or deficits.[4] Sometimes, these problems surface within a context of the greater opportunities that American life affords, or, of their being able to be more independent than they could be in their home country. At other times, there is the strain of having to be much more on one's own here, or, as a second-generation Indian-American, having to cope with immigrant parents in their stresses and struggles. Emotional conflicts can easily encompass all of these factors.

Narayan

I shall now give a few clinical examples to illustrate these points. Narayan had immigrated to the United States, as had many of his fellow graduates from their elite engineering college in India, because of the lack of jobs there at that time and the much greater opportunities here. And indeed, Narayan was able to obtain a research position at one of the very best scientific research centers in the United States where one is expected to do highly innovative work, the hallmark of American scientific creativity. Narayan liked being there a great deal, but although he could do routine scientific work very well, he was severely inhibited in doing long-term innovative research. This was why he came for therapy.

It took us many months to ferret out the sources of Narayan's inhibition and to free him to be more creative in his scientific work. To greatly condense the more than two years of twice a week psychoanalytic therapy, it emerged that to do the kind of innovative research that the center expected would mean not having results for a long time. One had to try one theory or another on a given problem, this method or another one, with many false starts and partial solutions, changing direction frequently, to come up with a new solution. It certainly was not a linear process.

In this context of uncertainty and ambiguity, Narayan felt extremely anxious. He needed results to confirm a sense of self and self-worth. Undoubtedly, the most inhibiting factor was his mother's attitudes as he was growing up. Narayan's family was part of a community where in his generation he was one of the only ones to have gone on to college. It was a middle caste community that didn't particularly value education. In this unlikely family and community context, Narayan emerged as a brilliant student throughout his schooling.

His mother, however, could not let well enough alone. She apparently felt that for Narayan to do well she had to constantly keep motivating him, using customary child rearing shaming techniques from their community. She always compared Narayan to some neighbor's child, who in her eyes always seemed to do better than Narayan in some way or another. How could he not do better, she constantly conveyed. Narayan thus felt no matter how well he did, it was never good enough. As a result, he needed the constant A's he received in his schoolwork to confirm that he was doing all right.

To do innovative research for long periods of time without immediate results created a sense of panic and shame in Narayan. He felt he wasn't doing well enough and was letting his mother and family down. This was not helped either by his father's attitudes, who as an army sergeant, was mainly interested in Narayan behaving properly and keeping everything in order. As we delved more and more into these parental attitudes, more particularly his mother's shaming of him, Narayan began to tolerate the uncertainties of creative, innovative research. He did this in gradual steps, starting with somewhat easier intermediate projects, and then built up to a major long-term one, where he eventually came up with a whole new way of developing certain communication processes that would save the industry very considerable sums of money.

In summary, if Narayan had remained in India at that time there would have been almost no opportunities to do the kind of creative scientific research that he could in his position in the United States. But this newer opportunity evoked severe inhibitions in Narayan that only could be dealt with in psychoanalytic therapy. Otherwise he would have had to seek a lower-level position. The inhibitions, themselves, were mainly related to a culture-specific kind of shaming technique in child rearing common to a particular South Indian middle-caste community. Other students whom Narayan knew at college from a Brahminical background had never been subjected to this kind of shaming.

Mrs. Kakkar

Mrs. Kakkar came for psychoanalytic therapy in New York City to resolve intensely distraught feelings about her mother who had died a couple of years previously. She and her mother had become bitterly alienated in her mother's last years after a lifetime of unusual closeness, companionship, and mutual support. Mrs. K. was baffled by what had happened. Both she and her mother were highly intelligent, cultured women with advanced degrees who were in the forefront of modernizing ideas for women in India. Her mother and her father, a forward-looking industrialist, had been deeply involved in the National Movement for Indian independence, and in Gandhi's and Nehru's programs for development once Independence occurred. At a dinner years ago when her father was still alive, the American ambassador to India commented to Mrs. K. that he had never talked with a more intelligent, knowledgeable woman than her mother.

"Why had everything between us gone so awry?" Mrs. K. exclaimed in session. The answer very gradually emerged after many detours into other issues in a three-year twice a week psychoanalytic therapy. The story encompasses life in the United States for Mrs. K. with her relationship with her husband, important sociohistorical factors involving a layering of the self in her mother, and a severe clash between the two.

Her difficulties with her mother apparently began when Mrs. K. separated from her husband in New York City six or seven years before coming to therapy. She and her husband had moved temporarily to New York City from New Delhi with their young daughter some years before so that he could further develop his import-export business. Living apart from their extended families and friends with whom they were so involved in New Delhi, she found her husband to be a very emotionally detached man who paid little attention to her and their daughter, instead thriving on work and entertaining clients. As he extended their stay indefinitely for business purposes, she found the relationship intolerable and asked for a separation. This is a more extreme version of what many immigrant Indian families find here when they are without the support and intimacy relationships of the extended family: once thrown upon their own in a way they never would have been in India, they find they do not particularly get along very well. Of course, there are many exceptions to this.

The first year of the separation was apparently quite acrimonious, but by the time Mrs. K. came for psychoanalytic therapy it had settled down a great deal. She had asked for a divorce, which her husband refused to give. With neither of them being United States citizens, she could only rely on his good will for child support, paying her daughter's private school tuition, and giving her some support as well.

By the time Mrs. K. had decided on a separation, her father had died. She felt he would have been fully supportive of her decision had he known the situation. Her mother was originally against the decision, as was an Indian psychiatrist she consulted in New York City. Indian women don't leave their husbands.

When Mrs. K. went ahead with the separation, her mother then insisted that Mrs. K. and her daughter return to their family home in New Delhi. If she had been living in India, this is exactly what she would have had to do.

But Mrs. K. had already tasted the possibilities of being an independent woman in New York City. American life gave her far more options than she would have had in New Delhi. Coming from a highly educated background, where she had already worked in publishing in New Delhi, she was easily able to get a good position in a publishing house, and to partake of the various cultural events in New York City, both Indian and American. She found this lifestyle far more preferable.

Her main anxiety was over the possibility that her husband would cut off the child support and the private school tuition, and later on, their daughter's college expenses. If he did, she would indeed have to return to India to the family home. She couldn't manage all of this financially, herself.

She then asked her mother to give her part of the house as her inheritance, where she could easily put in a kitchen and establish her own living quarters with her daughter. If she had this inheritance, she always knew that she would have a secure place to go to. The idea seemed a perfectly reasonable one to Mrs. K. Under the influence of Gandhi's and Nehru's ideas from the National Movement, legislation had been passed that daughters would inherit equally with sons, in contrast to practices of the past when only sons inherited. Moreover, her idea was not only in accord with the ideals of her father but seemingly those of her mother as well. How could such a modern woman as her mother not agree to this?

To Mrs. K.'s great surprise her mother refused. Her mother insisted that Mrs. K. could move back to the family house at any time, but her mother would not deed her any part of it. When Mrs. K. objected with the probability that her brother and his family would move into the house with his wife's aging parents, leaving little room for Mrs. K. and her daughter, her mother simply responded that it was the *dharma* (duty) of her brother to always look after Mrs. K. and her daughter. Mrs. K. would have nothing to worry about.

The more Mrs. K. pushed her mother for her rightful inheritance, feeling she really needed part of the house for her security, the more her mother refused. And as Mrs. K. became more adamant, a chasm of alienation and bitterness grew between them. Even before the mother died, Mrs. K.'s brother did move his family into the house, and a while later his aging in-laws, thus occupying most of the house. Mrs. K. simply could not understand how such a forward-looking, modern Indian woman as her mother could revert to the old morality and hierarchy of sons only inheriting, and daughters being left to be totally dependent on their brothers if their fathers were no longer living and they had no husbands to support them.

We spent many sessions discussing her and her mother's relationship from any number of angles, some of which were therapeutically quite helpful to Mrs. K., especially when it surfaced in the transference/countertransference relationship (see Chapter Five). I learned a great deal about Mrs. K.'s family and her mother's background over a period of time. Most relevant is that her mother had come from a traditional North Indian Brahmin community where Mrs. K.'s grandfather was Western-educated as an engineer, and wanted his daughter, Mrs. K.'s mother, to attain advanced degrees and become an educator, herself. Toward this end, he sent her to England to do graduate work, which was on the unusual side; and when she returned to India, he was instrumental in her becoming principal of a girl's school. Mrs. K.'s mother then met her father, a successful and influential industrialist interested in furthering the modernization of India. He was an excellent man to marry for those with modern views, and was readily accepted by Mrs. K.'s grandfather. However, since he was from a lower caste, Mrs. K.'s maternal grandmother never really accepted the marriage, and was never that hospitable when they visited her mother's family. Mrs. K.'s mother seemed to be stunningly different from her own mother, far more sophisticated, educated, and free-thinking in her views.

After learning all about the family background and a great deal more about the unusual family and social milieu in New Delhi in which Mrs. K. grew up, I suggested to her that perhaps she had never realized how deeply identified her mother was with her own very traditional Brahmin mother. This was not to deny that her mother had indeed acquired a very different outlook than her own mother in becoming far more educated, travelling a great deal, having at one time a professional life of her own, and living with a husband who was also very forward-looking with associations with some of the leaders of the National Movement. I suggested there was more of a layering of the self in her mother than Mrs. K. may have realized. That once Mrs. K.'s father had died and her mother, then older, was forced to be much more on her own, she may have reverted to her old identification with her own traditional mother. To the extent that this older self had resurfaced in her mother, it should be no surprise that she would have refused to give Mrs. K. part of the house, instead reserving it for her son only, and relying on his traditional sense of duty to take care of his sister in an emergency.

It took three years to reach this point of understanding, but it now made perfect sense to Mrs. K. She could only marvel how this older, traditional self of her mother could resurface in a woman who was so intelligently modern. For the first time in years, Mrs. K. felt at peace.

This tale is a strand in the larger fabric of social change in modern India, and how it impacts psychologically. Mrs. K. grew up in a family, who in those times had unusually modern views for their daughter to become highly educated, to have a career, and to choose her own mate. Mrs. K. took a further step toward independence and individualization by leaving a very unsatisfactory marriage in New York City, and then getting a professional position to support herself rather than returning to the family home in New Delhi with her widowed mother. This was obviously much more possible in the social and economic climate of the United States than in India. Her assertion of her rights as a daughter in modern India ran into a wall of opposition from her mother, who had reverted to an older identification with her own very traditional mother. The winds of change had blown unevenly in her mother's family: her mother's father had been Western-educated and had similar aspirations for his oldest daughter, while her mother's mother remained quite traditional, a not unusual combination in that era. For a psychoanalyst, it is extremely helpful to know not only the cultural self of a particular Asian patient, but equally important, how this cultural self is interwoven into the larger fabric of sociohistorical change within the patient's family background.

SUMMARY

The psychoanalytic relationship is discussed in terms of North American individualism and of the three psychosocial dimensions of Asian hierarchical relationships, with their variations in India and Japan. In the psychoanalytic relationship, normal selfobject ways of relating vary from Asians to North Americans, as do modes of communication. Culturally-related resistances, both North American and Asian, are then delineated. Culture also enters into the development of intense transferences, as illustrated by an Indian and a Japanese analysand. Two cases of Indians in psychoanalytic therapy illustrate Indian encounters with the culture of individualism. In one case, greater opportunities for creative scientific work in the United States brought out inhibitions and conflicts rooted in a particular Indian background. In the other case, the ability of a woman separated from her husband to function more independently in the United States brought about severe conflicts with her mother. In this case, knowing the sociohistorical background of an Asian society as it impacts on family relationships can be extremely helpful to a psychoanalyst.

ENDNOTES

1. They give examples of a professional Indian man working in New York City who has his family arrange a marriage for him, typical of his family culture and for many Indians here, but which is analyzed as his avoiding personal agency and making autonomous choices, which then results in his becoming irate at the analyst; of a Korean woman who is silent much of the time in her sessions because talking too much is very much frowned upon in Korean culture, but which the analyst treated as a resistance until realizing the value dissonance with free association; and of a

Cuban woman who believes from her culture that evil spirits will punish her for being in touch with forbidden negative feelings, thus making it difficult for her to be in touch with unconscious conflicts, a cardinal value of psychoanalysis.

2. These viewpoints emerged from two sources: a discussion of an earlier version of Chapter Six by Dr. Vamik Volkan, originally from Turkey but now living in the United States, at a Midwinter Meeting of the American Psychoanalytic Association; and published remarks by Dr. Ishak Ramzy, an Egyptian psychoanalyst who has lived in England and the United States (Jackson 1968).

3. One sometimes sees in the literature that it is impossible to work through intense anger of Japanese patients toward their mothers, as there is so much shame, guilt, and anxiety because the mother is such a powerful, self-sacrificing person (DeVos 1980; Jackson 1968). In this case, however, the strong anger toward the mother was eventually worked through to a very great extent.

4. This emerged from a conversation with Mrs. Loveleen Posmentier, an Indian psychoanalyst in New York City.

Chapter Nine

Sexuality, the Indian Extended Family, and Hindu Culture

INTRODUCTION

S exuality, the main protagonist of classical psychoanalysis, has been viewed in an eternal drama with its antagonist, the superego. The drama may vary with the individual players, but both the development and vicissitudes of sexuality and of the superego have been couched in universal terms. Oedipus, its tragic hero, has reigned supreme. In more contemporary Freudian psychoanalysis, new characters have entered the drama of sexuality, ones far more related to developmental ego formation, selfobject needs of the self, and early object relations—all embodying a more relational-oriented psychoanalysis than that of classical drive and structural theory.

What happens when the scene shifts from Mount Olympus to Mount Kailasa, the home of the Indian gods and goddesses? Or when the notions of morality change from the Categorical Imperative and the Sermon on the Mount, both highly universalistic, to that of *dharma* where proper behavior depends wholly on the context of relationships, the situation, and the specific natures of the persons involved? Or when kinds of child rearing, early object relations, and family structures are radically different? Psychoanalytic therapy in India enables us to assay the civilizational effects on the drama of sexuality from what Freud and other Western psychoanalysts have formulated.

INCESTUOUS FANTASIES

Before delving into the considerable variations in which sexuality may be played out in different civilizational contexts, I should first note from clinical experience that incestuous fantasies with punitive superego reactions—the hallmark of the classic formulations of the Oedipus complex—are indeed present in both Indian women and men. Incestous fantasies often surface through dreams, occasionally through conscious fantasies. Furthermore, Indian patients, both women and men, seem more open on the whole to bring up sexual fantasies and other associations to sexuality than even many of my liberated American patients—a point confirmed by Dr. B. K. Ramanujam (pers. com.) who has treated both Indian and American patients. And in fact, one long-term observer has commented that Indians will far more readily reveal the most intimate details of their sexual life than to mention anything about their involvement with spiritual practices (pers. com. Arthur Eisenberg).

I would like to cite a few examples simply to illustrate the surfacing of incestuous fantasies in Indian women. Shakuntala, an unmarried woman in her late twenties (highly unusual in Hindu communities where marriages are still usually arranged) who was involved for some years with a married man, Kumar, had the following dream. (For a fuller exposition of this case, see Roland 1988, pp. 154–174.) "Kumar drops off his youngest son at my flat and takes me in his car to a place with a large lawn and trees. We are about to kiss when a policeman comes over and insists we get out. I said, 'this is absurd, Kumar is simply my *maman* (maternal uncle),' but the policeman insists Kumar return tomorrow at 5 P.M. I am very uneasy." Her associations to the large lawn and trees were to her house where she grew up. The *maman* or maternal uncle represents a usual niece-uncle romantic attachment that is recognized in the culture; but she never had such an involvement with her *mamans*. This was clearly a diversionary tactic in the dream. Five P.M. reminded her of the exact hours of our analytic sessions. To her uneasiness over time, she associated being worried about Veena (Kumar's wife) because Kumar had recently spent a couple of unaccounted hours with Shakuntala.

I suggested to her the clear unconscious equation of Kumar with her father in the dream (the romantic involvement taking place where she grew up), that one important component of her relationship with Kumar is incestuous fantasies around her father, that the policeman (now equated with me) was her conscience, and her fear of her mother was now displaced onto Veena in the triangle. Shakuntala responded by recognizing the feeling of illicit love and its attraction. I felt at the time, but did not say, that Shakuntala's recent efforts to get me to lecture at her college were in part motivated by wishing to have me as the helpful person—thus offsetting any unconscious images of a projected, punitive conscience.

As Shakuntala had begun to differentiate herself from her mother as a result of our therapeutic work together, incestuous themes around her father and a punitive, maternal superego came to the fore—a not unusual progression in psychoanalytic therapy with women. Earlier, Kumar had unconsciously represented the mother who treated her specially as an infant and then deserted her for her brother; then, he was unconsciously equated with the father and brother whom Shakuntala had used to separate somewhat from her highly depressed mother who was engulfing her; and now Kumar was unconsciously the father-image with whom Shakuntala had incestuous fantasies with the backlash of a punitive, maternal superego.

Another example is Anjali, a second generation Indian-American, who was a social work student when I saw her in psychoanalytic therapy in New York City. Anjali had been quite close to a woman supervisor in an outpatient clinic in a New Jersey hospital where Anjali was doing her field placement. The supervisor was from a South American country, and Anjali felt they had much in common including a sensibility for family relationships and child rearing that often differed from the predominant North American ethos. When Anjali later shifted to the community social work unit, her supervisor was already there, but was clearly not as much at home as in outpatient psychotherapy. Anjali turned to learn from the new director of the unit who was highly dynamic and knowledgeable in community social work. He evidently took a strong interest in Anjali as an unusually capable student. At a key moment when he was praising her, she criticized him, alienating him for some time and souring an important developing professional relationship.

In analyzing this self-sabotaging act, it became evident that Anjali experienced her female supervisor as being unhappy over Anjali's relationship with the male director, something quite similar to her mother's jealous response whenever Anjali became close with her father. Anjali then unconsciously undermined her relationship with the director, as she had done for many years with her father over experiencing a jealous mother. Thus, an unconscious fantasy around a father-figure with a punitive superego clearly related to a jealous mother, and fear of the loss of the mother-figure's love, resulted in Anjali unconsciously sabotaging a valuable professional relationship.

But there were other problematic aspects to Anjali's relationship with the male director then simply an oedipal rivalry with her mother for her father's affections. These involved both her father's communal attitudes toward Anjali, and her growing up in the United States in an Indian immigrant family. Anjali, at the best of times, could not quite believe the director seriously thought very highly of her as a woman professional. This related to her father's attitudes and values from his Gujerati business community, where daughters are to be loved and cherished, then to have a good arranged marriage and have children, but never to have careers. Her father never encouraged her in the least in her desire to be a professional.

Even more distressing was her director's self-preoccupation from being under a great deal of stress because of harsh mental health care cuts in the hospital. She experienced his self-absorption as his not being at all interested in her, and began feeling increasingly insecure about herself as a competent social work student. It was only when I connected the director's stress with that of her father as a struggling immigrant when she was growing up, that her self-castigation and depression suddenly lifted. She vividly recalled how emotionally unavailable her father was for long stretches of time, as he was desparately trying to adapt to the expectations of American corporate life as an accountant, and how badly she had felt about herself then.

Another example is that of Joan, a married woman in her mid-twenties from a Christian community. (See Roland 1988, pp. 108–124.) For the first time in several months of three times a week psychoanalytic therapy, she told of a very close attachment in her college and graduate school days to a German priest, who used to come frequently to her house for discussions, and who greatly appreciated her. She said that her relationship with me seemed more similar to the one she had with him than to the relationship with her father, so that if I did not say much in session, she became upset. I had realized for some time that Joan had turned to her father, husband, former therapist, and now me to gain a kind of appreciation she had never received from her mother; but I had no idea until this session how the transference relationship with me was a mirroring one related to this German priest.

In the following session, however, it became apparent that the attachment to all of us men involved more than a mirroring selfobject relationship. When she told of a fantasy of her husband going out with another girl, then having dreams about this and becoming quite tense, I interpreted that in her attachment to us there must be some deep fantasy of winning out over other women and fearing retaliation. This theme continued the next day in session when she expressed feeling sad and defeated when some of the mothers removed their children from a special workshop Joan had started; in this case, the mother won out. I thus began to interpret an unconscious incestuous attachment and a punitive superego reaction.

In two Indian male patients in their early thirties whom I have seen in New York City, one from a Hindu community, the other Christian, incestuous fantasies readily surfaced. The former, the youngest of seven siblings, slept in his mother's bed until he was eleven. He was more consciously aware of sexual fantasies both about his mother and a favorite sister some twelve years older than was the other patient, whose incestuous fantasies occurred only in his dreams. When the former patient had women supervisors at work, he formed very close relationships with them, at one point with an inappropriate sexual interest and seductiveness that implied the presence of incestuous fantasies.

INDIAN OEDIPUS

For boys, the triangular relationship with mother and father is of an other order from that of Westerners. *The boy never loses his mother.* Beginning with prolonged, early symbiotic mothering with intense gratification and physical affection, often lasting to the fourth or fifth year if not beyond, it is expected that he remain deeply attached to his mother and deeply involved with his original family throughout life. The young child, boy or girl, sleeps next to his mother until the next sibling is born, and then with another sibling, aunt, or uncle, but almost never alone. Strivings for separation, autonomy, initiative, and self-direction—the hallmark of current American child rearing—are discouraged in the Indian context for dependence and interdependence. This is equally true for adolescence where there is no rebellion or striving to create an independent identity.

What effects does this close mother-son relationship have on the boy? Indian men incorporate much more of maternal-feminine qualities than is characteristic of Western men (Kakar 1978, 1989; Roland 1988), have a greater degree of bisexuality in terms of these more maternal-feminine components, and from clinical data are reported to have considerably less castration anxiety than Westerners, with Indian women having much less penis envy (pers. com. T. C. Sinha, former president of the Indian Psychoanalytic Society). The woman as mother looms much larger in the male Indian psyche than is characteristic in the West, so that women are unconsciously perceived as being very powerful—this being reinforced by the Hindu pantheon of extremely powerful mother goddesses. I should note that the maternal-feminine qualities in Indian men are highly adaptive, as superiors in Indian hierarchical relationships are expected to be highly empathic and nurturing toward their subordinates, much more so than in Western hierarchical relationships which are far more governed by contractual rights and obligations.

The structure of the Indian extended family reinforces this mother-son tie. Where the extended, multigenerational family traditionally takes precedence, and where the basic ties are structured around well-defined, complex hierarchical relationships both within and between sexes, the marital relationship does not assume the same importance or intensity that it does in the American nuclear family. The young wife traditionally becomes an integral part of her husband's family on the lowest rung of the ladder, usually encountering a mother-in-law rivalrous for her son's affections. (It is interesting to note the observations of Dr. Niti Seth, a psychoanalytic psychologist, that when a newly married woman is too easily accepted by her in-laws, her husband frequently experiences impotence. When she is treated as an outsider, it seems easier for her husband to unconsciously distinguish her from his incestuous fantasies of the women of his family.) In the patriarchal system, her status measurably increases when she has children, particularly sons, who are to see to her welfare in her older age. Thus, cultivating her sons' attachment helps to perpetuate a multigenerational extended family as well as serving her own welfare.

What role does the father play in the father-son relationship? The father is frequently no great competition for his son in the father-mother-sons triangle. Moreover, there is little evidence of intergenerational conflict or rebellion, either in the Oedipal stage or during adolescence, where the Western son frequently tries to outdo his father or other father-figures such as mentors. Competition among men in the Indian extended family is considerably downplayed in favor of interdependence, harmony, and cooperation; which is not to say that competition doesn't exist, particularly manifesting in envy among brothers, which I discuss in Chapter Eleven. Moreover, Hindu culture promotes strong idealizations of fathers and older brothers, where they and other male and female elders are viewed as partial manifestations of the gods and goddesses. The Indian son does not strive to topple the king and assume his throne. His position as prince is too greatly favored.

In the Indian family, the father is traditionally an overtly emotionally distant disciplinarian who formulates and embodies the ideals of the family (pers. com. B. K. Ramanujam); but psychoanalytic therapy reveals strongly covert father-son emotional ties. The son intensely needs his father not only for a masculine model to identify with, but as a structuring alliance to effect greater differentiation and partial separation from an engulfing maternal symbiosis (Kakar 1980). Throughout life, sons strive to earn the overtly distant father's respect, even after their fathers' demise; and in turn they try to reflect well on their fathers to enhance the latters' reputation and esteem.

Sexuality in teenagers is not experienced as a liberating force that enables them to begin establishing their autonomy outside of family relationships, as in contemporary America. Rather, sexuality is associated with even greater family enmeshments and obligations (Grey 1973), where marital partners are chosen by the family, or at minimum with family approval; and where marriage is considered as much between families as between husband and wife.

In folklore and in clinical practice, Indian men may complain of the voracious sexual appetite of women. This reflects the power of women in India where mother goddesses embody cosmic energy and activity—the male principle in the West. Indeed, in the cultural tradition there is fear that the loss of too much semen will result in debilitation. My clinical impression is that fear of women's sexual desires derives not so much from castration anxiety, but rather from fear of engulfment or of having to give over to the woman.

In Indian mythology, the Oedipus complex does not center on the son's murdering his father and marrying his mother. Rather it is on the jealous father's murderous impulses toward his son (Ramanujan 1983), only a subsidiary theme in the Oedipus myth. This obviously accords with the family structure in which sons are generally favored over husbands. An example is that of Parvati, Shiva's wife, taking a bath and instructing her oldest son, Ganesh, not to let anyone in. When Shiva, his father, arrived and Ganesh refused to let him enter, Shiva severed Ganesh's head. Later to placate Parvati, Shiva had it replaced, but by a turn of fortune it was an elephant's head.

Indian women's sexuality is shaped to a considerable extent by the morality of the extended family, which is deeply internalized into their ego-ideal. Paradoxically, there seems an easy acceptance of sexuality with little of the kind of repression generated by Puritan or Victorian values; while other internalized values strongly set the boundaries of sexual expression, much more so than in contemporary American society. An Indian girl's sexuality is extremely important to the honor and reputation of her original family, and later to the perpetuation of her in-laws family. And upon family reputation rests the marriagibility of herself, her siblings, and cousins. What occurs in public reflects far more on family reputation than what happens within the confines of the extended family. All kinds of flirtations and infatuations may go on between cousins and between nieces and uncles, as well as possible sexual affairs within the extended family; but as long as they do not cross the border into public display, the reputation of the family will not be damaged. Hindi movies exploit this old theme of the dual nature of women's sexuality by identifying the sexually loose woman who wreaks havoc in her family with Westernized Indian women who are free sexually; while the sexually circumspect girl is identified with traditional Indian women (Nandy 1979; Vatsyayan 1975).

I was struck while co-counseling a group of seventeen year-old college girls in Bombay that a surprising number of them felt extremely uneasy when they came each morning to the college. They felt that everyone's eyes were on them and that they would be judged harshly, especially by those they didn't know. I had expected that this projection must derive from internalized harsh criticism from their mothers and other women of the family. Rather it emerged that their reactions were generated by mothers pointing their finger at improper behavior of other girls, and then conveying how gossip about the other girl's behavior could damage her family's reputation. The lesson was not lost on these girls. By easily identifying with the other girl, and being in a stimulating co-ed environment, these students could feel deeply mortified and ashamed if they did anything improper in public. Their fear was of the unknown stranger who could gossip, not the critical voice of a trusted friend. There is in fact a saying that a woman's body has a thousand eyes on it, which reflects the extent to which they feel watched.

Within the extended family, there is also a strict morality for women that has been termed, "modesty/shame" (Das and Nicholas 1979). Married women must maintain a careful distance from their husbands' older brothers, their fathers-in-law, and their husbands' uncles; but are usually permitted a closer, more emotionally intimate relationship with any of their husbands' younger brothers. As a result of this family morality, there is far more separation of the sexes within the Indian extended family than within the American one. Traditionally, wives and husbands refrain from any displays of affection before other family members and may sit separately from each other at meals in a joint household.

Indian women in psychoanalytic therapy seem far more preoccupied with how they are getting along with their female in-laws than with their husbands. On the other hand, there is an increasing demand for a more equal relationship with their husbands in educated circles both in India and the United States. Second-generation Indian-American women who often arrange their own marriages are far more concerned about the marital relationship. Traditionally, Indian women tend to have their emotionally intimate relationships with the other women of the family as well as with their children. This is particularly true if they are living in a multigenerational joint household.

A striking example of this is Sa'ida, whom I originally saw in 1980 in psychoanalytic therapy because of typical mother-in-law/daughter-in-law conflicts (Roland 1988, pp. 174–179). She had been married for a couple of years, and was intensely upset much of the time with a truly difficult mother-in-law, who ordered her around, withheld permission for her to visit home, and gave many more gifts to her own daughters than to Sa'ida. They all lived together in a joint household from which there was no exit: it was understood when Sa'ida's marriage was arranged that since her husband was the oldest son, they would live with her in-laws. In one month of three times a week therapy, we were able to pinpoint unconscious transference reactions from problematic relationships in her original family to her mother-in-law that made it so difficult for Sa'ida to handle her. This helped her considerably.

Eleven years later, I also found Sa'ida distraught over her mother-in-law, but for remarkably different reasons. As a result of some complicated family business decisions, her in-laws directed her husband and Sa'ida to buy a large, luxury flat in a very good section of Bombay and move there with their two children. After they moved in, her mother-in-law would visit, but would refuse to stay overnight. Sa'ida and her husband were both deeply hurt and upset over this. Over the eleven years, Sa'ida and her mother-in-law had actually become very emotionally close to each other, the latter often depending on Sa'ida a great deal. It was a complete reversal of their earlier relationship, with considerable emotional intimacy that was not present when Sa'ida first saw me.

When we discussed this situation in a couple of sessions, Sa'ida mentioned that her mother-in-law had lost her own mother when she was six years old. I suggested that Sa'ida and her family's move to the new flat from the in-law's one must be experienced by her mother-in-law as an abandonment, one that resonates with her own mother dying when she was a child, even though she had sanctioned their move. I further suggested that Sa'ida take some time out from a busy professional life to have her mother-in-law over more and to spend a lot of time with her. This worked, and her mother-in-law then stayed over, healing what was becoming a major rift in the family.

Psychoanalytic therapy and social observations also reveal very strong father-daughter ties, as well as the daughter with her mother. The father seems characteristically less overtly distant from his daughters than from his sons, with the daughters often able to form an overtly closer relationship. Sometimes, as in the case of Sa'ida, the close relationship is with a much older brother, or it can be with an uncle.

Although the structure of the Indian family is generally patriarchal with young brides being integrated into their husband's households, the role of Indian women within the extended family is a very powerful one: arranging marriages and family alliances, performing the rituals for the well-being of the family, being involved in much of the decision-making, and such. Moreover, the philosophical principle of activity, energy, and power (*shakti*) is female in India in contrast to the West, with the goddesses being very powerful figures in the Hindu pantheon, and a plethora of female mythic figures to identify with. Thus, women in India have usually an identity of considerable strength and power, balancing the more overtly structural status of male patriarchy.

DRIVE THEORY AND INDIAN CHARACTER

The particular development of the Indian ego-ideal and superego, as they differ from the Western conscience, raises questions concerning classic psychoanalytic formulations of psychosexual development and character formation. It is pertinent to cite Mark Sylvan's (1981) application of classical formulations on oral character to his elaboration of Indian character and behavior. His application incisively illustrates serious problems in the theory of psychosexual development when the theory is postulated as being universal but is unreflectedly oriented toward childhood development in a culture of individualism; and when it does not take into account the specific development and functioning of the ego-ideal and superego, as well as of early object-relations involving the mother-child dyad, in radically different cultures and historical eras.

Sylvan sees the close childhood dependency relationship of Indians, and one can easily cite that of other Asians as well, as an extremely gratifying oral phase that condemns persons to inactivity and to demands for others to take care of them. In his view, there is a dominance of oral sadism that is pervasive in their relationships, and results in placation and compliance, where there is extreme difficulty in asserting any overt refusal to do something or to say, "no." Sylvan sees all of this as a reaction-formation against oral aggression.

Far more relevant than reactive oral sadism to the patterns of interpersonal behavior he mentions, such as compliance and never directly saying "no," is the Indian child's internalization of strong social values in his ego-ideal and super-ego during the latency and adolescent periods for expressing proper deference in formal hierarchical relationships. This is central to functioning in the extended family and other groups. Reaction-formation is indeed frequently present, but it is far more related to the strict latency-age superego resulting from the crackdown for proper behavior in hierarchical relationships than it is to the oral phase and oral sadism. The specific dictates and development of the conscience are thus far more central to subordination and related aspects of Indian character development and later behavior, as well as to the emphasis on certain defenses such as displacement and reaction-formation, than the vicissi-tudes of the drives. The very fact that Sylvan sees compliance and never directly saying, "no", (which is true of all Asians) in such a pejorative light reflects his own values of self-assertion and verbal expressiveness that are integral to West-ern individualism. Sylvan has not taken Freud's structural theory seriously as it is involved in cross-cultural work, not to mention the impact of culture on the conscience.

In like manner, early oral fulfillment and dependency does not condemn Indians to inactivity or extreme passivity, but rather to sensitized receptivity to others, and to expectations not only of receiving greater care from others, but also in identifying with the maternal caregiver to fulfill others' needs. In other words, this early symbiotic mother-child relationship, which may include other mothers of the extended family, results in far more interdependence than is characteristic of Euro-American relationships. It is essential for functioning in Indian extended family relationships. The pejorative ring to pronounced oral traits that seemingly condemn the person to inactivity or extreme passivity, derives more from a kind of Western symbiotic mothering that is highly incon-gruent to the predominant dictates of the separation-individuation process and individualism, and is therefore usually psychopathological, than to intense early libidinal gratification.

In Western cultures, this classical psychoanalytic model has a certain degree of clinical explanatory power. But largely, I would submit, this is because child rearing has been relatively of one piece, with but minor variations; that is, the intrapsychic internalizations of the early maternal relationship, as well as superego development, have been quite similar in Western societies. Classical psychoanalysts have not usually realized that their generalizations made on the gratification-frustration patterns of the drives at each of the psychosexual stages are closely related to the complex nature of the mother-child emotional rela-tionship and superego dictates.

From cross-civilizational psychoanalytic work it is evident that psychoana-lytic drive theory needs serious amending. The vicissitudes of superego and ego-ideal development and early object relations, all related to the culture, are just as or more central to character development, later behavior, and the kinds of defenses that are emphasized than those of the drives alone.

SPIRITUAL CULTURE AND SEXUALITY

Hindu spiritual culture oscillates between the erotic and ascetic. Sexuality and sensuality pervade the religious dimension through *bhakti* devotional practices, whereas its total opposite is expressed through renunciation and asceticism. I was particularly struck one day while attending rehearsals at a major Bharat Natyam school in Bombay that the dancer was at times extraordinarily sensuous in her subtle eye and facial movements, while at other times not at all. I assumed, approaching it as I did through my Western lens, that the striking sensuality related to secular dances. In actuality, the more devotional the theme, the more utterly sensual the dancer became. Sensuality was thus given full release in the service of aesthetic religiosity, while being properly contained in the aesthetics of the social sphere. As Barbara Stoler Miller (1977, 17) aptly puts it in her introduction to Jayadeva's *Gitagovinda*, "Jayadeva's verses . . . are explicitly sensual, and celebrate the sensual joy of divine love."

In the spiritual path of *bhakti*, Indian men frequently worship Krishna by identifying with Radha, his lover. This can be viewed reductionistically as spiritual practices fostering a regression to an early maternal identification. Or it can also be understood as these men drawing upon a powerful childhood identification with the maternal-feminine to participate in a devotional spiritual path.

Detachment, a major factor in spiritual disciplines, may involve the pervasively intense sensuality and sexuality of Indians. Since in India, sexuality connotes greatly increased familial obligations rather than personal autonomy as in the West (Grey 1973), the striving for *brahmacharya*, or sexual abstinence and renunciation in adulthood in the service of spiritual disciplines (in adolescence it is considered appropriate for the preparation for becoming a householder), can also be viewed as a step in the loosening of the intense personal attachments and obligations in extended family-communal relationships and a reaching toward personal autonomy in the spiritual sphere. In the case of Gandhi's striving for *brahmacharya*, Grey (1973) is appropriately critical of Erikson's (1969) emphasis on defensive motivation rather than a striving for competency and spiritual autonomy.

SUMMARY

This chapter explores sexuality and psychosexual development as it is shaped by radically different child rearing, family structures, ego-ideals and superego, and early object relations in Indian culture. Case vignettes of Indians in psychoanalytic therapy confirm the presence of incestuous fantasies and punitive superego reactions. The Indian Oedipus for the boy is delved into in terms of the various factors alluded to above. Women's sexuality is then discussed in the light of extended family morality and relationships. From an example of an attempted application of drive theory to Indian character, psychosexual theory as related to character formation is evaluated as needing serious reformulation for cross-civilizational analyses. The chapter concludes on the relationship between Hindu spiritual culture and sexuality.

Chapter Ten

The Spiritual and the Magic-Cosmic
in Psychoanalysis and Psychoanalytic Therapy

PSYCHOANALYTIC VIEWS

The spiritual as a core dimension of the human psyche has rarely been acknowledged in Freudian psychoanalysis, and only to a limited extent by neo-Freudian analysts. Enlightenment views demystifying religion and exalting a rational secularism and science were carried forth by Freud (1927) in his views of religion as an illusion to cope with the vulnerability of man's infantile helplessness. Psychoanalysis has usually denigrated spiritual experiences as either being regressive to the early mother-infant symbiotic relationship (the oceanic feeling[1]), or psychopathological in any number of ways (Masson 1976). Only a small handful of Freudian psychoanalysts have brooked this viewpoint.

In more recent years, two Catholic psychoanalysts, William Meissner (1984) and Anna Marie Rizzuto (1979), have used Winnicott's object relations theory to update the relationship between psychoanalysis and religion. By emphasizing Winnicott's positive views on illusion as central to early childhood development, and to symbolization in all of the realms of culture, including religion, they have developed a new psychoanalytic slant on religion, thus critiquing the Cartesian dualism inherent in Freud's pitting reality over illusion. Similar to Freud, both have generally steered away from any detailed consideration of spiritual experiences. Kakar (1991) has used their Winnicotian spin on illusion to justify viewing the "oceanic feeling" of great Indian mystics such as Ramakrishna as being regressive but in a positive way. Kakar thus continues the psychoanalytic tradition of reductionism on spiritual experiences but in a more sophisticated way.

The opprobrium attached by psychoanalysts to mysticism and the spiritual has been so powerful that one of the only Freudian analysts to contribute directly in this area, Marion Milner (1987), delayed publishing her paper on mysticism for a number of years, instead circulating it privately. Two of the main Freudian analysts who have directly acknowledged the realm of the spiritual are Wilfred Bion (1970) in his concepts of ultimate reality and the unknowable, and Erik Erikson (1958, 1969) in his work on Luther and Gandhi. There have obviously been others with a lower profile, such as Harmon Ephron, co-founder of the Flower Fifth Avenue Psychoanalytic Institute, and Margaret Brenman-Gibson, a close colleague of Erikson.

On the other hand, neo-Freudian psychoanalysts such as Karen Horney and Erich Fromm (Fromm, Suzuki, and DeMartino 1960) were much more open to the spiritual in their involvement with Zen Buddhism. The Horney group in particular were involved since the 1940s with Martin Buber and Hassidism,[2] with Zen Buddhism, and with an interest in Indian spiritual culture and leaders such as Krishnamurti.[3]

Much more recently, there has been a resurgence of interest in the interface between psychoanalysis and spirituality, mainly through psychoanalysts and/or psychoanalysts in training, who are seriously involved in Zen Buddhist or Burmese Vipassana Buddhist or Tibetan Buddhist meditation. In New York City in April, 1994, a two-day conference was organized on "The Suffering Self: A Dialogue Between Psychoanalysts and Buddhists," the first of its kind in the United States.[4] Over 500 persons applied to attend, far more than other psychoanalytic meetings ordinarily draw. Moreover, analysts or analysts-in-training, such as Nina Coltart (1992), Paul Cooper (1995), Mark Finn (1992), Jeffrey Rubin (1996), and John Suler (1993), are all actively writing on the interface between the process and theory of psychoanalysis and Buddhist meditation and theory. Other analysts such as Eigen (1995) and Leavy (1995) write in the broad area of psychoanalysis and mysticism. There have also been a few large conferences on Buddhism and psychotherapy, at which the Dalai Lama has occasionally spoken, and a literature on the subject by psychologists and psychiatrists involved in both, such as Brown (1986), Engler (1986), Epstein (1995), Goleman (1977), Kornfield (1977), and Wilbur (1986).

If the spiritual dimension in the human psyche has been treated cavalierly by psychoanalysis, then the magic-cosmic world of personal destiny as communicated by astrology, palmistry, psychics, the spirit world, and such are sheer anathema to the modern, scientifically-educated Western mind, including psychoanalysts and even South Asian specialists. There are to be sure countercurrents in the West, but they often assume a rank commercialization in the counterculture, related to notions of personal destiny and the magic-cosmic being completely denigrated as superstition by the dominant culture.[5]

On the other hand, there is a basic assumption by Hindus, and in one way or another by those in other Asian cultures influenced by Buddhism, Taoism,

Shintoism, and such, that the self is not only much more permeable in the social world than the Western individualized self, Asians having a more familial self; but it is also open to various invisible spheres and influences, and has a much longer time span to it. Thus, the self for Asians is open to the spirit world, to ancestors, to planetary influences, and to actions and experiences from past lives that impinge on the present, and by actions and experiences in the present that will impact on future lives. Moreover, Hindus assume that through astrology, palmistry, psychics, the spirit world, and such one can become aware of one's destiny; and through rituals and other means, one can partially alter it. All of this is totally foreign to the Western psychoanalyst; yet it can enter centrally into psychoanalytic treatment, especially with Hindu patients.

THE SPIRITUAL IN PSYCHOANALYTIC THERAPY

Of the twenty-five plus Indian patients I have seen in short and long-term psychoanalytic therapy and psychoanalysis in India and New York City, and of the variety of American patients I have worked with over thirty-five years, there have only been a small handful of each group who have been seriously and deeply committed to a spiritual quest. The difference between the overall group of Indians, particularly Hindus, and Americans is that all of the Indians assume there is a spiritual reality within themselves that can be realized if they make the effort. As one Moslem woman, a mother of three, mentioned in session one day in Bombay, "I know if I get up every morning at four A.M. and pray and meditate, I shall eventually see God. But I am just too tired to get up so early." This is in contrast to American attitudes of questioning the very possibility of such a reality, or simply considering it to be of no consequence.

It is implicitly assumed by Indians that the fundamental psychological goal in life is that of self-transformation to more refined qualities, gradually leading into a more active spiritual quest, often at a later stage in life, or in some future life. It is the person more actively engaged in such a quest that is the most respected. One friend upon returning from a pilgrimage had a hard time getting a taxi to take her home from the train station in Delhi in the wee hours of the morning; that is, until she mentioned, "Oh come on, I'm exhausted, I've just returned from a pilgrimage."

For those rare patients actively committed to ongoing meditation or other spiritual practices such as prayer and ritual, both an American and an Indian have reported the everyday, phenomonological self dissolving in the meditation experience. Shakuntala, an advanced mystic who had been asked by her guru to succeed her, had visions both as a teenager of a goddess moving, and when she was seeing me in psychoanalytic therapy in Bombay in 1977–78 of a famous early twentieth century sufi saint (Roland 1988, pp. 154–174). She further elaborated some of her spiritual experiences when I last saw her for some sessions in 1991. She related that she experiences God as light, white and yellow light, more intense than the sun. She described great spiritual leaders as manifestations of a light more intense than the sun, itself, or merged with this light. When I asked her about the frequency of her meditation—her lack of discipline had been a problem she had voiced in therapy sessions eleven years previously—she replied that her *mantra* is now with her constantly. It is apparently a very powerful one according to a noted swami, who has invited her to help run a hospital he is starting in the Himalayas for yogis.

The spiritual and psychopathology can have complex interactions, ones that are of a completely different nature than what have usually been written about by psychoanalysts. The spiritual and psychopathological are on two separate continua that can interface with each other in a variety of ways. There are, for instance, quite mature, sensible, self-aware persons who are not particularly oriented toward the spiritual. This is generally true of analysands who have completed a successful psychoanalysis. There can also be spiritually realized persons who are mature and sensitive in their relationships. On the other hand, there are those who may be well along the spiritual path but are sometimes beset by significant emotional problems, or who simply don't relate all that well to others. Their problems do not invalidate their spiritual experiences or practices, but they may complicate their journey, sometimes in important ways. Nor will their involvement in spiritual practices fundamentally alter their emotional conflicts or deficits as is sometimes thought, although it can often be of some assistance.

In summary, a person may be mature in his or her everyday functioning but may not be particularly attuned to or at all involved in realizing his or her spiritual potential. Or a person may be spiritually advanced but still have some knotty, unresolved emotional conflicts. Occasionally, a Zen master, a guru, or a swami has referred an emotionally troubled disciple to a therapist, while the disciple still continues his or her spiritual practices. Coltart (1992) observes that not infrequently Westerners seek a solution to their emotional distress through meditation when an experience of psychoanalytic therapy would be more to the point.

Of more relevance here are those who are both actively involved in some kind of spiritual practice, whether meditation or prayer, and who are also in psychoanalytic therapy or psychoanalysis. While it has been observed that meditation may be counterindicated for some persons who are deeply troubled, destabilizing them still further, or may be unconsciously used for defensive purposes, involvement even in simple centering exercises enables most people to withstand anxiety more easily in psychoanalytic therapy, enabling them to delve more deeply, more quickly into their emotional problems (Carrington 1977). Thus, those who are genuinely involved in spiritual practices may find that they make faster progress in their therapy, or from my observations, can better tackle long entrenched, highly disturbing emotional issues.

From quite another angle, emotional conflicts or deficits may indeed interfere with the development of a person's spiritual potential. Conversely, resolution of these emotional problems can enable a person to concentrate more fully on their practices. Shakuntala, who was very deeply involved in spiritual realization, had been unable to meditate or carry on her devotional practices in as disciplined a way as she felt was necessary because of psychological issues related to a depressed mother and an overly permissive father. She thus felt limited in the progress she could make. As these problems were partially resolved in the therapy, she seemed to become more committed to daily meditation.

Another patient, Ashis, had intense inner conflict over writing, which he considered his *sadhana* or spiritual discipline similar to Rabindranath Tagore (Roland 1988, pp. 25–47). I should mention parenthetically that another Indian patient and two American patients, all artists, considered their art as being closely related to the spiritual. Ashis's conflicts were related to deep-seated conflicts with a dominant father who foisted a high degree of Westernization on Ashis. That is, Ashis's father, who had a major position in the Indian Civil Service and had identified closely with British colonial values, foisted an ideal onto Ashis that he devote all of his energies to getting ahead and succeeding in work; in Ashis's circumstances, it was engineering which was considered highly prestigious. Meanwhile, his father denigrated Hindu culture and Ashis's literary-spiritual bent. Everytime Ashis went to write anything that was not primarily oriented toward career recognition, he suffered greatly because of internalized images of the father. The problem was partially alleviated through short-term psychoanalytic therapy, as was Shakuntala's, thus enabling each to become more involved in their spiritual disciplines.

Still another woman, Promilla, whom I worked with felt stultified in a marriage because her husband was not oriented toward the spiritual dimension as she was, even though he was a very fine and respected person in his own right. This issue became resolved in psychoanalytic work when it was traced to an unconscious displacement from a period in her early adolescence. During childhood, a venerated maternal grandfather, who was considered a holy man in her community, had taken great interest in Promilla developing her artistic talent. When he died in her early adolescence, the family then spent far more time in her father's family which was the more usual social pattern. That they had spent so much time earlier with this maternal grandfather was uncharacteristic in her North Indian community, but was sanctioned because he was so revered. The father's family, in contrast to this grandfather, was highly materialistic and mundane; my patient felt greatly stultified in their presence. It was this painful period of being in her father's family after the wondrous years with her grandfather that was being unconsciously projected onto her husband. As these memories were recovered through dreams and the material was analyzed, Promilla felt far more comfortable in her marriage, and was able to be more fully involved in her art— which she, similar to Ashis, considered a kind of *sadhana*.

American patients committed to the spiritual path have had similar experiences. A Catholic nun deeply involved in prayer and ritual, and well-known in her Order for conducting spiritual retreats, came for long-term psychoanalytic therapy because of intensely antagonistic relationships that had developed between her and some other important nuns. These relationships were gradually analyzed to be transference repetitions of childhood ones with her older siblings, who had been quite sadistic to her. Whereas the transference relationship with me was for the most part a selfobject one of a mirroring kind. Throughout the psychoanalytic therapy her spiritual practices proceeded unabated, and in fact seemed to deepen. As she worked out more of her knotty emotional problems and ways of alienating others, her retreats became far more well-attended. At one point, she was able to openly express and delve into major areas of her religious beliefs that she had strong doubts about.

Another American was deeply involved with an Indian guru who had instructed him in meditation. He struggled for a number of years in an intensive psychoanalysis to gradually work out of a highly withdrawn, schizoid position. In the early years of the analysis, my impression is that he partly used his meditative practices in the service of his schizoid aloofness. But in later years, the meditation actually enhanced his perseverance in working through his strong schizoid orientation to become far more emotionally related to others. Through this meditation, he became more and more known for his highly intuitive capacities in his work as a counselor in a college.

To show even more how the spiritual and psychopathology can be complexly intertwined, I shall turn again to the case of Shakuntala. When she came to see me in Bombay for therapy, she had been involved in a long-term affair with a married man, fending off efforts by her parents to arrange a marriage for her. She was in considerable conflict between the affair, marriage, and retiring to her aunt's ashram to become a guru. Through six months of short-term psychoanalytic therapy, particularly through the analysis of her dreams, we were able to delve into some of the unconscious motivation involving the married man she was involved with.

At one stage, when her boyfriend went back to his wife each time, he unconsciously stood for her mother who emotionally deserted her for her younger brother; at another stage, he unconsciously stood in for her brother and father who served to rescue her from her depressed mother; and still later, he unconsciously represented her father in an incestuous fantasy. At the same time during the therapy, Shakuntala and her boyfriend and his family went on a pilgrimage to the shrine of a holy man, who was her boyfriend's spiritual ideal, not her own. Afterward, she kept experiencing visions of the holy man, convinced that she and her boyfriend were devotees of this holy man in past lives. She saw no particular dissonance in the fact that there was a combination of unconscious conflictual motivation that drew her to this boyfriend and a spiritual twinship relationship with him from past lives.

This I may add is a manifestation of Indian metonymic thinking. In this kind of cognition, there is much more of a continuity and congruence than Western dualistic thinking. Thus, a book is not simply a symbol of the goddess of learning, Saraswati; rather, it is a partial manifestation of her. Shakuntala saw acceptable continuities between her past lives, psychopathology generated by conflictual family relationships, and the influences of the planets. These categories would create considerable dissonance for most Westerners.

THE MEDITATOR/PSYCHOANALYST

Psychoanalysts who are involved in meditation report an enhanced ability to work with their patients.[6] This encompasses a number of aspects. There seems to be a greater attentiveness to patients' associations, more easily observing Freud's call for evenly hovering attention, as well as Bion's attentiveness to the moment without memory or desire. For some, the analytic session, itself, becomes akin to a meditative experience.

Meditation also seems to enhance a person's intuitive capacities, something extremely valuable for an analyst. Coltart (1992) and others report a greater clarity to their clinical work with patients, with a fuller and more direct apprehension of the patient. One is more empathically in touch with the subtleties and nuances of patients' feelings in a self psychological mode. Correspondingly, an analyst can be more in touch with one's own reactions and attitudes as they arise in the intersubjective therapy relationship, more easily objectifying them, and then seeing how they relate to the transference in an object relations way of using the induced countertransference. There is also a greater ease in patiently staying with the unknown and the ongoing ambiguities of psychoanalytic work, or having more of a negative capability. There are further reports of greater spontaneity with greater courage and masterfulness in communicating and interpreting to the patient.

Does this mean that the meditating psychoanalyst is superior to other analysts who don't meditate? Not necessarily. There have always been informal discussions and comments in psychoanalytic circles over the psychological mindedness or intuitiveness and/or therapeutic personality of different analysts. These subjects are not usually discussed in the literature because they are so incredibly qualitative. There is no question that every analyst has to have considerable psychological mindedness and a therapeutic or healing personality

for good work to occur. But these qualities can vary significantly from one analyst to another. It is therefore impossible to assert that a meditating psychoanalyst is necessarily superior to those who don't meditate. What does seem
evident from all of the self-reports is that psychoanalysts who have become
involved with meditation observe that their own functioning as an analyst
improves considerably.

INDIVIDUALITY, IDENTITY, AND SPIRITUALITY

I have been struck that on those few occasions when I have been invited to
speak at a meeting connected with the topic of spirituality, one or another person inevitably asks me, "Do you meditate?" I would never be asked such a
question in India. Indians can be remarkably reticent on this subject. An
American publishing consultant, Arthur Eisenberg, who lived in India for
many years commented that Indians will much more easily comment on the
details of their sex lives to you than on any spiritual pursuits they may be
involved in. This reticence was confirmed by major social scientists at the Cen-
tre for Developing Societies in Delhi, the leading social science research center
in India, when asked how many of the people they know are involved in meditation or some other spiritual discipline. They replied that it is usually almost
impossible to know. I observed that Shakuntala, a lecturer in a Bombay university, was seen by other professors and administrators there whom I knew as a
social butterfly. They had no inkling whatsoever of her intense involvement
with the spiritual. Spiritual practices are so private in India that different
members of the same family will not know each other's *mantras*.

By contrast, most Americans I know who are involved in some kind of spiritual practice are usually quite open about it. My sense is that meditation,
prayer, or such becomes another major component in the self-creation of their
identity. Further, in the American culture of individualism, individuals' identity is central to their individuality and is to be expressed openly in the social
world. With Indians, on the other hand, involvement with the spiritual is actually a mode of individuating and separating themselves out of profound familial enmeshments, while still remaining connected to others. It, too, is part of a
deeply-rooted individuality, but one that is more kept to oneself.

MAGIC-COSMIC PERSONAL DESTINY AND PSYCHOANALYTIC THERAPY

I have found the magic-cosmic orientation to personal destiny to be ubiqui-
tously present in all of my Hindu patients, but only some of the time in Christian, Parsee, and Moslem patients with whom I have worked—almost all of
whom were highly educated with college and frequently graduate school degrees. Patients' concerns clearly focus around central life decisions involving

marriage and career, not around lesser preoccupations, with women on the whole being more involved with marriage and men more with career. All of my Hindu patients simply assumed that there was such a thing as personal destiny that was not only tied up with major life occurrences but also implicitly with self-trans-formations toward the ultimate realization of the spiritual self. They assumed a very different mode of cognition than is present in the more rational, causal, and logical mode of contemporary Western thinking. The magic-cosmic involves much more the assumption of influences from past lives and planets, synchronic-ities between events, and congruences between astrological charts as well as what is imprinted on the palm with everyday life occurrences.

In contrast to Western stereotypes of Indians having a passive attitude toward fate, I have found my patients to be extremely active in trying to accomplish what they wanted, using analyses and predictions from the magic-cosmic as aids in their endeavors. They seemed to take the attitude that while issues of destiny tied in to *karma* from past lives and planetary influences would ultimately affect what they could do, their efforts were still extremely impor-tant. They further assumed that personal destiny could indeed be ascertained through various means such as astrology, palmistry, psychics, and the spirit world—in direct contrast to the modern Western mind; and moreover, that destiny could also be modified by certain means such as rituals. In more than one case, their own therapy with me was seen as fulfilling or offsetting certain predictions.

I would like to cite a few examples to illustrate these observations. One Hindu woman, Sashi, in her early thirties who had a very high level position in India and was completing her doctorate at an Ivy League university, still very much wanted to be married. That she was not yet married was highly unusual for a Hindu woman of her age, in contrast to women in the United States now. Sashi had foregone an arranged marriage in her early twenties to go on with graduate school education and a top-level career; but by the time she felt ready to be married in her later twenties, her father had died, and her older brothers were not able to find a suitable mate for her since her prospective husband would also have to be equally well-educated with a similar high level position, and to be from the right family and community. He had to fit into her social sub-caste of highly educated, top career persons in Calcutta.

When I saw Sashi in New York City, she would have been in despair over being thirty-two and not married if it were not for consistent readings by both astrologers and palmists that she would have a very late but very good mar-riage. Sashi, using me as an empathic selfobject to fill in for absent family elders, then embarked in a systematic way to arrange her own marriage by plac-ing ads in the Indian newspapers and using her peer network. None of this worked. But when I ran into Sashi some two years after we had stopped working together, I learned that she had indeed gotten married to a man who met all of her standards, meeting him fortuitously on an airplane trip.

To refer to Shakuntala again, she was also very much involved with marital concerns, being unmarried in her late twenties and deeply involved with a married man. In her case, astrological charts predicted that it would be very difficult for her to get married since she is a *mangal* (born under the sign of Mars). Indeed, she did slip out of a couple of arranged marriages in her early twenties at the last minute. On one of those occasions, at an auspicious time to offset these adverse planetary influences so that Shakuntala could finally get married, the family priest had her go through the full wedding ritual, marrying her to one of the gods. In other cases I have read or heard about, it is usually to a tree or a pot. In Shakuntala's case, the ritual did not work as intended; Shakuntala became deeply involved in her spiritual life with this god.

It is not only women who are involved with the personal destiny of marriage through the magic-cosmic. Sailesh, with whom I worked in longer term therapy, was still unmarried in his middle thirties. Because of many problems in his family, he felt he had to arrange his own marriage, something that was not easy for him to do because of deep-seated emotional problems around women. Every time that he met or became involved with a new woman, he would consult astrologers both in India and New York City, as well as his family priest. I was struck that what the astrologers said about the nature of the particular woman and the interaction between Sailesh and the woman—the astrologers having no background data on the woman—was highly consonant with his own descriptions in sessions before he consulted the astrologers.

What was also striking was that there were definite differences in attitudes between Indian astrologers in India and those who had lived for awhile in the United States. The ones in America were far more concerned with how Sailesh and his prospective bride would get along in a number of ways. They individualized their analysis to a greater degree, realizing that the couple would be far more on their own in the United States than in India where they would be far more integrated into his extended family.

It was also clear that as Sailesh through the analysis became much more aware of how his problems with women were related to specific inner conflicts, he was able not to be so compulsively involved with astrological analyses. It is not that he abandoned what the astrologers had said. Far from it. But on an everyday level he wasn't nearly so involved with astrology. At a later point in the analysis when intense hateful transference feelings were manifested, he experienced the astrologers as persecutory objects who were telling him what to do.

With regard to career, Ashis regularly consulted a local palmist, who was an internationally noted scientist, whenever Ashis had important career decisions to make. These often related to his conflicts over developing the more spiritual side of himself. Many of the palmist's comments coincided with my own psychoanalytic interpretations. Rustum, a Parsee, was sent to college in the United States for a particular specialization that was equally good if not better in India because of advice from a trusted family astrologer (Roland 1988, p. 300).

But involvements with astrologers over career may not be solely confined to Indian men today. Promilla asked me whether I knew a good astrologer in New York City—I had no idea at the time of how to get hold of one—when she and her husband had to make some difficult career choices.

To my surprise, 17 and 18 year old female college students in a counseling group in Bombay repeatedly voiced their being involved in contacting the spirit world, often through Ouija boards. I wondered why they were doing this, and so asked two of my colleagues, a psychoanalyst and a social worker for their opinions. They analyzed this behavior as being motivated by these young women soon having arranged marriages where they would have little if any say as to whom they would marry and what kind of families they would then live in. While such young women do trust in their family's good judgment, nevertheless, marriage is still experienced as being totally out of their control. Thus, contacting the spirit world might give them more of an inkling of whom they would end up with and what kind of life they would have. According to my informants, it was an effort to gain some feeling of control in this area. Neither of my informants denied for a moment the existence of a spirit world. The social worker in fact commented that it is not good to contact the spirit world too often. An uncle of hers who had a special gift for contacting the spirits and did so died at a very early age.

It is obvious that involvement with the magic-cosmic is very much present in the Indian urban educated elite, whether in India or the United States, some of whom may occasionally come for psychoanalytic therapy. To work with these patients on these issues, it is incumbent upon the psychoanalytic therapist not to be reductionistic in the usual psychoanalytic mode as this will seriously cut off communication in highly important areas of the patient's inner life. Indians I have found will quickly sense whether a therapist is receptive to these areas. If the therapist isn't, then the patient will simply keep it all secret in a highly private self that is characteristic of Indians. Rather the therapist must ascertain what kind of interaction, if any, is present between the patient's psychopathology and their involvement with the magic-cosmic.

MYTHIC ORIENTATION

It had struck me while doing psychoanalytic research in South India that traditional women could be very much oriented to the use of mythology in everyday relationships. The divine and the demonic in the myths fit mundane existence in a metonymic way. And with such an abundance of mythology from the epics and *Puranas*, there is a great deal to draw upon to give meaning to life's experiences.

Occasionally, this has surfaced in psychoanalytic therapy with Indians in the United States. At one point in his therapy when Pradeep recalled his childhood yearning to have the kind of close relationship with his father his siblings seemed to have, he expressed his feelings through a myth from the *Mahabharata*. In this episode, a cousin of the Pandava brothers, the heroes of the epic, was longing to be trained in martial skills as were his cousins by Drona, an expert teacher. But because he was not a member of the royal family as they were, he was not allowed. Surrepticiously, he observed their archery lessons and became as expert an archer as his cousins. But when Drona learned of this, he had his thumb cut off. Pradeep's expressing himself through the myth was obviously both a yearning for closeness to his father, and a fear of castration if he learned from him. At that point in the therapy, the castration fear was largely displaced onto his father from his mother, who had forbidden Pradeep as a child from even walking in his father's shadow.

At a later point in the therapy, Pradeep had become a paramedic working in inner city ghetto areas. One day, he spent several hours with a family where one member had suffered an injury, but all of them were deeply distressed persons. Pradeep was very upset by their condition, but his steady presence seemed to help the family members considerably. He then had a dream that night of swallowing poison, which he immediately associated to the myth of Shiva swallowing poison to neutralize its effect, and prevent the destruction of the world by a demon. A psychoanalyst oriented toward object relations theory might well cast Pradeep's experience as one of containment (Bion 1970); but as an Indian, Pradeep could easily express his intense experience in a mythic image.

SUMMARY

After an introductory section which briefly delineates the older and newer psychoanalytic views on religion and the spiritual, and the still present dismissal of the magic-cosmic, the relationship of the spiritual to psychoanalytic therapy is delved into. Of particular relevance are the complex interactions between the spiritual and psychopathology, which are seen as two separate continua. Clinical examples illustrate these interactions. Psychoanalysts who are themselves involved in a meditative practices report on their own enhanced capacities to do psychoanalytic work. Cultural/psychological dynamics are then used to explain why Americans are far more open in expressing their involvement in spiritual practices than Indians are. The chapter concludes on the ubiquitous involvement of Indians, especially Hindus, with the magic-cosmic world of personal destiny as it manifests in psychoanalytic sessions; and the occasional mythic orientation of Hindus in psychoanalytic therapy.

ENDNOTES

1. The oceanic feeling is a term used by the noted French writer, Romain Rolland, in writing of spiritual experiences in his correspondance with Freud. Rolland was a follower of the great nineteenth century Hindu holy man, Ramakrishna. The term entered the psychoanalytic literature through this correspondance with Freud.

2. The interest of the Horney group since the 1940s in Hassidism, a major part of Jewish mysticism, came largely from a member of their group, Antonio Wenkart, a direct descendant through a rabbinical family of the Baal Shem Tov, the founder of Hassidism.

3. Other major psychoanalysts from the Horney group with interest in Indian spiritual culture were Harold Kelman and David Shainberg.

4. The conference was organized by the Metropolitan Institute for Training in Psychoanalytic Psychotherapy, a relatively small institute. Most major psychoanalytic institutes would not have touched this subject. Moreover, some established psychoanalysts interested or involved in Buddhism who were invited to participate were highly reluctant to make a presentation unless there were other well recognized psychoanalysts on the program.

5. These attitudes surfaced in a meeting of the Psychoanalysis and Anthropology Interdisciplinary Colloquium of the American Psychoanalytic Association in New York City in December 1991, where work on the tribal group, the Sora and their shamans, was presented by an anthropologist who had done field work among them. Some analysts asked the anthropologists, "you don't really believe in these shamans do you?"

6. Coltart (1992) and Rubin (1996) report this in their writings, as does Epstein (1995) for psychotherapists. This is supported by a variety of my own observations, including those of colleagues and a psychoanalytic supervisee involved in meditation.

Chapter Eleven

The Psychological and the Psychosocial in Indian Organizational Relationships

ASIAN AND AMERICAN MANAGEMENT THEORY

For over sixty years, American management theories have spread across the world on the unquestioned assumption of their universality. Only in recent years has there been any effort to recognize that American management theories reflect the highly individualistic cultural value systems and social patterns of the United States, and that these theories might not be so applicable to other cultures where the values are significantly different. (Gupta 1991; Hostede 1980). In India, it is increasingly seen that management and work relationships in Indian organizations are significantly different from those in America, or for that matter in Japan as well (Dayal 1977; Gupta 1991; Parek 1977; and Sinha 1980, 1988). For modernization and productivity to proceed in a far more optimal way than it now is, these writers are trying to frame an indigenous management theory and practice to be congruent with the basic psychology and social patterns of Indians as distinct from that of Americans or Japanese. They take into account the familial-communal self and familial hierarchical relationships of Indians in a way that has rarely been done.

Theorists such as Gupta recognize that unlike Japanese who have carried familial values and attitudes over into their various organizational groups through the *iemoto* master-disciple relationship, Indians are still mainly committed to the extended family as the psychological locus of their lives rather than the work group. As a result, loyalty to the organization is often at low ebb in India. Other more Western practices aimed at appealing to more individualistic motives for productivity within contractually-oriented relationships, egalitarian values, and organizational impersonality can still further alienate the Indian worker, resulting in lowered productivity.

These theorists all aim at transferring some of the familial values and attitudes to the organization in India through more personalized, caring relationships; a more sympathetic, nurturing father-figure; affiliative relationships with openness, trust, collaboration, and such; and tasks and roles clearly spelled out. On a more informal level, Ravi Kapur, a psychiatrist, sees that in many small organizations personalized, nurturing hierarchical relationships can easily be implemented, resulting in more effective work; but he questions whether they can be in larger ones. On the other hand, a senior manager in Tata Industries in Bombay related that these more caring, familial-type relationships can even be implemented in large organizations such as Tata if the senior management consciously puts them into practice. He, himself, usually keeps the door to his office open, lets it be known that he is available without appointment, and then first offers a coke when someone with a problem does come in.

Finally, it is recognized by Gupta and Sinha that Indian spiritual culture should find a way into organizational life as it is in Japan. This approach is mainly being formulated and practically implemented in India by S. K. Chakraborty (1987). He presents Vedanta and Sankyan philosophy in a relevant, modern way to Indian managers, as well as the practical use of simple yoga exercises. In essence, he aims at greater managerial effectiveness through personal self-transformation.

CASE EXAMPLES

I shall cite four case examples to illustrate aspects of the psychological and psychosocial in quite different kinds of Indian organizations. The first three examples will cite problems in an organizational setting with the underlying psychological and psychosocial factors that have caused the difficulties. Whereas the last case is of a different order, using a Western psychological paradigm, psychoanalysis, for enhancing managerial functioning. It is hoped that these case examples will shed additional light on psychological and psychosocial factors in Indian organizational relationships to assist in further framing an indigenous management theory and practice. Further, by enhancing an understanding of the Indian self within the organizational context it throws a different light on central psychological issues in Indian men.

Case Study 1

This problem in a successful computer company where the younger software personnel were leaving was related to me by Mrs. Sushma Sharma, a management consultant in Bombay. The company depended a great deal on these personnel, a majority of men and a minority of women, in their twenties from the more educated, modern families of Bombay. In terms of Indian-style managerial relationships, these younger persons definitely wanted strong managerial interest in themselves and their work, and to be treated with nurturance and respect—all now recognized as basic psychosocial aspects of traditional Indian work relationships. In Mrs. Sharma's terms, they needed and were treated with "carefrontation" if there were any problems, not the direct confrontations and criticism of Western managerial practices, which she holds to be too oriented toward individualism. These aspects of nurturing Indian hierarchical relationships in work settings have been cited by others as well (Gupta 1991) as central to successful Indian-style management. Furthermore, these younger professionals also expected to function in a more individualized way in which they could openly express their own views, needs, and wishes to the manager, manifesting the more individualizing changes of modernization in urban India.

In spite of the head manager, a man in his forties, treating the younger personnel with interest, care, and respect, as well as attending to their more individualized ideas and needs, after a year or two of training, many of them would leave. This is not common, and the manager was perplexed and dismayed. He contacted Mrs. Sharma to see what was going awry.

She found a subtle but important psychosocial aspect of Indian hierarchical work relationships that the manager had unwittingly abnegated. Besides going out of his way to treat the younger personnel well, he had some need of his own to be chummy with them, sharing his own problems, stresses, and difficulties. He related to them more as equals than as a superior at these times. This was causing the problem.

In Indian hierarchical relationships, besides the normal deference shown by the subordinate and the nurturance by the superior, the younger person has a strong need to idealize the superior, and to try to be as close as possible to the idealized other in order to identify with and take on the superior's better qualities (see Chapter Two for a fuller discussion of hierarchy by personal qualities). These idealizations are a subtle but profound part of Indian psychology for personal growth and self-transformation; although the negative side can sometimes be a denial of one's own self. By presenting himself as equal to the younger persons and sharing his problems with them, this manager unwittingly interfered with the idealization process, resulting in many of the younger staff leaving. When Mrs. Sharma pointed this out to him and he stopped doing it, far fewer left the company. Mrs. Sharma, herself, realized the importance of this issue when she found she had to stop sharing any problems of her own with managers she trained, as it interfered with their idealizations of her and therefore their relationship with her.

Case Study 2

The second case is of a Bombay professional consulting association in the management counselling field with strong ties to a similar but larger Scottish association, whose members have helped a great deal in their training. In 1980 when I first became acquainted with this association, it appeared that they were growing apace, had solid leadership, and would become an increasingly important part of the Bombay counselling field. But by 1991, this professional organization had suffered a serious decline, and was clearly in the doldrums with no apparent resolution for the future. Interviews with various members of the group, many of whom were no longer speaking to each other, clarified the factors that led to such a precipitous decline.

The initial factor that had profound consequences on the association was actually initiated by the head of the Scottish association. This man, apparently acting on the very best of intentions, believed that the Bombay group should be run by its most competent members, almost all of whom were junior members whom he had helped train. He and others of the Scottish association then arranged for two major structural changes in the association, both of them undermining traditional Indian hierarchical relationships for a more egalitarian ideology based on competence. The first change in the hierarchy was to make it possible for the Bombay group to certify its own new members, rather than having them apply to the older branch of their professional association in Bangalore. The Bombay organization thus became independent of the older Bangalore hierarchy.

The second structural change in the hierarchy was even more far-reaching, leading to more disastrous consequences. Ordinarily, in an Indian professional organization the more senior members are deferred to and have the authority to train and accept or reject applicants for membership. If a junior member is indeed perceived by the senior hierarchy as being very competent, he or she may be allotted much more responsibility than would ordinarily be accorded to his or her status in the hierarchy; while the junior member would still defer to those more senior. And indeed this had already happened with one of the gifted junior members by 1980.

But this Scottish leader felt that most of the junior members were better trained and more competent than the senior ones, and therefore should have the central authority in the group in place of the senior hierarchy. Because the Scottish leader was so influential he was able to bring this about. Almost all authority came to reside in the junior members who were now also independent of the Bangalore hierarchy.

What proceeded from this were two highly unfortunate consequences. The first was that the senior members of the Bombay group felt highly insulted at this loss of status and became totally alienated from the association, to the extent of refusing to attend any meetings, including the highly valued training sessions conducted by the Scottish association. But an even more insidious process was set loose by the undermining of the traditional hierarchy, a psychosocial process that is particularly Indian.

Among the junior members of the group, there was as I alluded to above, a gifted natural leader, Ravi, who at various times did a great deal to assist other junior members, especially one man, Pradeep, whom Ravi helped set up in his own consulting firm. In the familial terms of Indian organizations, Ravi was the oldest brother who was highly responsible, and on whom the younger brothers and sisters depended and deferred to. In turn, Ravi deferred to the more senior members of the association, although he happened to be more competent than almost all of them. As the older generation would gradually retire, it was clearly expected in 1980 that Ravi would assume leadership of the organization. At the time, there were several people in training and a growing interest in the association's approach, which would easily assure future members and continued growth. A few of the advanced students had almost as much training and experience as the junior members of the association. This was the status of the association in 1980.

As the formal hierarchy of the association was dissolved by the Scottish leader in the early 1980s, Pradeep, whom Ravi had helped the most, turned on him. From all of the information I could garner, Pradeep had tremendous envy of this "older brother," which was greatly compounded by Ravi's receiving a highly prestigious grant from abroad in the early 1980s. Pradeep then spread all kinds of pejorative information and rumors about Ravi to the Scottish association, as well as to the one or two senior members who remained, and to the older administrator of the Bombay group who had considerable influence. Pradeep thus forced Ravi to withdraw from the association, Pradeep then taking over the leadership role himself among the junior members, who now had central authority. He consolidated his position by the mid-1980s by refusing to accept almost all of the students who had completed the long training course.

He further refused to take in any new students, claiming that none of them measured up to the standards of the Bombay association. (One of these applicants then went to Scotland for training and was readily accepted.) And in these decisions, still another psychological factor seemed to play an important role. From my own talks with Pradeep, he conveyed a strong feeling of inferiority to the Scottish leader, a clear carryover of the effects of British colonial attitudes on Indians some forty plus years after Independence, where Indians were made to feel inferior to the British. Pradeep, much to his surprise, was accepted by the Scottish leader as were the other junior members whom the Scot had helped train. But Pradeep was not going to accept for training any other Indians who might be seen as inferior, and with whom he would have to associate. In other words, he had unconsciously projected the inferior Indian self-image of himself vis-à-vis the British onto new applicants whom he would then reject. The Bombay association was thus left with only a small coterie of junior members, with almost all of the senior membership alienated, with no new members in years, and with no students.

The issue of envy between younger and older brothers is by no means unknown to the Indian scene, especially in extended families. As the older generation of men retires, families not infrequently split up from fights among the brothers. However, in the case of this organization, it was the breaking up of the formal hierarchy by an outside influence, the Scottish association, that paved the way for the envy and destructiveness among brothers to break out. Otherwise, if the formal hierarchy had been left intact of the Bombay association to its parent Bangalore organization, and of seniority within the Bombay group, there was little way that this envy could have been manifested with such devastating effects. This exploration of envy and destructiveness among brothers in Indian organizations will be continued in the next case example.

Case Study 3

Vijay, a man in his early 50s, urbane and well-educated, came to me at his wife's urging for four consultations because of some continuing depression and passivity that has been interfering with setting up a new business, and has also been spilling over into family relationships. While his depression would get much more severe for a couple of days at a time after visiting his mother, he generally felt much better than a few years earlier. Then, he was so severely depressed that he was in a prolonged state of emotional paralysis that almost resulted in financial ruin.

What emerged from these four sessions is a horrendous family drama propelled by the destructive envy of three younger brothers. Vijay is the oldest son of an upper caste, North Indian family, whose father was highly westernized and identified with the British. His father sent Vijay away to English-style boarding schools in India from the time Vijay was five years old, a practice not uncommon for those British who could afford it but highly unusual for Indians. Vijay then went to England for high school and to an elite engineering college there. His father had the same road plan for three more sons, but soon found that Vijay was the only one for whom he could afford to do this. Thus, the younger sons all grew up at home, attending good schools and colleges in Bombay, while Vijay was always away at the more elite ones.

Moreover, when Vijay returned from England, his father was able to arrange a highly desireable marriage for his prized son to a woman from a very prominent, highly westernized, wealthy family, who was given considerable monies of her own. This alliance, of course, greatly enhanced the position of Vijay's family. This was a far better, much more prestigious marriage than any of his brothers had. It was therefore natural that these younger brothers had considerable resentment and envy of Vijay. But their envy was primarily fueled by the father's constant favoring of Vijay, rather than from the mother who had apparently little say in his education, and far less contact and involvement with him than with his younger brothers and sisters. This pattern generating envy goes against the usual psychoanalytic explanation which so centers around the early mother-child relationship. It also goes against the total centrality of the mother-son relationship in Indian development as elaborated by Kakar (1978). But it seems integral to the Indian extended family where fathers and grandfathers have traditionally determined the education and career choices of their sons, and often their daughters as well.

Shortly after Vijay's return to India, he entered into the family business, but with a training and expertise that his father didn't have. Although the business greatly prospered, in good part from Vijay's engineering know-how, Vijay always felt that his father was somewhat resentful of him for approaching things differently. The younger brothers as they got older entered the business. Apparently their envy and resentment of Vijay was present from the beginning causing friction, which his father then exploited to gain as much control as possible. In spite of this, the company prospered for a number of years.

As his father became older and ill, his brothers increasingly put their hands in the till of the family business, something Vijay refused to do. Then, as his father became seriously ill and finally died, the two youngest brothers made it increasingly impossible for Vijay to remain and run the company. Vijay finally pulled out of the business some time after the father died, deciding not to litigate for his share in the business to which he was entitled, expecting his brothers would give it to him. They gave him nothing.

Vijay then became deeply depressed and emotionally paralyzed. He was particularly bitter at his mother, who he expected would pressure his brothers for a fair settlement. She didn't, seemingly siding with them with whom she had lived for a number of years.

In desperation, Vijay went to his mother's house and went on a hunger strike until death, refusing to eat or drink, until he received his fair share of the business. It was a particularly Indian way of pressuring the family to undo a dreadful wrong by publicly shaming them. By the fourth day, the family doctor said that Vijay could indeed die if he continued his hunger strike because his not drinking would damage his kidneys. His mother then began pressuring his brothers. By the sixth day, the brothers agreed to a settlement, calling in his sister's husband, a lawyer, to write up a settlement. Vijay was to be given his fair share within a month.

The main settlement actually took ten months. And up to the time of the consultations with me, a few years later, Vijay had still not received a substantial part of the settlement. He blames his brother-in-law for being in league with his brothers (who had loaned him money unbeknownst to Vijay) and not writing up a truly binding settlement.

Over the last few years that Vijay pulled out of the family business, it has declined substantially—a not unusual result of envy and destructiveness among brothers. The three younger brothers have split up the company into different parts, and are just about able to earn a living from it, but not a very good one as before. Meanwhile, out of resentment over the brothers not willingly giving him his fair share, Vijay has pulled out of the family. The animosity that was directed at him by both his three brothers and two sisters is now apparently turned on each other, with considerable squabbling in the extended family. I have found it not uncommon that tensions and angers within the extended family can often be unconsciously channeled toward one member only (Roland 1988, pp. 69, 11–112, 259).

In the third session, I interpreted to Vijay that the severe depression that he had over being ousted from the family firm without compensation or support from his mother was an unconscious emotional repetition in the present of the childhood and adolescent experience of being constantly sent off to boarding schools in India from the time he was five years old. He was, in effect, the highly privileged oldest son who was emotionally deprived of growing up in his family. This must have generated repetitive feelings of abandonment by his mother. This interpretation came as a surprise to him as the family ideology always centered on his privileged status, not his ongoing childhood and adolescent deprivation.

He reacted by coming a half hour late to his final session, which signaled that the interpretation had considerable impact on him, including a possible wariness in facing these feelings of abandonment. However, he seemed more open than before to seeing one of the Bombay psychoanalysts. I was leaving the next day, which may well have been experienced as still another abandonment.

Case Study 4

This last study is that of a psychoanalytic approach to managerial relationships in a middle-sized firm, a leader in its field. The owner and managing director has an M.B.A. from Harvard University, and is very much oriented toward human relationships, his firm apparently being one of the few in Bombay to be so directed. He has tried to implement a philosophy of more equal senior and junior management relationships, first several years ago through a consultant trained in transactional analysis, and later through other modes of management training. For the last two years, he has hired Udayan Patel, a Bombay psychoanalyst, for meeting with managers in monthly groups of eight to ten each, with individual consultations as needed. The managing director confided in me that he found Udayan Patel's psychoanalytic approach far more helpful than the other methods he had previously used as it goes much deeper into problematic management relationships. I was invited by Mr. Patel to participate in two of these group sessions, and was referred five persons for individual consultations.

I shall first report on one group session where there was an emotionally charged interchange between one senior manager and three junior ones, which illustrates some of the psychological problems in Indian management relationships. Through seeing the senior manager and two of the junior managers involved in individual sessions, I was able to gain a greater understanding of their problematic interaction, and to some extent some resolution. I was in effect doing in a brief period what Udayan Patel had been regularly doing over a couple of year's time.

Group Sessions

Mr. Patel runs the group in the mode of psychoanalytic group therapy, encouraging the managers to express whatever is on their mind as well as their reactions to each other. From the very beginning he takes himself out of the role of someone who will help or guide them, simply saying that he is there to enable them to get to know themselves better. In effect, he relinquishes the image of a family elder who gives advice and guidance, which most Indians project onto therapists. Then he observes what conflicts emerge, particularly ones over autonomy and dependency.

This particular group of eight managers had met monthly for six times, and by Patel's account had not gotten into much depth. After I was introduced to them and some initial silence, one of the senior managers, Ahmed, a man in his fifties, spoke up that they should all go into their self-image more and share what each thinks of the other. If they are more revealing, they might be able to help each other. Ahmed, in effect, was taking the leadership role in the group.

Gradually, three junior managers, some twenty years or so younger than Ahmed, began expressing their feelings toward him. One of them, Rajiv, led off by saying that he was put off by Ahmed in last month's session when Ahmed stated that perhaps he shouldn't be with this group but rather with a group of senior managers. Two others chimed in that although they have a close, friendly relationship with Ahmed outside of work, during business hours he is very difficult to deal with. All three asserted that Ahmed is unapproachable at work, resulting in hurting their feelings and their responding by retreating from him in the office and having little to do with him.

Ahmed began complaining that as a senior manager he feels himself quite isolated at work, that junior managers are withholding all kinds of data he needs to make decisions with. He believes they are doing this because they are more loyal to another manager. As it became clear to Udayan and myself that there was an impasse in the communication between Ahmed and the junior managers, we began to intervene. We suggested Ahmed look at himself more to see what he might be unwittingly contributing to the problem. He felt the three junior managers were voicing their dissatisfactions with him to be spiteful, to get back at him before others in the group.

When I raised the question of why he had trouble seeing that the three junior managers were actually trying to get closer to him, and when Patel asked why he had trouble relating in the more equal senior-junior managerial relationship that the company encouraged, Ahmed began associating to his having very high standards of work, so that he often felt he was so busy he had no time to see anyone. He realized that all respected him for his expertise. The session which had become increasingly emotionally charged ended with Ahmed beginning to delve into his own problematic behavior that contributed to the impasse with the junior managers.

To summarize, in this psychoanalytically oriented group session with its emphasis on free expression, at the invitation of a senior manager, three junior managers went out on a limb by expressing poignantly their problems with him, whom they experienced as being too self-involved at work to have anything to do with them. They handled their hurt over what they experienced as his lack of caring in a characteristic Indian way: not cooperating with him in any number of ways, rather than directly speaking to him about the problem. Ahmed experienced their non-cooperation as disloyalty to him as a superior and as their favoritism for another superior. He initially experienced their expressing this problem in junior-senior managerial relationships in the group session as a spiteful attack on him before others, implying the ordinary injunction in Indian hierarchical relationships that juniors should never be directly critical of a superior. It was very difficult at first for him to see the junior managers as genuinely wanting a better relationship with him.

After the group session was over, Ahmed and one of the junior managers who had spoken up, Anthony, both wanted to see someone for individual consultations. Udayan Patel suggested they should see me. I had already begun seeing Rajiv, another of the junior managers involved, before the group session occurred, which may have helped him speak out about Ahmed. I shall now report on their individual sessions to show what light a more in-depth psychological analysis sheds on their particular problematic interaction in the company, how the problems derive from their personal histories, and further problems they were having that impinged on their functioning at work. I shall start with Ahmed first, and then with Rajiv and Anthony.

I should first mention that I was struck by all five members of the firm I saw in consultations as being very open with me and having an expectation that I would be helpful to them, even though I was there as a complete stranger. I was apparently associated with a more caring administration, and clearly there were familial attitudes involved that I as the psychological expert would be like the helpful, caring familial elder.

Ahmed

Ahmed immediately expressed in session that he was in a bitter conflict with his father, an elderly, self-made, wealthy Muslim businessman. Although he was his father's favorite, he had not wanted to go into his father's business, as his older and younger brothers had, because he experienced his father as far too possessive and controlling. Not being the oldest son, he was allowed some leeway. Ahmed went to college, then to Germany for further technical training, and upon returning worked in a very good position at a major company. His father had supported all of this and was very proud of his accomplishments. Similar to his brothers, Ahmed had lived at home with his wife and children in a joint household, but he was more independent of his father than his brothers were because he worked in another firm.

Some thirteen or so years ago, Ahmed had an opportunity for an excellent position with his firm by transferring to New Delhi. He went with his immediate family, and his father never forgave him for leaving home. Just nine months later, he had a heart attack and returned home to Bombay to recover. When he was better, his doctor vetoed his returning to New Delhi because of the periodic power outages: if he had another attack, they might not be able to contact the doctor or hospital. He, nevertheless, decided to move away from his father's home stating that he did not want his wife and daughter to be subject to his father's possessiveness, criticism, and temper outbursts—obviously projecting onto them his own feelings about his father.

His father reacted by disowning Ahmed. Ahmed will only inherit a bare minimum of the family property when his father dies. Ahmed is now not getting any extra rupees or jewelry as his brothers are, although he has made it clear to the extended family that he needs help for his daughter's wedding and for his living expenses because of poor health. Ahmed is now very bitter and angry toward his father.

It was apparent in sessions that Ahmed has an obsessive-compulsive personality with perfectionistic standards, trying to control considerable anger. As his rage has mounted toward his father, his obsessive-compulsive defenses with perfectionistic standards have intensified, resulting in Ahmed's increasing unapproachability at work and at home, as well as more temper outbursts at home. This seems to be an unconscious identification with his father, who has similar traits. It is just this kind of problem that led to the impasse in his relationships with the junior managers over not being available to them at work. His perceiving the junior managers as more loyal to another senior manager than himself seems to be a projection of the loyalty his brothers have to his father. His work problems are further compounded by being unable to delegate responsibility to anyone under him because he feels everything has to be done perfectly and others won't do it as well as him. While I interpreted some of the unconscious connections between his highly problematic managerial relationship and his problems with his father, it became apparent that Ahmed needed regular psychoanalytic therapy. He desperately wants help, and with the advice of Udayan Patel, I referred him to one of the junior psychoanalysts, which he readily accepted.

It is evident from these sessions with Ahmed that a highly problematic relationship with an overbearing, critical father, together with Ahmed's own obsessive-compulsive personality, make it very difficult for this very intelligent and capable senior manager to work well with junior managers, especially in a company where caring and equality in management relationships are prime considerations. It is evident, too, that the role of the father in Ahmed's personal problems as well as in his career difficulties is a central one. This contradicts the downplaying of the role and influence of the father in much of the Indian psychoanalytic literature (Kakar 1978). Because it was felt by senior administrators in the company that it might take some time in personal therapy for Ahmed to work out his problems, he was transferred to a position with much less contact with junior managers.

Rajiv

Rajiv, a friendly, lively junior manager in his early thirties was one of those involved in the interchange with Ahmed. He came to me for three sessions before the group meeting and another three sessions afterwards for obsessional thinking that is interfering in his work. He becomes preoccupied with the thought that when something bad happens, it is because of what he has done. He then follows certain compulsive rituals to avoid bad occurrences: e.g. he must bow to all shrines he passes, or he cannot drink water when he first comes to work. Or when he took a different route home one day, it caused his father-in-law's heart attack. This obsessional thinking began three years previously when he became head of regional sales with greatly increased responsibilities. His responsibilities also increased at home at that time when he had a child and his wife stopped working. His general mood was anxiety over expecting the worst.

I found Rajiv has had a very poor relationship with a successful but highly critical father who had no confidence in him. The more critical his father was, the worse he did in school, and the more critical his father became. He did so poorly he ended up at a second rate school and college. While in college and for two years afterwards, he worked for a maternal uncle in his printing business who had confidence and interest in him. Rajiv thrived and things turned around for him. We also found that earlier he had done good work at school when he had an interested, concerned tutor. And at this firm he has done quite well through having an interested boss and coworkers.

The main problems he experiences at work are two-fold besides his anxiety. One was failing at a new assignment because he had not asked others for advice and information on how to do it. The other is procrastinating on decisions when he is dealing with a company that has no confidence or trust in him or in his firm and its products. If people are unbending, he hates them. Rajiv is very much living out his old problematic relationship with his father in these situations, whom he never approached for advice and experienced as not having any confidance in him. His anxiety evoked by increased responsibility is probably related to inner fears of his father's old criticisms.

Rajiv responded well to my connecting his current-day problems and anxiety with his old relationship with his father. It is highly likely that through these interpretations, and through my presence at the group session, that he was able to become more assertive by being the first junior manager in the group to express his complaints about Ahmed. And in fact after the group, he was very much impressed by a coworker saying, "why didn't you discuss your feelings at the time with Ahmed?" when Rajiv and others felt Ahmed was so unavailable during work hours. It had never occurred to him that he could ever approach a superior in this way.

He now sees that some persons like Ahmed are not as unbending as his father, that he can have a dialogue with them and be much more direct. He further realizes that he doesn't have to fall back on his old reactions of noncooperation, apathy, and withdrawal—which left Ahmed in a state of isolation and annoyance that Rajiv and others were not giving him the data he needed for certain decisions. In a later session, we found that Rajiv's noncooperation, which was so apparent in his reaction to his father's criticism, had deeper roots with his mother and can manifest itself in not dressing appropriately when he and his wife go out. He easily feels dominated by his mother and his wife, which he handles either by noncooperation or becoming harsh and crude toward them. Nevertheless, while problems with his mother are present, I have a distinct impression that Rajiv's main problems as a manager stem from unconsciously displacing old reactions from a highly problematic relationship with an overcritical, untrusting father.

Anthony

Anthony, a pleasant man with a seemingly sunny smile, came with the problems of either over-explaining things to his subordinates at work and his wife, or always having a smile on his face so that the managing director and other superiors are unable to fathom what he thinks or where he stands on various issues. Anthony seems much more aware of his over-explaining than his constantly smiling. In the two sessions we had, it became apparent that similar to Ahmed and Rajiv, Anthony has had an extremely difficult relationship with his father. In his case, his father was an extremely strict, scolding, lecturing man.

Anthony remembers being humiliated by his father when he was thirteen by his father grabbing him from a concert that he went to with his friends, saying that if Anthony wants to continue to live at home he always has to obey; otherwise, he can leave. Anthony inwardly vowed never to obey his father, but always did so secretly while presenting a conforming appearance. As an example, his father only permitted him to go away to college if Anthony would do well, which he promised. But once there, he went on drugs and generally did poorly in his schoolwork for the first year and a half.

Anthony is well aware that in any situation he will conform outwardly, but in hidden ways he does as he pleases. His relationship with Ahmed is a case in point when he felt Ahmed was unapproachable. He was friendly to Ahmed but gave him nothing. Whereas with subordinates and his wife, he unconsciously identifies with his lecturing father. At one point he was about to leave the firm because he felt humiliated by something the managing director said in front of Anthony to a dealer. It was only when a friend suggested he first speak directly to the managing director before leaving that he even considered doing so. The managing director then explained why he had to say what he did, further telling Anthony that he later told the dealer that Anthony was one of his best men. It was obvious that Anthony felt that superiors could not be talked to directly, as with his father. It is also clear that from these two sessions he was becoming more aware of displacing reactions to a critical father onto managerial relationships in the present, both to superiors and subordinates.

It is apparent from the impasse in the firm between Ahmed and the junior managers that on one level they experience Ahmed's obsessional preoccupation with work as an uncaring, rejecting attitude of a father-figure; which they react to by a noncooperative emotional withdrawal and withholding of data that Ahmed needs, thus interfering with the functioning of the company. On another level that emerged in individual sessions, it became clear that the reactions of both Ahmed and the junior managers were deeply inscribed by highly problematic relationships with their own fathers, with whom they all felt that there was little communication or mutuality. Through the group and individual sessions, part of this vicious circle between them began to be reversed.

The psychoanalytically oriented experience with these three managers, one senior and the other two junior, suggests that there needs to be far greater depth psychological exploration of the father-son relationship than has appeared in the psychoanalytic literature on India. Similarly, the second and third case study also call for greater in-depth psychological study of envy and destructiveness among brothers. The experience with these managers also indicate, at least in this particular company, that with a caring, concerned stance of the administration, managers are quite willing to delve into their own problematic attitudes and behavior to try to resolve them. A psychoanalytic approach that connects current difficulties in managerial interactions with past problematic familial relationships seems to be of substantial help.

SUMMARY

Indian management theorists have begun developing an indigenous management theory to supplant the current reliance in India on American and Japanese theories that do not well suit Indian organizations or psychology. Four case examples illustrate the psychological and the psychosocial in hierarchical relationships in diverse Indian organization. The first example is of a successful company where talented younger members were prematurely leaving because of their manager relating in too egalitarian a way, thereby interfering with the former's idealization needs. The second example is of a near collapse of a highly promising counselling association because its British teachers undermined the formal Indian hierarchy, setting loose envy and destructiveness by a younger member. The theme of envy and destructiveness by younger brothers is continued in the third example, where a highly competent, favored, and better educated oldest brother was edged out of the family business by younger brothers and then not compensated. The fourth example is of a highly successful mid-sized company where psychoanalytically oriented group and individual sessions with managers have been of great assistance. From group and individual sessions with a senior and two junior managers, the psychodynamics of a highly problematic interaction between them is delineated. From most of these examples, there is clearly a need for a much greater psychoanalytic elaboration of the relationship between fathers and sons, and between brothers than has appeared in the current psychoanalytic literature on India.

Insight-Oriented Psychotherapy
and the Chinese Patient

MAY TUNG, PH.D.

"Insight-oriented psychotherapy" and "Chinese patient" are terms that may appear contradictory to those mental health professionals who are interested in cross-cultural issues concerning the Chinese. They must by now be familiar with the interdependent and situational nature of Chinese life (Hsu 1985; Lin and Lin 1981; Sue and Zane 1987). Furthermore, there is a wealth of literature regarding somatization of the Chinese (Cheung 1985; Kleinman and Kleinman, 1985; Tseng 1975). Lin (1985), however, has pointed out that the number of well-trained, psychoanalytically-oriented Chinese psychotherapists is so small that insight-oriented psychotherapy has not been adequately tried with Chinese patients. It may therefore be premature to assume that it does not work with this population. Roland (1988) utilized clinical examples to show how, with some modifications, psychoanalytic psychotherapy can be used with at least some Asians.

It seems evident that in considering the application of insight to psychotherapy, the first question be: "Insight into what?" Some kind of road map, as it were, is necessary to give us an overview of the relevant areas to be explored. This paper is an attempt to chart such a map, exploring the topics of the world of the Chinese "self," and of characteristic Chinese defense and coping mechanisms. Issues raised are illustrated by clinical examples, some from reports in Chinese psychiatric journals, and some from case histories of Chinese-Americans in therapy in this country.

THE CHINESE "SELF"

Popular Chinese creation stories named P'an-ku as the creator who, in turn, had come into existence by way of cosmological evolution (Williams 1976). Human beings are depicted as having come either from parasites on P'an-ku's body or from clay figures which he made in large supply (Eberhard 1965). Thus, the Chinese view concerning the origin of human species is in sharp contrast to that of the Christian West, which views man made in the image of God, unique and well defined.

The core of the Western definition of self, then, is reflective awareness. The issue of boundary applies to components within a system of the self; conflict is among these components, and is therefore intrapsychic (Johnson 1985). In summarizing the world of a Chinese self, Hsu's (1985) concept of psychosocial homeostasis is useful. Instead of stressing personality, which is an individualistic concept, Hsu delineated the affective involvement of individuals with other people, gods, and objects. The Chinese are rooted in their kinship system, called by Hsu "intimate society and culture" (p. 28). The people who occupy this region for any individual are stable, and their accessibility is predictable and automatic. In contrast, Westerners are expected to leave this region of origin in order to find their own identity in a self-created world where relationships are voluntary and conditional. Thus, the Eastern definition of intimacy is the extent to which one can depend on the other (Roland 1988). The Western definition is the extent to which one can feel safely undefended regarding one's innermost world.

Implied in the intimate region of the Chinese kinship system is that the structure predates the individual. This system is maintained by the durability of roles and regularity of the social order. A Chinese father-son story illustrates the absolute nature of this social order (and is especially interesting when compared to the story of Oedipus). In the Chinese story, a famous warrior leaves his pregnant wife to conduct a distant campaign for his emperor. He is away for 18 years. On his way home he meets a young man to whom he loses a marksmanship competition. The warrior immediately drives an arrow into the young man's heart, killing him, because no one is supposed to be superior to the warrior. The young man, it transpires, is his son, whom he had never seen before. The warrior justifies his act by asserting that the son had violated his cultural role, first by not recognizing his own father, then by daring to defeat him (Bond 1986). The story implies that, without exception, role distinctions must be adhered to at all times.

During my ten years of practice as a Chinese-American psychotherapist in San Francisco, the differences between Western and Chinese worlds of the self have been broadly reflected in the way of life of my patients. Most of the Caucasian patients are from out of state; they live away from their families, with whom they have only occasional contact. All the Chinese patients, whether American-born or foreign-born, live near their families of origin. Many of them work for their parents, or for relatives or family friends. Some of them live in parental properties, and unmarried adult children frequently live with their parents.

DEFENSE AND COPING MECHANISMS

The characteristic coping and defense mechanisms of a culture are important in this context insofar as they reveal a people's psychological makeup and patterns of pathology. From these can be gleaned directions to be taken in treatment. Hsu (1983) pointed out that, while repression is more representative of cultures that emphasize internal control and individual responsibilities, suppression is more applicable to cultures of external control and situation-centered behavior. The contrast between situation and individual centeredness was discussed by Roland (1988), who used the terms "universalistic" as more characteristic of the West and "contextual" as characteristic of the East. Johnson (1985), characterizing Eastern and Western systems of perception and experience, called them "monotheistic" and "polytheistic," respectively. These terms suggest that, in the West, certain types of behavior are right or wrong under all circumstances; the ideal is a land governed by law. In the East, on the other hand, whether behavior is considered right or wrong depends on the circumstances and people involved; actions are compartmentalized, and there are clear guidelines as to what constitutes appropriate behavior in particular situations or relationships. For example, humor is considered inappropriate in formal settings or in speaking to an elder. One is expected to do what is right in a particular situation regardless of one's feelings (Hsu 1985). The ideal is the endurance and stability of the social order as, in nature, one season forever follows another in certain order. In terms of individual behavior and adjustment, value is attached to rational control, compromise, and patience.

Appreciation of these basic contrasts in emphasis will enable us to understand that a Westerner can be "psychologically hurt" (Hsu 1985, p. 121) by circumstances that would not have the same effect on an Easterner, and vice versa. This understanding will, in turn, affect the clinician's views of what constitutes an appropriate intervention in psychotherapy. An example of clinical work with a Chinese-American may illustrate this point:

David, an Asian-born professional man in his 40s, sought help for a profound depression of one year's duration. His symptoms included significant weight loss, insomnia, inability to concentrate on his work, and general loss of interest in life. David's own explanation was in terms of guilt feelings toward his wife's death. When she had had to go to the hospital with what proved to be her final illness, David had been too busy at work to take her. Their son did so instead. David's life history showed no indications of childhood trauma or previous psychiatric problems. His marriage had been primarily duty-bound, as were most other aspects of his life. As therapy progressed, the only significant material that emerged was his life-long wish to be a teacher, a profession not known for its financial rewards. Being the eldest son of a Chinese family he had felt responsible for providing for his parents. He became an engineer, worked diligently and strenuously, and was financially successful. As we were reviewing his life, David reported a dream in which he was in an airplane with colleagues on the way to a construction site. As the plane landed he realized that he was in the middle of Paris, which was bustling with color and gaiety, a far cry from the dusty construction site he had expected. By the time David had this dream, he had already gained enough self-understanding to recognize the message from his unconscious, and we shared a moment of humor. David's therapy lasted only eight sessions. He began to sleep and eat normally, then resigned from his firm and went to Asia. Eight months later, he called to express thanks for the treatment. He had been traveling, doing free-lance consultations, and writing a text book on his engineering specialty for schools in Asia.

This case of bicultural psychotherapy combined the Chinese value of filial responsibility, doing what is right for one's parents, with the Western value of individual pursuit. The wife's sudden death was like an unexpected stop signal, jolting him into realization of the pointlessness of continuing in the same direction. He was at a loss. Without the cultural knowledge of how essential it is for an eldest Chinese son to be filial, this man's course of action in life could easily be misdiagnosed as neurotic dependency, or even masochism. In China, on the other hand, he might be considered selfish for wanting fulfillment of his own wishes. Of course, if he lived in China, he might not have experienced such a bicultural conflict in the first place. But even if he wanted such changes, there would be much more social pressure there for him to stay put. Alernatives would be far fewer, and a fling in Paris definitely not an option!

CLINICAL EXAMPLES FROM CHINA

Increasing Asian immigration to North America has brought with it a growth in the Asian patient population in this country. In working with these patients, it is important for the clinician to understand the cultural roots that are firmly planted, even in second and third generation Asian-Americans. On the continuum of individual/situation orientation and affective/cognitive emphasis, case histories from China can exemplify that end of the continuum at which situational and cognitive elements are culturally dominant. By referring to the source, we may acquire some fundamental knowledge.

Psychotherapy is still rare in Chinese psychiatry. In case records of psychotherapy from Chinese psychiatric journals of the 1980s, the most prominent feature is the pivotal role of rational, cognitive, common-sense understanding. Chinese psychotherapy invariably takes the form of the doctor explaining to the patient that the symptoms or preoccupations presented are illogical and abnormal. Common sense, reasoning, and objective reality are cited as "evidence." The treatments prescribed combine medication, specific behavioral homework (e.g. keeping a diary), desensitization exercises, and a few "talk" sessions with the doctor to reinforce the prescription. The goal is symptom removal (Tan 1988; Yang 1983; Zhao 1987).

Reflected, but not explicitly stated, in these records is the kindly and supportive, but directive and parent-like position of the doctor, who patiently guides the child-patient to see reason. This impression of the therapeutic relationship is consistent with the family orientation of the Chinese.

A departure from this therapeutic attitude, although more in content than style, is the work of Zhong You-bin,[1] a Beijing psychiatrist, who is considered to be China's authority on Freud. He had found Freud's emphasis on child experiences a familiar concept to the Chinese, illustrated in Chinese folktales and proverbs. By means of self-analysis ("Just like Freud himself did!"), he concluded that Freud's concepts were applicable in his own practice. The core of his psychotherapy is to explain to his patients that their current difficulties are rooted in their childhood and therefore no longer appropriate for an adult. He instructs them to recall childhood trauma, often with the help of family members, and to trace how certain behavioral and thinking patterns were established. He has been successful in treating some severe pathologies in just a few sessions. In essence, the style remains uniquely Chinese, addressed mainly to the cognitive and rational rather than to the affective and unconscious. However, what is new about Zhong's approach is his use of a different content—childhood experiences—and the fact that he requires more participation from the patients and their families in working on recollection and understanding. In other words, his approach is a form of structured and guided insight, reminiscent of the therapeutic process described in Bellak's intensive brief psychotherapy (1983, p. 39).

Though Zhong has published many of his successful cases, for our purpose, the following two case examples that he recorded as failures (Zhong 1988) are more relevant as illustrations of how cultural style can be an asset as well as a limitation in any treatment:

Y was a female high school teacher in her 40s. Her difficulties began when she graduated from high school with superior grades. She was refused college entrance because her father had been classified as an "intellectual" which often meant being regarded as a "reactionary rightist" in China's political climate of the late 1950s. Y worked in a factory before becoming a high school teacher, which did not require a college degree in certain parts of China. From depression in her late adolescence, her difficulties escalated to phobic preoccupation with cancer and obsessive-compulsive ritualistic washing of everything in sight. She had 13 sessions with Zhong within one year. She understood and agreed with the doctor's explanations but terminated treatment after only a minimum degree of improvement.

In this case, as in all others from China, nothing was said about affective aspects such as her many losses, great sadness, and other emotional injuries. Unlike other Chinese therapists, however, Zhong acknowledged "more deep-seated reasons" for her resistance. In his second failed case:

Z was a female factory worker in her mid-30s. In her background were an aggressive, intrusive mother and a quiet, passive father. When her father died, she became depressed and gradually developed obsessive-compulsive cleaning and washing behavior. Within a period of nine months she had ten sessions with Zhong. At each session, Z talked incessantly leaving little opportunity for the doctor to do so.

Zhong correctly identified this form of resistance as "the best defense is offense." He further conceptualized this case in terms of Z's need for these symptoms as a defense against her situational stresses. In other words, the symptoms were the lesser of the two evils. This interpretation, accurate or not, is the only one implying unconscious motivation that I have come across in case histories from China. As in the first case, no mention was made of any intervention on the affective level or of addressing the unconscious. The possiblity that Z had adopted with the doctor her mother's strategy of being always on the offensive to avoid being dominated in the way her father had been—a matter of transference—was not discussed. Whether and how transference interpretations should be made in psychotherapy with Chinese patients is another complex issue (addressed later in the paper). In both of Zhong's cases, guidance and explanations were apparently not enough. Chinese people do not openly challenge authority, in this instance personified by the therapist; they just stop coming. Thus, one must be careful not to overstate the effectiveness of the authoritative approach in treating Chinese patients.

These clinical examples from China raise important issues—the role of affective, irrational, and unconscious material, and the nature of the therapeutic relationship—all key concepts in psychodynamic psychotherapy.

CLINICAL EXAMPLES OF CHINESE-AMERICANS

To explore some of these issues, two case histories of Chinese-Americans seen in therapy in San Francisco are illustrative:

Lynn

Lynn was a third generation Chinese-American woman. She was in her mid-20s when she began therapy, and attended sessions once a week, with rare cancellations, for almost six years. Her presenting complaints were mainly in somatic terms: hyperventilation, insomnia, night sweats, severe stomach aches with no organic basis, and general nervousness. She had to be driven everywhere, and displayed agorophobic symptoms in such places as resaurants and supermarkets. In the first session, she reported a recurrent dream of huge spiders and spider webs that she associated with death. She described herself as pessimistic, and believed that she was born that way.

Lynn was the oldest of three children, and the only girl. Her childhood was marked by an elderly father, a paranoid mother, frequent parental fights, and beatings by her mother. Her father was disappointed that his first child was a girl, which is a common Chinese reaction. Lynn's wish to continue her father's work repeatedly met with strong objections from both her father and his contemporaries in the business.

In the initial sessions she dwelled mainly on her many painful memories, although she first had to be given permission to do so and assured that she was not being selfish to think of herself (a typical Chinese attitude), and that her feelings were understandable. She was greatly relieved to be told that her pessimism was learned, rooted in her childhood experiences, and could therefore be unlearned.

Hyperventilation was greatly reduced within a month of starting therapy. After working through her fears of being condemned or criticized by the therapist, she began to deal with her sense of worthlessness and guilt. For example, in the fifth month of therapy, she talked one day about the fact that her father was vague and distant, and that she always felt disapproval from him. Later in the session she mentioned that her worst fear was that "God will come to me before I'm ready" and she would be condemned to "eternal suffering." When the therapist commented on the similarity between her perception of her father and her perception of God, she was able to see that her anxiety about God was related to her experiences with her father. This insight into the fact that her problems were "inside" herself, gave her a degree of freedom. The following week, she reported a dream of being on horseback. She wanted the horse to go in one dirction, but "he had a mind of his own," and overtook another horse to gallop across the San Francisco-Oakland Bay Bridge. She felt good: "We won!" This dream of her aspirations and innate power was used repeatedly as a metaphor in the course of her treatment.

In her eighth month of therapy, she experienced two episodes of severe stomachache in one week. In the therapy session she was able to associate her symptoms with her pain at her father's unfair treatment of her and "the way I am," meaning she was "unclean." She recalled how her mother used to tell her that she was "no good" because she was not a boy.

There were continuous indications of increasing self-awareness and more realistic assessment of her life situation, as well as the evolution of skills to bring about changes. Lynn used psychotherapy not only to remove symptoms but also for growth. The fact that she had been deprived of adequate parenting made long-term psychotherapy even more beneficial.

Barry

Barry was a married Chinese man in his late 20s when he began therapy. He saw the therapist once a week, with rare cancellations, for four years and ten months. He was the younger of two sons, born and raised in Asia, and came to the United States to attend college. Depression was his presenting complaint with no somatic component except moderate overweight. The core conflict was his fear of his father, for whom he worked. All his life Barry had been convinced that the father favored the older son, a common Chinese phenomenon. With this conviction as a base, Barry construed detailed "evidence" of slights, deception, and conspiracy against him on the part of his father and brother. His intelligence and his compulsive style lent themselves to "documenting" these conjectures so well that they reached paranoid proportions. While Barry managed the office in San Francisco, his father and brother basically lived in Asia. They were in regular telephone communication several times a week. The three were so close knit that they could have been living and working under the same roof. In his relationship to his wife Barry was rigidly controlling, though extremely dependent on her emotionally. They lived a guarded life and did not take a vacation until his second year of therapy for fear his father would think him irresponsible.

There was no evidence of abuse or neglect in Barry's early life. It appeared that while his father and three siblings were all outgoing and verbal, Barry had always been introverted, awkward, and "out of it." Only after some years of therapy and the experience of fathering a child somewhat like himself did he appreciate the anxiety he had caused his parents. They had kept him under close surveillance as a young child to insure his safety. For instance, they would come into his room to check up on him, even when he had locked the door; they would also look through his belongings while he, on his part, pretended to be asleep. (In Chinese family life, while emotions are considered to be private, property is not, so that searches such as the ones by Barry's parents would not be viewed as extreme.) Since they never explained or even mentioned their actions, Barry grew up assuming that something was wrong with him.

Two other features in Barry's background are relevant. First, he was brought up by his widowed maternal grandmother (a frequent practice in Chinese families) who was herself an unhappy and suspicious person. Second, instability and unrest prevailed in Asia during Barry's childhood; he recalled, for instance, anxiety and fears of kidnapping when his father went on business trips. Thus, suspicion and caution were also endemic in this larger context.

It was understood in the family that Barry and his brother would grow up to work for their father. Despite feeling unnoticed and undervalued, Barry always had a deep love for his father, often fantasizing great achievements that he would dedicate to him. During therapy, he realized that his desire to please his father was, in part, competitive. In working for him, he often felt that his father got all the credit. He felt unable to really "see" himself. As he put it, he wanted a sense of himself as a whole tree (an individualistic goal) and not just as a branch (a Chinese view). Even though he felt suffocated in the family business, however, Barry saw the outside world as a fearsome jungle. For many years, he had a recurrent dream of being literally glued to a spot from which he could not pull himself up. Ambivalence toward his father coiled through therapy. In the third year of therapy he had enough money to purchase a house on his own. He thought his father would be pleased; instead, his father was cool toward the project. It was obvious that he felt Barry should have honored him by asking his advice. Barry reclaimed his father's interest by skillfully involving him in a financial arrangement. This experience taught Barry how difficult it would be for him to become independent in the Western sense. Purchasing a house independently would have been praiseworthy for a Caucasian-American, but in Chinese culture, fathers must be consulted at all times. For Westerners, to stay with one's parents much beyond adulthood is undesirable. For Chinese, to leave one's parents is a serious offense.

Toward the end of his third year of therapy, Barry went through two months of extreme depression, during which time he played with the idea of resigning from the family business, much like a person preparing to plunge from a great height. The depression lifted just as abruptly as it had started, as if a fever had broken. Retrospectively, Barry felt that it had been his last flirtation with independence before finally committing himself to the family business; after resolving to stay, he looked almost light-hearted and happy—in his own metaphor, he had just come out of incubation.

Equipped with more self-knowledge and awareness of his bicultural life situation, Barry was able to make decisions that gave him a sense of self-worth and freedom.

DISCUSSION

It is clear, then, that Chinese tradition persists, even with vastly different pathologies and lengths of exposure to the West. In this section three key issues regarding insight-oriented psychotherapy and the Chinese patient will be addressed: the "territory" of psychological exploration, the therapeutic relationship, and the role of didactic teaching.

Therapeutic Territory

The main difference between the latter two Chinese-American cases and insight-oriented psychotherapy with middle-class Caucasian-Americans is in terms of the "territory" of exploration. The term "insight" in this context is usually limited to an intrapsychic sense, as in Johnson's (1985) definition of the Western self, the locus of control residing in the individual self. Since the boundary of the Chinese self is vastly different, so must be the application of insight. For most Chinese-Americans, therapeutic explorations are never far from the family sphere. The core conflict is worked out directly with the original cast of characters.

The energy and emotional investment of Chinese-Americans are permanently centered on this original cast. Emotionally, they need not be as mobile as their Caucasian counterparts. Therapy with Caucasians, on the other hand, deals mainly with patterns of transference distortions. Because they have to create their own structures and conditions in each new encounter, these patterns persist from one relationship to the next. Slater (1970), while discussing dependence and independence, described American society as having: " . . . fewer 'givens,' more ambiguous criteria, less environmental stability, and less social structural support, than any people in history. (Within this fluid culture the) mobile individual must travel light, and internalized controls are portable and transistorized, as it were" (pp. 21, 23).

This is a graphic image of a highly charged, compact, and enclosed bundle of energy. For this group, each new involvement becomes of central importance for that time period. In other words, the territory of psychological significance is directly related to the next issue.

Therapeutic Relationship

When the new involvement of the Caucasian patient is the therapeutic one, then that is the matter of central importance, the present focus of energy for that patient. My own therapeutic work with Chinese-American patients has seemed to lack the intense patient-therapist relationship of my work with Caucasian-American patients. Coming from a psychodynamic background, where transference interpretation is of central importance, I feared having overlooked something, or possible interference from my own countertransference. At the same time, my Chinese patients seemed much less concerned about their dependence on me as the therapist than did many of my Caucasian patients. The Chinese patients as a whole were also less likely to tolerate or benefit from frequent sessions—say, twice a week—or from long-term work. These phenomena may be related, but no literature has discussed them except in terms of frustration and bewilderment at the tendency for Chinese people to be "underserved" in mental health services.

In Hsu's (1981) analysis of family structure and emotionality, he observed that a deeper emotional involvement between parents and children obtains in a Western, exclusive, nuclear family because the parents are the sole authority figures in a child's life. In the Chinese extended family, parent-child relationships are "diluted" by frequent exposure to other significant adults, often of equal authority over the children.

Typically, the Chinese patient in therapy continues to be centrally involved in the original extended family; the therapist is of only peripheral importance.

Space does not allow a full description of the typical formation of a Chinese support network, but in terms of that network, the professional relationship with the therapist is functional and pragmatic; it does not define or threaten the patient's concept of self-worth.

In comparison, dynamic or psychoanalytic psychotherapy with Caucasians entails hundreds of hours working on issues involving one's family of origin, especially the parents. The very concept of transference is based on the pivotal role of the parents. Perhaps the culturally necessitated separation and independence from them further intensify these earlier ties, leaving little opportunity for resolution. In the absence of real parents who can be dealt with directly, this intensity is transferred onto the therapist. The complexity of this transference is increased by the Westerner's cultural ambivalence toward dependency needs, and the consequent suspicion that therapy may lead to dependence on the therapist. A recent Hawaiian study (*Harvard Mental Health Letter, 1990*) of ethnic differences in marital status and psychiatric symptoms reported that, after correction for age, the correlation between psychiatric symptoms and unmarried state disappeared for Filipino and Japanese Hawaiians, but not for white and native Hawaiians. The authors speculated that the two former groups receive from their extended families support that substitutes for the protection of marriage, while the latter two do not. Thus, it seems appropriate to allocate a seconday role to transference analysis in working with Chinese patients. Emphasis on this aspect of psychotherapy sometimes frustrates these patients, disrupting the flow of their work because it is basically unimportant, even irrelevant, for them. Further detail with regard to Chinese styles of therapeutic relationship can be found in articles by Hsu (1985) and Tung (1984).

Didactic Teaching

The role of didactic teaching, which applies to cognitive understanding, is of unique importance to the Chinese population. Again, space limits do not allow a more detailed discourse on the relation of Chinese cognition to learning and functioning. Liu (1986) spoke of the "respect superiors" rule of Chinese life style. Pillsbury (1986) discussed the differences in styles of learning between East and West, representing the former as passive, with the responsibility for initiation being the teacher's. The Chinese typically prefer the teacher to outline the parameters of action. In the case of psychiatric treatment, a rational explanation, direction, and even justification from the therapeutic authority is consistent with the external locus of control of the world of a Chinese self, where situational givens have to be noted alongside subjective reactions.

Although two of the Chinese-American cases, those of Lynn and Barry, used substantially affective and unconscious material, cognitive understanding was necessary to establish a working relationship. Because the therapist occupies a peripheral and functional role in Chinese patients' lives, it is not enough to rely on the transference. It is necessary to help them to see how therapy is relevant in terms they find familiar. Lynn, for example, was "taught" to explore her feelings by being told that her pessimism was learned and could be unlearned; and that, while the Chinese tend to perceive self-analysis as being selfish, it is hard work of eventual benefit to the patient and the family. In Barry's case, much discussion of cultural differences was necessary to clarify his bicultural dilemma and misunderstandings.

It is also extremely valuable to discuss and concede importance to the experience of being uprooted that both the patient and patient's parents have usually undergone. These experiences often have a direct correspondance to fragmented self-identity.

CONCLUSION

The applicability of insight-oriented psychotherapy for the Chinese patient appears to be twofold. On the specific level of somatic expression of distress among the Chinese, Lynn's case demonstrates that "liberation" of suppressed material is effective in dealing with somatic symptoms, and can lead to better integration and functioning. In this sense psychodynamic insight-oriented psychotherapy should be particularly appropriate for some Chinese patients. More generally, psychodynamic principles are only partially based on knowledge of such human conditions as the power of the emotions and the unconscious. However, a great deal of the approach, at least as it is practiced in the West, is based on cultural values, belief systems, and life styles. With modifications appropriate to the patient's personal world—be it unicultural or bicultural— the basic principles have the potential for broad applications. When the cultural-dynamic dimension is combined with psychodynamics, the approach can only enrich psychotherapy for everyone.

ENDNOTE

1. In Chinese names the family name comes first, again consistent with the emphasis of family over the individual.

Koreans Abroad in Therapy

WALTER H. SLOTE, PH.D.

The data elicited during psychotherapy sessions constitute one of the richest, and I may add, one of the most neglected sources of data about a culture and its members. As both a practicing psychoanalyst and a psychoanalytic anthropologist, I deal with both conscious and unconscious material. This includes repressed data that is not available to consciousness, or may only be partially available and thus adds a dimension that is not usually addressed in sociocultural research.

The concerns that patients bring to psychoanalysis are not unique. They represent psychological considerations that are inherent in all mankind, but in addition, they reveal psychosocial data that is specific to their own culture. Although the problems presented are always personal, they are also usually reflective of issues innate in the culture. Because those who seek therapy are troubled they tend to be less inhibited, and thus the restraints in exposing one's inner feelings are lessened. The fact that the person seeking psychotherapy comes with a problem to be solved does not detract from the validity of the data, although it may be distorted. However, this is a factor in all clinical research; the fact is that everyone, to one degree or another, tends to modify perception. In this case, it is the therapist/researcher's job to distinguish between what is idiosyncratic, meaning true for only that person, and what is consensually valid, meaning applicable to most members of the culture.

In addition to therapy with Koreans and other Asians, the sources of the observations that I shall be presenting come also from my own research both in Korea and with Koreans in the United States, as well as personal relationships with Koreans.

The primary issue that I shall address in this paper, and a central focus of both my research and therapy, is that of the second generation. I refer to those problems that arise before the immigrating group is integrated into the host community. Entry problems are confronted by everyone who enters a new society, but the conflicts that arise between the old and the new generation and their resolution, plus the implications for succeeding generations, are faced only by those who are either born in the new country or who come when they are young. It is the children who are of the greatest concern because it is they who represent the future. As such, there are two considerations that I consider of primary importance: 1) Confucianism—the philosophical, social, and moral standards that it encompasses in contrast to those values found in the United States; and, 2) acculturation and the interpersonal relationships and value system in the Korean family.

It is the family, especially the parents, who are the primary transmitters of the culture. Although others also play a crucial role, such as certain significant adults, peers, and the pervasive social atmosphere, it is the mother and father, especially during the early developmental years, who are most responsible for indoctrinating the children into the mores, values, and social parameters of the world in which they live.

Historically speaking, those problems currently experienced by Koreans replicate those faced by a number of their predecessors: the need to accommodate to a value system and to stylistic forms quite different from their own; resistance on the part of earlier migrants and established minorities; prejudice, hostility, and envy—the latter a particular factor for the Koreans because of their industriousness, diligenece, intelligence, unity, and rapid success. Although the basic problems faced by the Koreans are not very different from those of other ethnic and nationality groups, what is different, and this holds for all, is the unique nature of the particular people, the problems they faced in the homeland, their aspirations, and the qualifications that they bring with them.

It seems to me that the immigrant wave most similar to the Koreans was that of the Jews, particularly the East European Jews who came to the United States primarily between 1880 and 1920. As with the Koreans, they brought with them an elevated set of religious and moral values, and close family ties in which the children were the primary focus. Not only have they succeeded, they have made major contributions to science, the arts, and American society. Freed from the chains that bound them in the past in inhospitable societies, they have flourished. I think that this will also be the destiny of the Koreans in the coming decades; in fact, it has already begun.

The Koreans bring a heritage of hard work, a deep respect for education, a strong moral commitment, the centrality of the family, and a highly defined code of ethical conduct. As laudable as these qualities may be, they are also the source of dissonance with the host culture: the problem is not the fact of morality, it is the nature of that morality; it is not the centrality of the family, it is the nature of the relationships and the commitment of family members to each other; it is not the ethical code itself, it is the components of that code that conflict both with certain aspects of human nature in a world that has dramatically changed in the present era, and with the standards that are held by the Western world. And there, in the words of Shakespeare, lies the rub.

All of which brings us to Confucianism, a core issue. Although Buddhism, Taoism, Folk Beliefs, and Christianity all play their roles, it is Confucianism that is the primary determinant in the Korean's adaptation to America (Slote and DeVos 1996).

Confucianism is a body of ethical principles which have historically shaped the social and political structure of the Confucian countries: China, Korea, Japan, and Vietnam. Confucianism has been the major determinant in establishing the personal perspective, the *Weltanschauung*—the worldview—and, to a great extent, the internalized sense of being of its members. It has established criteria for modes of conduct, interpersonal relationships, moral and ethical values, and it specifically concerns itself with authority on all levels. As a consequence it is a primary determinant of individual perception, of ideation and thought processes, and it establishes acceptable and unacceptable standards of emotional expression.

Beyond this, however, it must be recognized that Confucianism was founded upon a patriarchal, authoritarian base. The system was rigorously hierarchical and its members were thrust into stereotypic categories. This included assignment of status, role, and propriety. Behavior, meaning sanctioned behavior, was precisely defined and adherence was demanded. Confucius, Mencius, and later revisionists were all very precise on this as a central ethic. Confucius stated, ". . . it is by rules of propriety (*Li*) that character is established" (Confucius 1960a, Book VIII, Chapter ii). "Look not at what is contrary to propriety; listen not to what is contrary to propriety; speak not what is contrary to propriety; make no movement which is contrary to propriety" (Confucius 1960a, Book XII, Chapter i, 2).

Thus, individual differences were regarded as discordant intrusions upon the matrix of society. "To subdue oneself and return to propriety is perfect virtue" (Confucius, 1960a, Book XII, Chapter i, 1). Moreover, not only was Confucian dogma explicit, it was also enforced throughout the life sequence, although greater latitude was permitted as one grew older, and this held true for both women and men.

Confucian authoritarianism has endured, and it is only during the present era that it has been significantly challenged. This is primarily due to the influence of Western democracy and its focus on individualism, egalitarianism, and autonomy. Although the Western model may be far from ideal, it has exerted a dramatic influence on all Asian countries, as it has elsewhere. It is in this sense that East Asian Confucianism and democracy and individualism as found in America collide. They are diametrically opposed: one proclaims equality and individuation; the other, conformity and adherence to tradition in which everyone has an assigned role which is superimposed from above. Historically, this did not acknowledge, as it has in the West, that each person is unique and that it is his nature, his talent, and his particular being that defines him, not his place in a structured society.

The Koreans are a people in transition. The old ways are still deeply ingrained. This particularly holds true for the older generations; traditional patterns are increasingly being questioned, and rejected, by the youth. The issue is personal freedom and self-determination versus a codified life style that has endured for millennia. The young Asians that I see in consultation are confronted with a very serious dilemma. They proclaim their love for their parents and most feel loved. They do not want to give up the security of the family, and they do not want to hurt their parents. In fact, they seem to feel quite protective of their mothers and fathers. They are confused. Their parents are equally confused. On the one hand, they see their beloved children as headed for destruction and purgatory; on the other, the freedoms they themselves see in Western societies are very beguiling, and often very threatening. Thus, not only is there an intergenerational conflict, but both parents and children are conflicted within themselves as well. Ultimately there will be, and to some extent there already is a resolution between the two generations, but it is far from fully achieved.

There have been two recent waves of Korean immigrants: the first, those who came to the United States in the 1950s and 1960s to study and remained, and those, by far the larger, who came since 1965 and who shall be our primary concern here. Before either of these groups arrived, Koreans had been "imported" as laborers for the plantations in Hawaii and the farms in California. Moreover, a small number came to study before and after World War I, such as Syngman Rhee who got a Ph.D. from Princeton. Some were permitted to remain, even though the immigration laws in those years were designed to keep Asians out. My wife's father was among this group. He was brought over as a young man by the Methodist Church. Two of his children were born in Korea (the first and third), two in the United States (the second and fourth) which gives you an idea of how he shuttled back and forth while acquiring two university degrees in the United States—seven in all, including those from Korean and Japanese universities. He settled permanently in the United States in 1934. This was atypical and only possible because he was a minister and the church certified that his services were needed in the United States. Incidentally, as a little girl my wife knew some of the families whose fathers came as laborers (their wives were probably brought over as picture brides) because they were members of her father's congregation. I have been told that their children have done remarkably well both in business and in the professions.

Those Koreans who came as students in the 1950s and 1960s, and who remained because professional jobs were then not available at the level of their expertise in Korea, now consider themselves an elite. "Koreans who came here as students and then were educated here, they are completely like Americans; they have no differences really. However, those recent immigrants are different from the rest of us. We Koreans here in the United States always compare the two: those educated in this country and then the immigrants. They (meaning 'we') are two different people, actually." They speak of being more American than Korean, and it is quite true that to a great extent they have entered into the mainstream of American life. Many, perhaps most, are highly successful. They are often married to Korean women who also came here to study, indicating that originally both probably came from affluent families. The wives whom I know, except for those who have professions (and a number of them do), devote themselves to the home and the children, much as they would have had they remained in Korea. Their children, most of whom were born here (the second generation), are usually very Americanized. It is they who are the transitional generation, the bridge leading to a change in identity, a sense of self from "I am a Korean" to "I am a Korean-American" to, for some, "I am an American." Many marry Caucasians. With rare exceptions, these marriages are arranged by the children themselves. Moreover, many second generation children also marry other Koreans of their own choice. Relatively few marriages seem to be arranged by the parents. This situation would be quite different in Korea where arranged marriages are the rule rather than the exception.

Their children, the third generation (and there are now third and occasionally fourth generation Korean-American children in the United States), not infrequently have begun to lose a sense of their Korean heritage. Although all immigrating groups bring their past with them, family memory usually exists only for three generations. The fourth generation has a minimal feeling of connectedness to their roots, which is sad because one's self-image encompasses the past as well as the present. The major Korean immigration is of recent origin, and therefore the past is still very much a part of current life, as it is for their children, because the parents tend to pass it on. Although many new émigrés periodically return to the homeland with the children, thus renewing their sense of Koreanness, it is questionable as to how long this will hold true for succeeding generations.

Many of the recent émigrés, both men and women, are well educated. Although a large number of the men are professionals they frequently find that they face barriers that they did not anticipate, such as formidable licensing examinations, a dearth of jobs, or simply that the level of their education and experience in Korea does not qualify them for employment here. As a result, they are forced into what they consider humiliating jobs. Inasmuch as in Korea one's sense of personal worth is particularly dependent on status, this can result in a serious loss of face and self-respect—a significant psychological issue. Its effect may extend beyond the work place and into the home, affecting the father's relationships with his wife and children and the consequent interpersonal balance of the family.

Moreover, it is true that due to insecurity, the language barrier, and the reassurance of being with one's own, most recent arrivals do tend to cluster together, and it does tend to isolate them. This is scarcely a new problem. Over fifty years ago, Harold Fields, a distinguished expert on the refugee experience, wrote, "The refugee who settles down in an area in which his own nationals are concentrated finds the process of assimilation slow. His native tongue is spoken, home customs and ceremonies are retained, his life becomes an experience of self-centered occupation in a foreign land. He suffers from the faults of ethnic cohesion. His capacity for putting the past behind him, and living in the present and for the future, becomes circumscribed" (Fields 1938). This is certainly true, but in a new world, in which one feels alienated and insecure, it is natural to seek the company of one's own and to stay with that which is familiar.

The family throughout the modern and emerging world is under tremendous stress. The format of the past is being challenged everywhere. The family was once easily defined: a father who worked, a mother who bore the children and devoted herself to the home, and children, many or few, performing their assigned tasks. I am no historian, but I would think that there is probably more questioning into the concept of family, meaning what constitutes a family— duties, responsibilities, role assignments, etc.—than in almost any previous period in time. Thus, the Korean family, having emigrated to the United States, is confronted not only by a dramatically different set of attitudes and values, but by standards which are in the process of change.

The family is at the heart of all Confucian societies, and in Korea certainly no less than elsewhere. Traditionally, it has been defined by its value system: the generational sequence; the bonding between parents and siblings; the security brought to its members by a complex but highly effective extended family system; the common core of intensely structured values; an ethical code and a morality widely disseminated and known to all; a role definition in which everyone had a specified assignment; industriousness; discipline; and the elevated poition given to learning—all of which are extremely valuable and relevant for modern life. The ethical and moral code established by Confucianism determined both a personal and a societal superego, and one which, to a great extent, meshes with Judeo-Christian morality as found in the West.

Beyond this, however, traditionally the Confucian family system was arbitrary. Its members were thrust into stereotypic categories that included assignment of status, role, and behavior. In the past, individual differences were not only disregarded, but were essentially not considered. Confucianism was based upon authority and hierarchy. Highly structured, everyone was subservient to, or superior to, everyone else, i.e., father, mother, elder brother, younger sister, etc. All were forced into a set behavioral and attitudinal pattern.

Although the Korean family is gradually modifying and adapting itself to an increasingly egalitarian perspective, the substance of Confucianism, particularly in terms of interpersonal relationships and ethical values, is still present. This issue of form versus substance is of great consequence: adherence to many Confucian practices may have died out, but inherent patterns remain and have been maintained. This, as we shall discuss later, is the basis for much of the conflict that takes place between Korean parents and their children in America, where tantalizing alternatives to the restrictions in the Korean home are offered.

All Confucian societies are male dominant; however, within the home it is the mother who is the primary force. It is she who runs the household and brings up the children, who nurtures, supervises and sanctions. In general, the father is a feared and distant figure who, following the model set by his own father and his father's father before him, had been admonished to teach, direct, and discipline the children. In the past, displays of affection were permitted toward the little ones, especially the girls—at least until they entered puberty, but not otherwise. My sense is that this is changing. As restraints have lessened, fathers in Korea seem to be increasingly free to care for the children and to be warm and affectionate to them in public, but this applies only to the young children. Nevertheless, all my male informants, the products of previous generations, carried the image of their fathers as stern and remote. Though the fathers often acknowledge the desirability of change, they are uncomfortable in reaching out to the children and so they tend to revert to the old pattern of distance, discipline, and instruction. This is not how one establishes a companionable and affectionate relationship.

Moreover, Korean children, especially the adolescents and young adults, are acutely aware that American fathers are different, that they play with their children, join in their activities, that they openly express affection, that they find pleasure in simply being with them and try to be friends rather than authorities. Only recently, a second year law student, during a widely ranging discussion around our breakfast, said that he and his father had never talked openly and candidly together, nor had he seen much of his father because his father worked long hours and slept much of the time during the weekends. He added that as a result he really didn't know his father, which he deeply regretted and resented. Furthermore, he said that although he had many Korean friends, none had a relationship with their father different from his. My impression is that this paradigm is essentially universal. Certainly it is true for the young men that I see in consultation.

The proper stance for a Confucian husband was, and is, to suppress affect, to restrain emotion, to be detached, and to remain aloof, thus constructing a barrier that the wife found difficult if not impossible to penetrate. To do otherwise would be to act improperly, regardless of how he might feel. This also meant that the love and affection that every human needs was denied—a great sacrifice imposed on the men. Not surprisingly, there was also an impressive body of hostility that existed between husbands and wives. It was mostly suppressed although, not infrequently, it broke out into the open.

The women were equally deprived of the love and affection for which they searched. They felt it deeply because they were more aware of the loss. Repeatedly, Korean wives said that what they missed most in their marriages was "romance." Although they may have had an elevated sense of romance based on the American media, the fact that they talked about it at all, and then with such deep feeling, defined their longing for far greater intimacy with their husbands than they had found.

Consequently, the primary emotional tie was, and to a great extent still is, between mother and son, not husband and wife. This is a condition that has perpetuated itself from one generation to the next. The mothers turn to the children, especially the sons and in particular the eldest son, for the comfort and devotion they do not find with their husbands. Thus, for the son, the mother tends to remain the most significant woman throughout life, a classical Oedipal situation. The result is that most Confucian males, particularly in the past, were not able to replace the mother with a woman of equivalent significance. The difference between East and West in this respect is that in East Asian societies it is culturally positive: supported, maintained, and reinforced; in the West it is culturally negative: it is considered abnormal and tends to be denigrated.

A son's tie to his mother, prolonged long past the normal developmental sequence as defined in the West, resulted in a dependency which later, particularly after the mother's death, was transferred to the wife. The catch was that it could not be acknowledged and had to be suppressed. The man had a role to play, and it did not include any show of uncertainty and inadequacy. Thus he was faced with seminal intrapsychic conflict, one that tended to remain unresolved. There always were exceptions, of course, but the overall effect was that everyone suffered: wives, husbands, and children.

Moreover, the mothers, deprived of affection elsewhere, were extremely possessive of the sons. Once the son married, the young wife, even though she might be subdued and self-effacing, represented a serious threat to the mother/son tie, and this was one of the sources (though not the only one) of the distressing mother-in-law/daughter-in-law conflict which has been well documented elsewhere.

Mothers-in-law could be very punitive and hostile to their daughter-in-law. The young wives were intimidated, and they feared the older women's unjustified attacks. However, it was not just resentment of their mothers-in-law that resulted. On a deeper level they were furious with their husbands for rejecting them in favor of their mothers and not protecting them at a time when they needed understanding and support. They were able to express their feelings about their mothers-in-law to other women and receive substantiation, because the mother-in-law issue is openly acknowledged. But it was much more difficult to reveal their despair over their marital relationships, their unhappiness, and their increasing conviction that their husbands would never change. They felt betrayed, desparately alone, with no one to turn to.

The following verbatim consultation with a young wife dramatically focuses the issue: I am very confused. I don't know what to do with my life. I'm unhappy. I'm not even sure whether I love my husband. I don't think he loves me. I have a lot of problems with my in-laws. My mother-in-law is an evil person. In a couple of years my husband has to go back to Korea, and we will be expected to live with his parents because he is the first son. I don't want to live with them. Recently my in-laws visited us from Korea and stayed with us for a couple of months. It was hell (emphasized). Right after they left for Korea I was hospitalized with a kidney infection (hostility introjected). I almost died. I cried all day and night in the hospital. My doctor said that I should see you, but I am afraid that when my husband and my in-laws learn that I am seeing a therapist, they will say I am crazy. I am scared of them. Originally, I was naive of my mother-in-law. I tried to be affectionate and open to her about everything in my life. I related to my in-laws as though they were my real parents. But my mother-in-law twisted everything that I said to her and she put me in the most difficult situations. She is a wicked woman. I feel that she is trying to destroy my relationship with my husband. During their visit my husband joined her and put me down. He humiliated me in front of his parents. I was abused mentally for two months. I am thinking about leaving him, but I don't have any place to go. I am scared. I can go back to my parents. I spoke to my mother who said to me that I can come back to them if I am unhappy with my marriage. She would take care of me.

They maintain control from thousands and thousands of miles away. They continue to tell my husband how to treat me. My husband reports every event to

them. They expect me to call them every so often but I have nothing to say. Not
long ago I received a package from my father-in-law. It was a copy of a book on
moral guidance for women written 500 years ago. I was angry (said with vehe-
mence) with my husband about it and he was no comfort to me. He disregarded
my feelings. My husband is *very* attached to his parents, especially to his mother.
He seems to listen to everything that they say and to depend on them. He listens
to his mother more than he listens to me.[1]

This was a distraught young woman who may well have overstated the
problem, but the essence of her profound unhappiness is clearly established.
She is not alone.

The majority of Koreans, especially those who have arrived recently, try to
hold on to the traditions and values of the past. The parents attempt to bring up
their children in America in the same manner that they themselves were raised
in Korea. Living in this environment at home, and in quite another outside the
home, the children are caught in a conflict between Confucian and American
values. Forced into a world of opposites they are confronted with a true
dilemma. The ultimate question for them is: how does one reconcile the two?

As complex as this is for the children, it is equally so for the parents. Confucianism may preach a message of superior male status, but as those of us know
who have lived in a Korean household, the family is centered around the children. In all Confucian societies, and perhaps particularly so in Korea, the children are infinitely precious. Not only does the future of the family depend upon
them, the future of the lineage, especially in *"yangban"* families,[2] rests on their
shoulders as well. Add to this the love the parents feel for their young ones, and
their deep concern that their lives should turn out well. Moreover, most first
generation Korean men, unfamiliar with the new world that they have entered,
handicapped by language and social form, find that they must limit their personal goals. However, their aspirations can be realized through the accomplishments of their children. Yale and Harvard, Columbia and Princeton are well
within reach of these highly intelligent, talented offspring if, in the eyes of the
parents, they are brought up properly.

Every culture carries an image of what constitutes good parenting, and the
Korean Confucian image does not mesh with the American. Nor, for that matter, with that held by the rest of the Western world. To further complicate the
matter, times have changed—the world moves on—not only for the Koreans in
America, but also for the Koreans in Korea. And, may I add, for Americans as
well.

The overriding issue for both children and parents is freedom. For the children it brings release from onerous cultural and parental restrictions; for the
parents it represents new but intimidating opportunities. It is not only the

children who are torn between the old and the new; it is the parents as well. Even though on the surface the older generation may hold tightly to their past and deny the new, on a deeper, subconscious level the freedom offered in America is perceived as desirable, although they may not be able to admit it.

It must be recognized, however, that Confucianism, burdensome as it may have been, brought with it a deeply felt sense of security: everyone knew their exact place in the social schema, the precise path that they were assigned to tread, and the specific personal parameters that existed for them. Nothing was left to chance or improvisation. On the other hand, except for the law which codifies every social system, democracy presents shifting guide posts. Democracy is not an unmixed blessing; it also brings insecurity, anxiety, and fear (Fromm 1941).

It is also important to realize that freedom, as practiced in America and elsewhere, can lead to a sense of alienation from one's fellow man, to a sense of not being an integral part of a broader community nor, for that matter, a family. This was never true for Confucianism. The Korean family offered a solid base. One's sense of belonging was never challenged. Everyone was always a part of a well defined whole. There were few, if any, "outsiders." This is one of the reasons that the family in Korea has remained so powerful a force.

As turbulent as the battle within the home may be, ultimately the children are in the more powerful position, because under no circumstances are the parents willing to lose them. Before positions are irretrievably frozen, I find that the parents will compromise. The adult children whom I know and with whom I have worked are usually the more flexible by far, and they sincerely attempt to work out a modus vivendi. But pushed to the ultimate in matters of great consequence, such as marriage or career, they will usually balk and refuse to make further concessions. It is at this point that the parents usually concede. I have found only one exception, and in this instance the parents were paranoid and actually drove their only son out because he married a woman of whom they disapproved (who is, incidentally, a very fine person).

CONCLUSION

It would appear that sociopolitical systems that result in governance have to be related to the historical era and the evolving nature of the people whose lives they effect. Thus, although the mesh between those governed and the system that governs them may be effective for one time period, it may not be so for another. With the advent of Jeffersonian democracy and the influence of Western thought, we have increasingly witnessed major changes in the aspirations and patterns of behavior throughout the world.

This specifically includes Korea, as well as the other East Asian nations. The future of the Confucian societies will be determined as it unfolds. The issue is process—evolving process, which will determine its own goals and achieve-ments. Yet the constructive components of Confucianism: the centrality of the family; the crucial importance of the children; the emphasis upon education and learning; a respect for moral values; a commitment to hard work, and an intrinsic acknowledgement that gain comes only through effort (together with an unanticipated entrepreneurial spirit) will provide a solid base wherever the future may lead. As we have seen in these past few years, the Koreans have pros-pered dramatically, and their achievements have been impressive.

ENDNOTES

1. Case presented with permission of Dr. Mia Kim.
2. These are upper-class families, usually of noble lineage.

References

Akhtar, S. 1995. A third individuation: Immigration, identity, and the psychoanalytic process. *Journal of the American Psychoanalytic Association*, 43:1051–1084.

Allen, D. 1991. Indian, Marxist, and feminist critques of the "modern" concepts of the self. In *Culture and self: Philosophical and religious perspectives, East and West*, ed. by D. Allen and A. Malhotra. Boulder, CO: Westview.

Atwood, G. and R. Stolorow. 1984. *Structures of subjectivity: Explorations in psychoanalytic phenomenology*. New Jersey: The Analytic Press.

Bellak, L., and H. Siegel. 1983. *Handbook of intensive brief and emergency psychotherapy*. New York: C. P. S. Inc.

Bernstein, D. 1993. *Female identity conflict in clinical practice,* ed. N. Freedman and B. Distler). New Jersey: Jason Aronson.

Bion, W. 1970. *Attention and interpretation*. New York: Basic Books.

Bond, M. and K. Hwang. 1986. The social psychology of Chinese people. In *The psychology of Chinese people*, ed. by M. Bond, 213–266. New York: Oxford University Press.

Boucher, S. 1988. *Turning the wheel: American women creating the new Buddhism*. San Francisco: Harper and Row.

Brown, D. 1986. The stages of meditation in cross-cultural perspective. In Wilbur, K. J. Engler, and D. Brown. *Transformations of consciousness: Conventional and contemplative perspectives on development*. Boston and London: Shambhala.

Cabaniss, D. L., M. A. Oquendo, and M. B. Singer. 1994. The impact of psychoanalytic values on transference and countertransference: A study in transcultural psychotherapy. *Journal American Academy of Psychoanalysis*, 22:609–622.

Carrington, P. 1977. *Freedom in meditation*. Garden City, New York: Anchor Press/Doubleday.

Caudhill, W., and D. W. Plath. 1974. Who sleeps by whom? Parent-child involvement in urban Japanese families. In *Japanese culture and behavior*, ed. by T. Lebra and W. Lebra, 277-312. Honolulu: University Press of Hawaii.

Chakraborty, S. K. 1987. *Managerial effectiveness and quality of worklife: Indian insights*. New Delhi: Tata McGraw-Hill Publishing Company Limited.

Chang, H-C and G. R. Holt. 1995. Debt-repaying mechanism in Chinese relationships: An exploration of the folk concepts of *pao* and human emotional debt. *Research on Language and Social Interaction*. 27:351–387.

Cheung, F. 1985. An overview of psychopathology in Hong Kong with special reference to somatic presentations. In *Chinese culture and mental health*, ed. by W. S. Tseng and D. Wu. Orlando, Florida: Academic Press.

Clarke, C., C. Peach, and S. Vertovec, ed. 1990 *South Asians overseas: Migration and ethnicity*. New York: Cambridge University Press.

Coltart, N. 1992. The practice of psychoanalysis and Buddhism. In *Slouching towards Bethlehem*, 164–175. New York and London: Guilford Press.

Confucius. 1960. *Book VIII*, chapter ii.

———. 1960. *Book XII*, chapter i, 2.

———. 1960. *Book XII*, chapter i, 1.

Cooper, P. 1995. Affects and affect states: A case study on the integration of Buddhist analytic meditation and psychoanalysis. Unpublished paper.

Daniels, R. 1990. *History of Indian immigration in the United States: An interpretive essay*. New York: The Asian Society.

Dayal, I. 1977. *Change in work organization*. Delhi: Concept Pub.

Desai, P., and G. Coelho. 1980. Indian immigrants in America: Some cultural aspects of psychological adaptation. In *The new ethnics: Asian Indians in the United States*, ed. by P. Saran and E. Eames, 363–386. New York: Praeger.

Deri, S. 1984. *Symbolization and creativity*. New York: International Universities Press.

DeVos, G. 1980. Afterword to *The quiet therapies*, by D. K. Reynolds, 113–132. Honolulu: University Press of Hawaii.

Doi, T. 1973. *The anatomy of dependence*. Tokyo: Kodansha International Ltd.

———. 1986. *The anatomy of self: The individual versus the society*. Tokyo: Kodansha International Ltd.

Dumont, L. 1986. *Essays on individualism*. Chicago: University of Chicago Press.

Eberhard, W. 1965. *Folktales of China* (3rd revision). Chicago: University of Chicago Press.

Eigen, M. 1995. Stones in a stream. *Psychoanalytic Review*, 82:371–390.

Engler, J. 1986. Therapeutic aims in psychotherapy and meditation. In Wilbur, K., J. Engler, and D. Brown. *Transformations of consciousness: Conventional and contemplative perspectives on development*. Boston and London: Shambhala.

Epstein, M. 1995. *Thoughts without a thinker: Psychotherapy from a Buddhist perspective*. New York: Basic Books.

Erikson, E. 1946. Ego development and historical change. In *Identity and the life cycle*. New York: International Universities Press. Reprint 1959.

————. 1950. *Childhood and society*. New York: W. W. Norton.

————. 1958. *Young man Luther*. New York: W. W. Norton.

————, 1963. *Childhood and society*. 2nd ed. New York: W. W. Norton.

————, 1968. *Identity, youth, and crisis*. New York: W. W. Norton.

————. 1969. *Gandhi's truth*. New York: W. W. Norton.

Ewing, C. 1991. Can psychoanalytic theories explain the Pakistani woman? Intrapsychic autonomy and interpersonal engagement in the extended family. *Ethos*. 19:131–160.

Fields, H. 1938. *The refugee in the United States*. New York: Oxford University Press.

Finn, M. 1992. Transitional space and Tibetan Buddhism: The object relations of meditation. In *Object relations theory and religious experience*, ed. by M. Finn and J. Gartner. New York: Praeger.

Fisher, M. P. 1980. *The Indians of New York City: A study of immigrants from India*. New Delhi: Heritage Publishers.

Freud, S. 1923. The ego and the id. *Standard edition*. 19:13–59. London: Hogarth Press, 1953.

————. 1927. The future of an illusion. *Standard Edition*, 21:5–56. London: Hogarth Press.

————, 1930. Civilization and its discontents. *Standard edition*. 21:64–148. London: Hogarth Press, 1953.

Fromm, E. 1941. *Escape from freedom*. New York: Rinehart.

Fromm, E., D. T. Suzuki, and R. DeMartino. 1960. *Zen Buddhism and psychoanalysis*. New York: Harper and Row.

Gilligan, C. 1980. *In a different voice*. Cambridge: Harvard University Press.

Goleman, D. 1977. *The varieties of meditative experience*. New York: Dutton.

Gonzales, Jr., J. L. 1992. *Racial and ethnic families in America*. Dubuque, Iowa: Kendall/Hunt Publishing Company.

Grey, A. 1973. Oedipus in Hindu dreams. *Contemporary Psychoanalysis*. 9:327–355.

Grolnick, S. and L. Barkin, ed. 1978. *Between reality and fantasy*. New York: Jason Aronson.

Gupta, R. 1991. Integrating employees and organization in the Indian context: The need for moving beyond American and Japanese models. *Political and Economic Monthly*, May.

Hagman, G. 1996. Flight from the subjectivity of the other: Pathological adaptation to early parent-loss. In *Progress in self psychology, volume 12*, ed. by Arnold Goldberg. Hillsdale, New Jersey: The Analytic Press.

Harvard Mental Health Letter. 1990. *Marriage and psychiatric symptoms: Ethnic differences*, December, p. 7.

Heimann, P. 1950. On countertransference. *International Journal Psycho-Analysis*, 50.

Hofstede, G. 1980. *Culture's consequences: International differences in work-related values*. Beverly Hills: Sage Publications.

Hong, B. 1985. Politeness in Chinese: Impersonal pronouns and personal greetings. *Anthropological Linguistics*. 27:204–213.

Hsu, F. L. K. 1981. *Americans and Chinese: Passage to differences* (3rd Edition, 76–120). Honolulu: University of Hawaii Press.

———. 1983. Suppression versus repression: A limited psychological interpretation of four cultures. In *Rugged individualism reconsidered*, ed. F. L. K. Hsu, 104–129. Knoxville: University of Tennessee Press.

———. 1985. The self in cross-cultural perspective. In *Culture and self: Asian and Western perspectives*, ed. A. Marsella, G. DeVos, and F. L. K. Hsu, 24–55. London: Tavistock Publications.

———. 1985. The Chinese family: Relations, problems, and therapy. In *Chinese culture and mental health*, ed. W. S. Tseng and D. Wu, 95–112. Orlando, Florida: Academic Press.

Jackson, S. W. 1968. Aspects of culture in psychoanalytic theory and practice. *Journal American Psychoanalytic Association.* 16:651–670.

Jensen, J. M. 1988. *Passage from India: Asian Indian immigrants in North America.* New Haven: Yale University Press.

Johnson, F. 1985. The Western concept of self. In *Culture and Self: Asian and Western perspectives*, ed. A. Marsella, G. DeVos, and F. L. K. Hsu, 91–138. London: Tavistock Publications.

Joseph, B. 1985. Transference: The total situation. *International Journal Psycho-Analysis.* 66:447–454.

Kakar, S. 1978. *The inner world: A psychoanalytic study of childhood and society in India.* Delhi: Oxford University Press.

———. 1980. Observations on "the Oedipal alliance" in a patient with a narcissistic personality disorder. *Samiksa.* 34:47–53.

———. 1982. *Shamans, mystics, and doctors.* New York: Alfred A. Knopf.

———. 1989a. The maternal-feminine in Indian psychoanalysis. *International Review of Psycho-Analysis.* 16:355–362.

———. 1989b. *Intimate relations: Exploring Indian sexuality.* Chicago: University of Chicago Press.

———. 1991. *The analyst and the mystic.* New Delhi: Viking by Penguin Books India.

Khandelwal, M. S. 1995. Indian immigrants in Queens, New York City: Patterns of spatial concentration and distribution. In *Nation migration: The politics of space in the South Asian diaspora*, ed. P. van der Veer. Philadelphia: University of Pennsylvania Press.

Kirschner, S. R. 1992. Anglo-American values in post-Freudian psychoanalysis. In *Psychoanalytic anthropology after Freud*, ed. D. H. Spain, 162–197. New York: Psyche Press.

Kleinman, A. 1985. Somatization: The interconnections in Chinese society among culture, depressive experiences, and the meanings of pain. In *Culture and depression*, ed. A. Kleinman and B. Good, 429–490. Berkeley: University of California Press.

Kohut, H. 1971. *Analysis of the self.* New York: International Universities Press.

———. 1977. *Restoration of the self.* New York: International Universities Press.

———. 1984. *How does analysis cure?* Chicago: University of Chicago Press.

Kornfield, J. 1977. *Living Buddhist masters*. Santa Cruz: Unity Press.

Kumar, R. 1993. Communicative conflict in intercultural negotiations: The case of American and Japanese business negotiations. Unpublished paper.

Kurtz, S. 1992. *All the mothers are one*. New York: Columbia University Press.

Lachmann, F. and B. Beebe. 1995. Self psychology: Today. *Psychoanalytic Dialogues*, 5(3): 375–384.

Leavy, S. 1995. Roots of unitive experience. *Psychoanalytic Review*, 82:349–370.

Lichtenstein, H. 1977. *The dilemma of human identity*. New York: Jason Aronson.

Lin, T. Y. 1985. Mental disorders and psychiatry in Chinese culture: Characteristic features and major issues. In *Chinese culture and mental health*, ed. W. S. Tseng and D. Wu, 369–393. Orlando, Florida: Academic Press.

Lin, T. Y. and M. C. Lin. 1981. Love, denial, and rejection: Responses of Chinese families to mental illness. In *Normal and abnormal behavior in Chinese behavior*, ed. A. Kleinman and T. Y. Lin, 387–401. Norwell, Massachusetts: D. Reidel.

Liu, I. M. 1986. *Chinese cognition in the psychology of the Chinese people*, 73–105. New York: Oxford University Press.

Lo, Kitt. C. 1958. *Cooking the Chinese way*. London: Arco Publication Co.

Mahler, M., F. Pine, and A. Bergman. 1975. *Psychological birth of the human infant*. New York: Basic Books.

Markus, H. and S. Kitayama. 1991. Culture and the self: Implications for cognition, emotion, and motivation. *Psychological Review*. 98:224–253.

Marriott, M. 1990. Constructing an Indian ethnosociology. In *India through Hindu categories*, ed. M. Marriott, 1–40. New Delhi, London: Sage Publications.

Masson, J. M. 1976. The psychology of the ascetic. *Journal Asian Studies*, 35:611–625.

Mazumdar, S. 1991. Asian American and Asian studies: Rethinking roots. In *Asian Americans: Comparative and global perspectives*, ed. S. Hune, H. Kim, S. Fugita, and A. Ling. Pullman: Washington State University Press.

Meaders, N. 1996. The transcultural self. In *Immigrant experiences: Personal narrative and psychological analysis*, ed. P. Ellowitz and C. Kahn. Teaneck, N.J.: Farleigh Dickinson University Press.

Meissner, W. W. 1984. *Psychoanalysis and religious experience*. New York and London: Yale University Press.

Miller, B. S., trans. and ed. 1977. *Love song of the dark lord, Jayadeva's Gitagovinda*. New York: Columbia University Press.

Milner, M. 1973. Some notes on psychoanalytic ideas about mysticism. *The suppressed madness of sane men*. 1987. London: Tavistock Publications.

Mitchell, S. 1988. *Relational concepts in psychoanalysis: An integration*. Cambridge: Harvard University Press.

Nakane, C. 1970. *Japanese society*. Berkeley and Los Angeles: University of California Press.

Nandy, A. 1979. The double in Hindi films. *Times of India*. October 14.

Nelson, Benjamin. 1965. Self-images and systems of spiritual direction in the history of European civilization. In *The quest for self-control*, ed. S. Z. Klausner. New York: Free Press.

Noy, P. 1969. A revision of the psychoanalytic theory of the primary process. *International Journal Psycho-Analysis*. 50:155–178.

Oatey, H. 1988. Chinese and Western interpersonal relationships. In *Intercultural Communication: What it means to Chinese learners of English*, ed. H. Wenzhong. Shanghai: Shanghai Translation Publishing House.

Okano, K. 1994. Shame and social phobia: A transcultural viewpoint. *Bulletin of the Menninger Clinic*. 58:323–338.

Pareek, U. 1977. Culture and organization designing. Proactive or reactive strategy? *Vikalpa*, 2(4), 303–308.

Pillsbury, B. 1986. *Medical learning in North America: A handbook for Chinese visiting scholars in the United States and Canada*. San Francisco: U. S. China Education Institute.

Ramanujan, A.K. 1983. The Indian Oedipus. In *Oedipus: A folklore casebook*, ed. L. Edmunds and A. Dundes, 234–261. London: Garland Publishing.

————. 1990. Is there an Indian way of thinking?: An informal essay. In *India through Hindu categories*, ed. McKim Marriott, 41–58. New Delhi, London: Sage Publications.

Ramanujam, B. K. 1989. Technical factors in psychotherapy in India. Unpublished paper.

Rizzuto, A. 1979. *The birth of the living God: A psychoanalytic study*. Chicago and London: University of Chicago Press.

Roland, A. 1972. Imagery and symbolic expression in dreams and art. *International Journal Psycho-Analysis*. 53:531–539.

————. 1988. *In search of self in India and Japan: Toward a cross-cultural psychology*. Princeton: Princeton University Press.

Rubin, J. 1996. *Pathways to transformation: An integrative study of psychoanalysis and Buddhism*. New York: Plenum Press.

Rycroft, C. 1968. *Imagination and reality*. New York: International Universities Press.

Sanjek, R. 1989. *Worship and community: Christianity and Hinduism in contemporary Queens*. Flushing, N.Y.: Asian/American Center, Queens College.

Schafer, R. 1983. *The analytic attitude*. New York: Basic Books.

Shweder, R.A. and E. J. Bourne. 1984. Does the concept of the person vary cross-culturally? In *Culture theory: Essays on mind, self, and emotion*. ed. R. Shweder and R. LeVine, 158–199. Cambridge, Melbourne, New York: Cambridge University Press.

Sinha, J. 1980a. Power structure, perceptual frame, and behavioral strategies in dyadic relationships. Unpublished paper presented at the International Association for Cross-Cultural Psychology, Bhubaneswar.

————. 1980b. *The nurturant task leader: A model of the effective executive*. New Delhi: Concept Publishing.

————. 1988. Reorganizing values for development. In Sinha, D. and H. S. R. Kao (eds.), *Social values and development: Asian perspectives*. New Delhi: Sage Pub.

Slater, P. 1970. *The pursuit of loneliness*. Boston: Beacon Press.

Slote, W. and G. DeVos, eds. 1996. *Confucianism and the family in an interdiscipli-nary, comparative context.* New York: State University of New York Press.

Spitz, R. 1959. *A genetic field theory of ego formation.* New York: International Uni-versities Press.

Stolorow, R. and G. Atwwod. 1992. *Contexts of being: The intersubjective foundations of psychological life.* New York: Analytic Press.

Sue, S. and N. Zane. 1987. The role of culture and cultural techniques in psy-chotherapy. *American Psychologist*, 42:37–45.

Suler, J. 1993. *Contemporary psychoanalysis and Eastern thought.* Albany: State Univer-sity of New York Press.

Sylvan, M. 1981. Reply to Alan Roland's paper on "Psychoanalytic perspectives on personality development in India." *International Review of Psycho-Analysis.* 8:93–99.

Taketomo, Y. 1982. The reticent father: Some thoughts on Japanese culture and conflict. *Journal of the American Academy of Psychoanalysis.* 26:12–14.

———. 1986. *Amae* as metalanguage: A critique of Doi's theory of *amae. Journal of the American Academy of Psychoanalysis*, 14:525–544.

———. 1989. An American-Japanese transcultural psychoanalysis and the issue of teacher transference. *Journal of the American Academy of Psychoanalysis*, 17:427–450.

Tan, Y. C. 1988. *Notes of a Chinese psychiatrist.* Beijing: Quonzhong Publications. (In Chinese)

Tseng, W. S. 1975. The nature of somatic complaints among psychiatric patients: The Chinese case. *Comprehensive Psychiatry*, 16:237–245.

Tung, M. 1984. Life values, psychotherapy, and East-West integration. *Psychiatry*, 47:285–292.

Uba, L. 1994. *Asian Americans: Personality patterns, identity, and mental health.* New York: The Guilford Press.

Vatsayayan, K. 1975. In the performing arts. In *Indian women*, ed. D. Jain, 291–300. Delhi: Publications Division, Ministry of Information and Broad-casting, Government of India.

Wadley, S. 1980. Hindu women's family and household rites in a North Indian vil-lage. In *Unspoken worlds: Women's religious lives in non-Western cultures*, ed. R. Gross and N. Falk, 94–109. New York: Harper and Row.

White, M. 1987. *The Japanese educational challenge: A commitment to children.* New York: Free Press.

Wilbur, K., J. Engler, and D. Brown. 1986. *Transformations of consciousness: Conven-tional and contemplative perspectives on development.* Boston and London: Shambhala.

Williams, C. A. S. 1976. *Outline of Chinese symbolism and art motifs* (3rd edition). New York: Dover Publications.

Winnicott, D. W. 1951. Transitional objects and transitional phenomena. In *Col-lected Papers.* New York: Basic Books.

———. 1958. The capacity to be alone. In *The maturational processes and the facili-tating environment*, 29–36. London: Hogarth Press, 1965.

————. 1960. Ego distortion in terms of true and false self. In *The maturational processes and the facilitating environment*, 140–152. London: Hogarth Press, 1965.

————. 1965. *The maturational processes and the facilitating environment*. London: Hogarth Press.

Yang, H. Y. 1983. Phobia and its psychological treatment. *Chinese Journal of Nervous and Mental Disease*, 9:102–103. (In Chinese).

Yang, M. M-H. 1994. *Gifts, favors, and banquets: The art of social relationship in China*. Ithaca, New York: Cornell University Press.

Young, L. W. L. 1994. *Crosstalk and culture in Sino-American communication*. Cambridge: Cambridge University Press.

Zhao, G. Y. 1987. Eight cases of anxiety disorders and obsessive compulsive behavior. *Chinese Mental Health Journal*, 1:236. (In Chinese).

Zhao, G. Y. 1988. Fear of height and "treatment dependency." *Chinese Mental Health Journal*, 2:90. (In Chinese).

Zhong, Y. B. 1988. *Chinese psychoanalysis*. People's Publication of Lian Nin. (In Chinese).

Index

Agoraphobia: case of Lynn, 180
Ahmed: problems in management relationships, 167–168; problems with his
   father, 169–170
Akahisa: rebellion against maternal expectations, 80
Albert: ethnic layering of the self, 92
Alka: multiple mothering and selfobject
   relationships, 113–114
Amae: entitlement, 124; in Japanese,
   15–17; psychopathology in Japanese, 17;
   transference with Keigo, 78
Americans: artistic creativity and Japanese,
   52–54; changes in attitudes towards
   Asians, V, VI; child-parent communication, 56; comparison with Japanese on
   child rearing, 55–57; comparison with
   Japanese on decision-making, 49–50; ego
   boundaries, 18–19; experiential sense of
   self, 35; in Asian spiritual hierarchies,
   41–43; interface with Indians and Japanese, VII, VIII; management theories, 159;
   misunderstanding of Indian-Americans
   in corporations, 35; misunderstanding
   with Japanese in corporations, 45, 48–51;
   negotiations with Japanese, 50, 58; reactions to Indian intimacy, 34; spiritual
   practices and identity, 152
Andrew: sociohistorical holocaust trauma,
   96–97

Anger: in Japanese patients toward the
   mother; transference and anxiety in Asian
   patients,
Anglos: discourse compared with Chinese,
   61; miscommunication with Chinese, 59
Anjali: relationship with her father,
   135–136; unconscious rivalry with her
   mother, 135
Anthony, 168, 171–173
Artistic creativity: Japanese and American
   comparison, IX, 52–54
Ashis: emotional conflicts and spiritual discipline, 149
Asians: psychoanalytic understanding of,
   VIII
Asok: problematic use of the magic-cosmic
   world, 75; seeking advice and guidance
   in the transference, 76
Astrology: Asian involvement in, 146–147;
   career choice, 155; marriage, 154; Western views of, 146. *See also* Magic-cosmic

Barry: Chinese-American in psychotherapy,
   181–183
Bhatt, Geeta: analysis of conflict in Indian-
   American families, 39–40
Bicultural self: conflicts between first and
   second generation Indian-Americans,
   37–38; conflicts in second generation
   Indian-Americans, 37–38; ego psycho-

logical analysis, 43; in second generation Indian-Americans, 36–38; Indians in the United States, IX, 27, 31

brothers: envy in Indian relationships between, 163–164

Buddhism: emotional problems in the United States, 41–42; meditation and psychoanalysts, XII; psychoanalytic institutes, 157

Calvinism: roots of individualism, 5

Career: comparison of Indian and American women, 40

Carl: intercultural misunderstanding, 34

Character-formation: in Indians, 141–143; influence of culture on, XI

Child rearing: Japanese and American comparison, 54–57; Japanese maternal expectations, 57

Child-parent relationship: social change in Korean-Americans, 196–197

Children: conflict in Indian-American families, 40

Chinese: comparison of self with Americans, XIII; comparison with Anglos, 59; defense mechanisms, 177; family emotions and expectations of sons, 182; family relationships and psychotherapy, 184; hierarchical relationships, 64; immigration to the United States, VI, XVI; interface with Americans through language, IX; locus of control of the self, 185; self, nature of, 63, 175–176; communication by silence, 115; thinking of oneself, 181; topic-comment linguistic construction, 62; tradition in the West, 183. *See also* Chinese-Americans

Chinese-Americans: in psychotherapy, 177–178, 180–183; therapeutic territory, 183–184. *See also* Chinese

Colonial attitudes: internalized by Indians, 163

Communication: by metaphorizing situations and objects, 112; by silences among Asians, 108–109, 115; child-parent relationship in Japanese and Americans, 56; Chinese social cooperation, 64; conflict between Japanese and American modes

of, 85; conflict in Indian families, 38; empathic sensing among Japanese, 80–81; in American-Japanese educational relationship, 52; in Japanese and American intercultural marriages, 53–54; Japanese private self, 48; problems between Americans and Indians in a spiritual hierarchy, 42–43; variations by Indians and Japanese in psychoanalytic relationship, 120; varying with ego boundaries and kinds of individuality, 19–20. *See also* Miscommunication

Conflict: handling of, in Indian and Indian-American families, 38, 39–40; in the cultural self, X

Confucianism: conflicts with American individualism, XIII, 190; contrast with American values, 188; Korean family, 192–193; nature of, 189; ritual, self, and social interaction, 63–64

Conscience: character development in Indians, 142; Chinese collective, 63; Indians in the United States, 27; Kant's concept of, 7–8; perfectionistic, in Japanese, 79–80; Reformation, 7

Construction: Chinese topic-comment linguistic, 62

Corporations: decision-making process, Japanese and American, 49–50; Japanese and American misunderstandings in Japanese, 45, 48–51; Japanese in American 51; Japanese interface with Americans, IX; misunderstandings between Indian-Americans and other Americans, 35; negotiations between Americans and Japanese, 50; training by Japanese and Americans, 50. *See also* Management relationships

Creative process: Japanese and American comparison, 45, 52–53

Countertransference: and meditation, 151; Keigo and his mother, 125; projective identification and individualism, 9–10

Cultural anthropology: reexamination of individualism, VII, 79

Cultural expectations: in psychoanalytic relationship with Indians and Japanese, 79

Cultural hurdles: Chinese and British, 60;

Chinese and British differences in world-view and personal engagement, 63; Chinese and British differing grammar and language structure, 62

Cultural ideals: Japanese 48

Cultural/psychological: continuum of normality/psychopathology, 73; interface of Indians with Americans, 25; interface of Japanese with Americans, 46

Cultural self: conceptualization of, 84–85; ethnic layering of, 91–92; in psychoanalysis, 83–84; in the transference, 88–89; psychological conflict, X, 85–86, 90–91; regional self of Lucille, 97–98. *See also* Culture; Self

Culture: and transference XI, 122–125; in clinical psychoanalysis, IX, X; in psychoanalytic relationship, X; influences on psychoanalysis, VIII; relationship to self psychology, X, XI. *See also* Cultural self; Norms; Values

Cultural values: personal psychopathology, 77–79. *See also* Culture; Norms; Values

Daughter-father relationship: in Indians, 141

Daughter-in-law: behavior and expectations with in-laws

Daughter-in-law/mother-in-law relationship: in Koreans, 195–196

Daughter-mother relationship: Mrs. Kakkar, 73–74

David: Chinese-American in psychotherapy, 177–178

Decision-making: American and Japanese comparison, 49–50; in Japanese groups, 47

Defenses: Eastern and Western comparison, 177

Deficits: and the spiritual, 148–149. *See also* Depression; Emotional conflicts; Psychopathology

Democracy: social change in Koreans, 197

Dependence: American and Japanese comparison on child rearing, 56; cultural expectations in Indians and Japanese, 79; in exchange for esteem, 33–34, 120; in hierarchical intimacy relationships, 32;

in Japanese, 15–17; Indian receptiveness to, 142

Depression: case of Z, 180; in a Chinese man, 177–178; in Barry, a Chinese-American, 182, 183; in Vijay, 164–166. *See also* Deficit; Emotional Conflicts; Psychological Conflict; Psychopathology

Depressive position: relationship to individualism, 10

Destiny, personal: in psychoanalytic therapy, 152–155

Detachment: related to sexuality and spirituality in Indians, 143

Dharma: Indians in the United States, 27

Discourse: Chinese foregrounding background information, 65; Chinese style of, 64; Chinese worldview, 63; Chinese and British comparison, 60

Doi, Takeo: dependency relationships, 15–17; dual-self structure, 15; individualism, 15–16; psychoanalytic relativism and universalism, 15–17

Dolores: layering of the self, 99–100

Drive theory: critique of, as applied to Indians, 142–143; influences of culture on, XI

Dualism: emotions and rationality in Western culture, 8; in the psychoanalytic process, 8; in Western culture, 6

Economics: changes in American attitudes towards Asians, VI; roots of individualism, 6

Education: and marriage in Indian-Americans, 38; Asian hierarchical expectations in, in the United States, 30; Asian immigration, VI; in psychotherapy with Chinese, 185–186; Korean-Americans, 191–192

Egalitarian: comparison with Confucianism, 193. *See also* Equality

Ego boundaries: American in an Indian setting, 74; Asian and American comparison, 18–19; in hierarchical intimacy relationships, 32; psychopathology in Asians and Americans, 19

Ego-ideal: in Japanese, 5; Indian deference

in hierarchical relationships, 142; Japanese standards and psychoanalytic therapy, 79–80; Japanese-Indian-American comparison of the, 48; Yoshiko's vulnerability to criticism, 85–86

Ego psychology: use of, in psychological universalism, 14–15

Emotions: in Chinese, 182; Western philosophical assumptions concerning, 8

Emotional conflicts: and the spiritual, 148–151. See also Depression; Obsessive-compulsive; Psychological conflict; Psychopathology

Empathic attunement: Asian patients with the psychoanalyst, 118; differing contents of, across cultures, 109–110; differing modes of, across cultures, 108–109. See also Empathic sensing; Empathy

Empathic sensing: Japanese nonverbal communication, 80–81. See also Empathic attunement; Empathy

Empathy: in hierarchical intimacy relationships, 32; in Japanese intimacy relationships, 48; Indian interface with Americans, 33; of psychoanalyst with Asian patients' value dissonances in the United States, 85–86. See also Empathic attunement

English: Indian English, 44

Enlightenment: influence on psychoanalysis, XII; modes of reasoning, 6; roots of individualism, 5–6; views of religion, 6, 145

Entitlement: in Japanese, 124. See also Amae

Envy: among Indian brothers, XIII, 163–166

Equality: child-parent communication in Americans, 56; Indian-American women, 40. See also Egalitarian

Erikson, Erik: critique of individualism, 11; self-creation of identity, 11; sociocultural and sociohistorical factors in personality and psychopathology, 83–84

Erotic: relationship to spirituality, XI

Ethnic self: dissonant parental values, 93–94; layering of, in Graziella and Albert, 91–92; layering of the self, X

Evolutionism: relationship to psychoanalysis, 13; in work of Sudhir Kakar, 13–14

Ewing, Catherine: psychological universalism, 14–15

Family: attitudes in Indian management relationships, 168–169; Chinese, 176; Chinese and Western comparison, 184; conflict and communication in Indians, 38; Confucianism and Koreans, 189–190; description of Korean, 192–195; envy among Indian brothers, 164–166; Indian extended, and Oedipus Complex, 136–139; Japanese and American intercultural marriages and child rearing, 54–57; Japanese i.e., 58; Korean, 188; women in Indian extended, 139, 141; social change in Korean-American, 192–197; values and attitudes in Japanese and Indian organizations, 159–160. See also Family reputation

Family reputation: as selfobject in Asians, 106; Indian college girls' sexuality, 139; resistance to psychoanalytic therapy, 121; sexuality of Indian women, 139–140. See also Family

Fate: Indian attitudes towards, 153

Father: in Japanese child rearing, 56–57; social change in Korean families, 193

Father-daughter relationship: in Indians, 141

Father-son relationship: in Chinese, 182–183; in Indians, 138, 169–172

Feminism: Lucille and layering of the self, 98–100; reexamination of Western culture and individualism, VII

Filipinos: immigration to the United States, VI,, XVI

Frank: dissonant ethnic encounters in the self, 93–94

Freedom: social change in Korean-Americans, 196–197

Freud: assumptions of individualism, 8; critique of rationality, 7

Futia, Christine: Indian-Americans in corporations, 35

Geeta: parental attitudes towards education and marriage, 38

George: value dissonances in an intercultural marriage, 81–82

Gopal: family reputation and we-self esteem, 76

Graziella: cultural self and laundry compulsion, 90–91; ethnic layering of the self, 91–92

Group therapy: transference repetition of an Indian man in, 76

Harmony: in Chinese food, 65–66; in Chinese hierarchical relationships, 64–65

Hierarchical intimacy relationships: ego boundaries in, 32; in psychoanalytic therapy, 119–120; interface with Americans, 33; nature of, in Asians, 32; we-self in, 32. *See also*

Hierarchical relationships; Hierarchical relationships, formal; Hierarchy by personal qualities

Hierarchical relationships: American-Asian interface, 41–43; Japanese and American interface, 29–30; Asians in psychoanalysis, 118–120; Chinese, 64; comparison with American individualism, 27–28; formal hierarchy of Indians, 28–31; Indian expecations, 76; Indian work setting, 161; Indian-American men in families and at work, 39; interface of Indians and Americans, 27–35, 29–30; Japanese we-self and communication, 4; Japanese hierarchy, 46–48; selfobject relationships and self-esteem in Asians, 103–104; two poles of Japanese hierarchy in Keigo's transference, 78; Western undermining of Indian, 162–163, 164. *See also* Hierarchical intimacy relationships; Hierarchical relationships, formal; Hierarchy by personal qualities;

Hierarchical relationships, formal: Japanese decision-making, 47; Japanese in American corporation, 51; Japanese work group and mentor-disciple relationship, 46–47; Japanese and Indian comparison of public and private selves, 48; reciprocal expectations in Indians, 28–29. *See also* Hierarchy by personal qualities; Hierarchical intimacy relationships; Hierarchical relationships

Hierarchy: Indian cultural notions and American egalitarianism, 31

Hierarchy by personal qualities: attitudes and relationships, 31–32. *See also* Hierarchical intimacy relationships; Hierarchical relationships; Hierarchical relationships, formal

Hunger strike: Vijay, 165

Husband: Indian-American hierarchical expectations, 39, 40; in Korean Confucian family, 194

Hyperventilation: in Lynn, Chinese-American, 180,181. *See also* Emotional conflicts; Psychological conflict; Psychopathology

Idei, Yoshiko: 55

Idealization: Asian relationship with psychoanalyst, 119; by personal qualities of the superior in Asians, 105–106; in Indian hierarchical work relationships, 161; in Japanese hierarchical relationships, 79; mentorship and psychoanalytic relationship with Japanese, 79; psychological goal of Asian idealization, 105–106

Identity: Chinese-British comparison, 63; self-creation of, 11; spiritual practices, 152

i.e. Japanese family: structure of, 46–47

Iemoto: Japanese mentor-disciple relationship, 47. *See also* junior, senior, subordinate, superior

Immigration: Asians in the United States, VI; changes in, law, VI; Chinese in the United States, VI, XVI; Filipinos in the United States, VI, XVI; Indians and bicultural self, IX; Indians in the United States, VI, 25–26; Japanese in the United States, XVI, 53; Koreans in the United States, VI, 188, 190–191; Vietnamese in the United States, VI

Indians: attitudes towards the spiritual, 147; attitudes towards personal destiny, 153; conscience (*dharma*) in, 27; ego boundaries of, 18–19; encounters with American individualism, 125–130; experiential sense of self, 35; immigration to the United States, VI, 25–26; sexual and incestuous fantasies of men and women, 133–136; management theories and practices, 159–160, 161; psychological adaptation in the United States, 26–27; spiritual practices, 152; variations with Japanese in psychoanalytic relationship, 119–120; women's sexuality and family reputation, 139–140. *See also* Indian-Americans

Indian-Americans: conflict in experiential sense of self, 35–36; cultural misunderstandings in corporations, 35; education, 43–44; immigrant generation and bicultural self, IX, 27; interface of hierarchical relationships with American individualism, IX; interface with other Americans, VII, VIII, IX, 25, 30; second generation and bicultural self, 36–38; women and marital relationship, 39–40. *See also* Indians

Individualism: as related to American artistic creativity, 52; Calvinism, 5; comparison with Indian hierarchical relationships, 27–28; D. W. Winnicott, 11–12; depressive position, 10; economics, 6; Erik Erikson, 11; historical roots of, 5–7; Indian-Americans, 27; interface with Indian hierarchical relationships, IX, 42–43; Jurists, 5; Koreans in the United States, XIII, 190; Margaret Mahler's separation- individuation and, 10; reexamination of, VII; Reformation, 5; relationship to psychoanalysis, VIII, 7–13; relationship to self psychology, XI, 101–103; Romanticism, 6; self-contained individual in psychoanalysis, 8; self-creation of identity, 11; Social Contract, 5; transitional objects and phenomena, 11–12; verbal expression in Americans, 55. *See also* Individuality; Self-contained individual

Individuality: as related to *ma* in Japanese art, 52–53; private self in Indians and Japanese, 19; spiritual practices, 152. *See also* Individualism

Insider relationships: in Indian hierarchical relationships, 34

Intercultural encounter: Yoshiko in American corporation, 85–86 Intercultural stress: Asian patients, 81; Yoshiko, 85–86

Interdependence: in Chinese relationships, 65. *See also* Dependence

Intersubjectivity: critique of the isolated individual mind, 12

Intimacy: American reactions to Indians, 33–34; Eastern and Western definitions of, 176; Indian experiences with Americans, 33

Ira: negotiations with Japanese, 50

Japanese: artistic creativity, 45, 52–53; avoiding therapy as admission of failure, 121; child rearing in marriages with Americans, 54–56; decision-making, 47, 50; demanding entitlement, 124; ego boundaries of, 18–19; formal hierarchical relationships, 46–48; immigration to the United States, XVI, 53; in American corporation, 51; intercultural marriages with Americans, 46, 53–54; interface with Americans, VII VIII, IX; management theories, 159; mentor-disciple relationship, 47; misunderstandings with Americans in corporations, 45, 48–51; problems in we-self esteem, 110–111; resistance-analysis, 4; students in American art schools, 52; truth and self-esteem, 50–51; variations with Indians in psychoanalytic relationship, 119–120

Joan: incestuous fantasies and punitive superego reaction, 136

Junior: and senior in Indian hierarchy, 162; in management relationships, 166–168. *See also* Subordinate

Jurists: roots of individualism, 5

Kakar, Sudhir: evolutionism, 13–14; Indian-Western comparison, 13–14

Kakkar, Mrs.: divorce and living in the United States, 127–128; expectations of advice and guidance in psychoanalytic therapy, 75–76; magic-cosmic world of personal destiny, 74; evaluating normality/psychopathology, 73–74; sociohistorical change in India, 126–130; transference reenactment, 74

Keigo: evaluating normality/psychopathology, 77–79; negative transference and acting out, 124–125; perfectionistic conscience, 80

Klein, Melanie: critique of individualism, 9; self-contained individual, 10

Kondo, Akahisa: comments on individuality in Japanese, 52

Kohut, Heinz: critique of individualism, 12; fulfillment of individualism, 12–13

Koreans: families in American individualism, XIII, 190; family, nature of, 188; immigration to the United States, VI, 188, 190–191; social change in the United States, 190; value dissonance in communication in psychoanalysis, 121. *See also* Korean-Americans

Korean-Americans: conflict between generations, 190, 197; immigrants, 188–189; social change, 192–197. *See also* Koreans

Kudo, Kunio: comments on Japanese and Western art, 52

Language: Chinese, 66; Chinese construction, 62; Chinese discourse compared to Anglos, 61, 65; cultural assumptions and expectations, 59; dropping topic pronouns in Chinese, 63; Japanese respect, 47–48

Lucille: regional cultural self, 97–98; social change and career, 98–99

Lynn: Chinese-American in psychotherapy, 180–181

Ma: in Japanese art and creativity, 52–53

Madhu: praise and self-esteem, 38

Magic: attitudes of Enlightenment rationality towards, 6

Magic-cosmic: Asian involvement in, 146–147; in psychoanalytic therapy with Asians, 152–155; Mrs. Kakkar and the, 74; psychoanalysis and the, XII; transference in Asok, 75; Western views of the, 146

Mahler, Margaret: Romanticism and individualism in her theories, 10

Management relationships: in Indian computer company, 160–161; in Japanese corporations with Americans, 49–51; problems in, because of Indian father-son

conflicts, 169–173; psychoanalytic approach to, in India, 166–173

Management theories: American, Indian, and Japanese, 159–160

Manisha: Americanization, 26

Manoj, negative transference and anxiety states, 123–124; problem in idealizing selfobject relationship, 112–113

Marilyn: sociohistorical trauma, 95–96

Marital relationship: in Indian families, 137, 140; in Indian-American families, 39–40. *See also* Marriage

Marriage: and education in Indian-Americans, 38; child rearing in Japanese and American intercultural, 54–57; communication in Japanese and American intercultural, 54; conflict in Indian-American, 39, 40; a cause of envy among Indian brothers, 164; personal destiny, 153–154; second and third generation Korean-Americans, 191. *See also* Husband; Marital Relationship; Wife

Marty: truth and self-esteem, 51

Marxism: reexamination of Western culture and individualism, VII

Maternal-feminine: bisexuality in Indian men, 137

Meaders, Nobuko: attaining of a transcultural self, 53

Meditation: American and Indian comparison, 152; over-meditation in a teenager, 75; psychoanalysis and, 151; psychoanalysts involved in, XII, 151–152; psychoanalytic therapy and, 148–149, 150; spiritual experiences, 147–148

Meena: value dissonances in intercultural marriage, 81–82

Mentor: Japanese hierarchy and psychoanalytic relationship, 79. *See also* Senior; Superior

Mentor-disciple relationship: nature of Japanese, 47. *See also* Junior; Senior; Subordinate; Superior

Metonymic thinking: as contrasted with Western dualistic thinking, 151

Miscommunication: between Americans and Indians in a spiritual hierarchy, 42–43; between Chinese and Westerners,

59–60, 66. *See also* Communication
Misunderstanding: between Americans and
    Indians, 34, 43
Mothers: American and Japanese compari-
    son, 55–57; in Confucian societies, 193
Mothering: multiple, and selfobject rela-
    tionships, 113–114
Mother-daughter relationship: Mrs. Kakkar,
    73–74
Mother-in-law/daughter-in-law relation-
    ship: in Koreans, 195–196
Mother-son relationship: in Korean fami-
    lies, 194–195
Mysticism: Karen Horney group, 157; psy-
    choanalytic views of, 145–146
Mythic orientation: as manifested in psy-
    choanalytic therapy, 156

Narayan: different sources of psychological
    conflict, 87–88; problems in doing cre-
    ative science in the United States,
    125–126
Narcissism: different transformations of,
    across cultures, 115
Narratives: clinical and theoretical in psy-
    choanalysis, 9
Negative capability: meditation and psy-
    choanalysis, 151
Negotiation: American and Japanese, 50;
    Chinese flexibility in, 65; Japanese and
    Americans in corporations, 58
Niti: handling of family discord, 38
Noncooperation: in Indian management
    relationships, 168; Rajiv 171
Norms: of dependence in psychoanalytic
    relationship with Asians, 79; psycho-
    analysis and individualism regarding
    Asians, 72 *See also* Culture;
    Normality/psychopathology; Norms;
    Values; Value Orientation
Normality/psychopathology: Asian and
    American comparison, X, 72;
judgments in psychoanalysis, 71; and the
    spiritual, XII; value orientation of Amer-
    ican psychoanalyst with Japanese patient,
    77–79. *See also* Emotional conflicts;
    Norms; Psychopathology; Values

Object relations theory: critique of individ-
    ualism, 9
Obsessive-compulsive: Ahmed, 169–170,
    172; Case of Z, Chinese, 180; Rajiv's son-
    father relationship, 170
Oceanic feeling: spiritual experiences and
    Freudian attitudes towards, 145, 157
Oedipus Complex: in Confucian families,
    194; in Indian men, 137–139; in Indian
    women, 133–136; Indian and Western
    comparison, XI; self-contained individ-
    ual and the, 8
Omoiyari: concerned empathy in Japanese, 55
Orality: relationship to Indian character-
    formation, 141–142
Outsider relationships: in Indian hierarchi-
    cal relationships, 42; Indian and Japanese
    comparison, 34

Palmistry: Ashis, 154–155; Asian involve-
    ment in, 146–147; marriage, 153–154;
    Western views of, 146
Patel, Udayan: psychoanalytic management
    consulting, 166–168
Penis envy: in Indian women, 137
Personal destiny: Asian involvement in,
    146–147; Mrs. Kakkar, 74; psychoanaly-
    sis, XII; Western views of, 146
Personal self: conceptualization of, 84
Pradeep: brother relationship, 163; mythic
    orientation, 156
Prakash: cultural self in the transference,
    88–89
Prayer: psychoanalytic therapy, 150
Private self: as related to *ma* in Japanese art,
    52–53; individuality and modes of com-
    munication in the, 19–20; Japanese and
    Indian comparison on the, 48; secrets in
    psychoanalytic therapy, 121; therapeutic
    relationship with Japanese, 4. *See also*
    Public self
Projective identification: induced counter-
    transference and individualism, 9–10
Promilla: emotional conflicts and spiritual
    aspirations, 149–150
Protestantism: Margaret Mahler's theories
    and individualism, 10; roots of individu-
    alism, 5

Psychic ability: Mrs. Kakkar's daughter, 75

Psychoanalysis: and the spiritual, 20, 145–146, 150; Buddhist meditation, XII, 146; cultural influences on, VIII; cultural roots of, 5–7; differentiating psychopathology in Asians from a different normality, 73; ignorance of Asian psychological makeup, 72; in Indian management relationships, 166–173; Indian brothers, XIII, 163–164; Indian father-son relationship, 138, 169–172; judgments of intercultural encounters and normality/psychopathology, 71–72; magic-cosmic world, 20, 146–147; meditation and the magic-cosmic, XII; new model for, with Asians, 18–20; philosophical assumption of, 5–7; relationship of, to individualism, VIII, 5–13; sociohistorical change in new paradigm of, 20; understanding Asians, VIIII; values working with Asians, X. See also Psychoanalytic relationship; Psychoanalytic therapy

Psychoanalyst: involved in meditation, XII, 151–152

Psychoanalytic group therapy: Indian management relationships, 167

Psychoanalytic institutes: Buddhism, 157

Psychoanalytic process: Cartesian dualism and self-contained individual, 8

Psychoanalytic relationship: Asian and American comparison, XI; Asian variations according to hierarchical relationships, 118–120; dependency for esteem exchange with Asian patients, 120; North American cultural assumptions, 117–118. See also Psychoanalysis; Psychoanalytic therapy

Psychoanalytic relativism: Takeo Doi, 15–17

Psychoanalytic research: across cultures, 187

Psychoanalytic therapy: and the spiritual, 147, 148–151; Indian encounters with American individualism, 125–130; Indian managers, 164–166, 169–172; personal destiny, 152–155; working with Asian patients' stress of intercultural encounters, 85–86. See also Psychoanaly-

sis; Psychoanalytic relationship

Psychological conflict: differentiating between, from cultural values and problematic family relationships, 86–88; sociocultural and sociohistorical factors in, 83–84. See also Emotional conflict; Psychopathology

Psychological (psychoanalytic) universalism: and variability, 16–17; anthropological relativism versus, VIII; Catherine Ewing's use of ego psychology in, 14–15

Psychopathology: and self psychology, 101–103; relationship to the spiritual, 148–151; sociocultural and sociohistorical factors in, 83–84; variations of, in Pakistanis and North Americans, 15. See also Deficits; Depression; Emotional conflicts; Obsessive-compulsive; Psychological conflicts

Psychotherapy: Cultural roots of Asians, 178; in China, 178–180; research data in different cultures, 187; with Chinese-American patients, 179–180. See also Psychoanalysis; Psychoanalytic therapy

Public self: Japanese, 4; Japanese-Indian comparison, 48. See also Private self

Rajiv: problems in management relationships, 167–168, 170–171

Rationalism: Freud and rationality, 7; relationship to individualism, 6; relationship to religion, 6; secondary process thinking in psychoanalysis, 7; Western denigration of astrology, palmistry, and such, 74–75. See also Dualism; Enlightenment; Reason; Universalism

Ravi: brother relationship, 163

Rawn, Monica: attunement to Hindu patient, 118

Reaction-formation: relationship to latency-age superego in Indians, 142. See also Emotional conflicts; Psychological conflict; Psychopathology

Reason: Western dualism and universalism, 6–7

Reformation: roots of individualism, 5

Regional self: psychological conflict, X, 97–98. See also Cultural self

Relativism: and psychological (psychoanalytic) universalism, VIII, 16–17; Takeo Doi's theory, 15–17. *See also* Universalism

Religion: demystification in Sudhir Kakar's work, 14; Enlightenment rational attitudes towards, 6; Freud and Winnicott's views of illusion and, 145. *See also* Spiritual

Repression: in Western cultures, 177

Resistances: advice and guidance in Indians, 121–122; analysis with Japanese, 4; Asian and American comparison, XI; cultural and idiosyncratic, 120–122; private self and secrets in Asians, 121

Rhetoric: Chinese and British comparison, 61

Rituals: Confucian, in relationships, 63–64; Rajiv, 170; routines of everyday talk, 64

Romanticism: in Margaret Mahler's theories, 10; roots of individualism, 6

Sa'ida: daughter-in-law/mother-in-law relationship, 140–141

Sailesh: involvement with astrology, 154

Sashi: personal destiny, 153–154

Secondary process: Enlightenment rationality, 7

Secrets: Asian secrecy in psychoanalytic therapy, 74; resistance in psychoanalytic therapy, 121

Self: Chinese and Western comparison, XIII, 175–176, 183; Chinese interpersonal embeddedness, 63; conflict in Indians' experiential sense of, 35–36; development of, in American and Japanese child rearing, 56; ethnic layering of, and psychological conflict, X, 91–92, 98–100; father-son relationship in Chinese, 176; I-self in American individualism, 4; Japanese we-self, 4; locus of control in Chinese, 185; problems in psychological universalism, 15; transcultural, in a Japanese, 53; true self/false self and individualism, 12; Western cultural meanings of, 3

Self-contained individual: critique of, by Erik Erikson and D. W. Winnicott, 11; drive and structural theory and the, 8; in

psychoanalysis, 9; Oedipus Complex and psychoanalytic process, 8. *See also* Individualism

Self-creation of identity: American artistic creativity, 52; individualism, 11

Self-direction: true self/false self, 12

Self-esteem: centrality of esteem in Asians, 103–106; enhancement of, by dependence exchange in Asian hierarchical intimacy relationships, 104–105; enhancement of, by family reputation, 106–107; enhancement of, by idealization, 105–106; praise in Indian child rearing, 38; relationship of, to objective truth in Asians and Americans, 50–51, 104. *See also* We-self esteem

Self-identity: fragmented in Chinese-Americans, 186

Self psychology: Asian psychological makeup, XI; critique of individualism, 12, 101; cultural patterning of selfobject relationships, 107–108; fulfillment of individualism, 102; individualism and, XI; problem in use of induced countertransference, 115; psychopathology of individualism and North Americans, 12, 101–102; reciprocal selfobject relationships, XI, 107. *See also* Self-esteem; Selfobject relationships

Selfobject relationships: Asian psychological makeup, XI; failure of, in Indians, 111–114; failure of, in Japanese 111; family reputation as, XI, 106–107; high levels of empathic attunement and esteem in Asians, 103–106; idealizations in Asians, 105–106; indirect communication in Asians, 104; multiple mothering in Indians, 113–114; reciprocity and cultural patterning of, 107; separation-individuation and, XI, 109. *See also* Self-esteem; Self Psychology

Senior: and junior in Indian hierarchy, 162; Japanese managers with Americans, 49; management relationships in India, 166–168. *See also* Superior; Mentor-disciple

Separation-individuation: culturally specific selfobject relationship, 109; Romanticism and individualism, 10; selfobject relationships, XI

Sexuality: abstinence in Indian spiritual disciplines, 143; communication by Indians, 152; in Indian teenagers, 138; in Indian spiritual culture, 143; in women cross-culturally, XI; incestuous fantasies and superego reactions in Indian women, 133–136; male fear of Indian women's sexuality, 138; sexual fantasies in Indian women and men, 134

Shakuntala: astrological predictions, 154; emotional conflicts and spiritual disciplines, 149, 150–151; incestuous fantasies and superego reaction, 134–135; metonymic thinking, 151; secrecy in spiritual discipline, 152; spiritual experiences, 147–148

Shame: cultural self of Graziella, 91; in Japanese, 51; Lucille and regional self, 97–98 Sharma, Sushma: problems in a computer company, 160–161

Social constructionism: reexamination of Western culture, VII

Social Contract: roots of individualism, 5

Social change: Koreans in the United States, 190, 192–197; women and layering of the self, 98–100

Social etiquette: in Indian hierarchical relationships, 28; in Japanese hierarchical relationships, 47–48

Sociocultural: conceptualization in psychological conflict and psychopathology, 83–84; ignored in psychoanalytic therapy, 90; in transference/countertransference with Graziella, 91

Sociohistorical: change in Mrs. Kakkar's family, 130; change in new psychoanalytic paradigm, 20; conceptualization in psychological conflict and psychopathology, 83–84; ignored in psychoanalytic therapy, 90; in psychoanalysis, 5; in the transference, 88–89; trauma and psychoanalysis, 94–97

Son: eldest in Chinese family, 177–178

Son-father relationship: in Chinese, 182–183; in Indian families, 138, 169–172; in Koreans, 193–194

Son-mother relationship: in Korean Confucian families, 194–195

Spirit world: Indian female college students, 155

Spiritual: Americans in Asian hierarchical relationships, 41–43; experiences of Shakuntala, 147–148; Indian assumptions of the, 147; interaction of the, with psychopathology, 148–151; normality/psychopathology and the, XII; psychoanalytic views of the, 145–146; relationship to the erotic, XI. See also Meditation; Spiritual practices

Spiritual practices: individuality and identity, 152. See also Meditation; Spiritual

Subordinate: Americans in Asian spiritual hierarchies, 42–43; Asians in American education, 30; Asians in American hierarchical relationships, 29–30; expectations in Indian hierarchical relationships, 28–29; in hierarchical intimacy relationships, 33; in problematic Indian management relationships, 172; Japanese hierarchical relationships and Keigo's transference, 78. See also Junior

Sunil: intercultural misunderstanding, 34

Superego: categorical imperative, 7–8; cross-cultural studies, 8; gender, 8; Indian deference in hierarchical relationships, 142; in Japanese, 5; punitive reactions to incestuous fantasies in Indian women, 133–136; transference reactions of anger and anxiety in Asian patients, 123. See also Ego-ideal

Superior: expectations in Indian hierarchical relationships, 28–29; in hierarchical intimacy relationships, 33; in Indian work relationship, 161; in North American settings, 29–30; in problematic Indian management relationships, 172; Indian swamis and American disciples, 42–43; Japanese hierarchical relationships and Keigo's transference, 78. See also Mentor; Senior

Suppression: major defence in Eastern cultures, 177

Sushma: conflict in experiential sense of self, 35–36

Therapeutic relationship: Chinese-American and Caucasian-American comparison, 184–185
Therapeutic territory: Chinese and Western comparison, 183–184
Training: Japanese and American comparison on, in corporations, 50
Transference: analysis with Chinese, 185; and meditation, 151; Asian and American comparison, XI; influence of culture on, XI, 122–125; negative, and anxiety states in Asian patients, 122–125; repetition and spiritual practices, 150
Transference-resistance: Japanese cultural attitudes, 78–79
Transitional objects and phenomena: fulfillment of individualism, 11–12
Truth: relationship to self-esteem in Japanese and Americans, 50–51

Udayan: problems in early selfobject relationships, 111–112
Unconscious: use of, in sociocultural research, 187
Universalism: in Western culture, 6–7
Universalism, psychological (psychoanalytic): and variability, 16–17; anthropological relativism versus, VIII; Catherine Ewing's use of ego psychology in, 14–15

Values: American psychoanalytic, toward magic-cosmic world, 74; American rationalism and denigration of reincarnation and psychic abilities, 75; dissonances between American psychoanalysts and Asian patients, 117, 130–131; in Japanese and American marriages and child rearing, 55; Indian and American comparison of, 30; Indian patients' expectations for advice and guidance in psychoanalysis, 75–76; of Western psychoanalysts with Asians, X. See also

Norms; Normality/psychopathology; Value orientation
Value dissonances: Asians patients in American relationships, 81–82
Value orientation: American psychoanalyst and intercultural stress of Asian patients, 81–82; internalized high standards of Japanese, 79–80; Japanese communication by empathic sensing, 80–81
Vietnamese: immigration, VI

We-self: in hierarchical intimacy relationships, 32
We-self esteem: dependency in Asians, 33–34; family reputation and, 76–77; problems of, in Asians, 110–111
Western culture: definition of self, 176; reexamination of, VII. See also Culture
Westernized: Indians, 164
Wife: battering in Indian-American families, 39–40; Japanese in American intercultural marriage, 53–54, 57; Korean Confucian family, 194. See also Marriage; Women
Winnicott, D. W.: critique of self-contained individual, 11; fulfillment of individualism, 12
Women: Indian and American comparison, 40; layering of the self in sociohistorical change, 98–100. See also Marriage; Wife
Work: Asians in North American hierarchies, 29–30
Work group: Japanese attitudes towards outsiders, 47; Japanese functioning in, 47
Wright, Rosemary: Japanese and American comparison on artistic creativity, 52–53

Yoshiko: cultural self of, 85–86; intercultural encounter, 85–86; interface with American corporation, 51